Conflict of Interest in Policing

SYDNEY INSTITUTE OF CRIMINOLOGY SERIES NO 26

Series Editors: Chris Cunneen, University of New South Wales

Mark Findlay, University of Sydney

Julie Stubbs, University of Sydney

Titles in the Series:

Aboriginal Perspectives on Criminal Justice Cunneen, C (ed) (1992)

Doing Less Time: Penal Reform in Crisis Chan, J (1992)

Psychiatry in Court Shea, P (1996)

Cricket and the Law Fraser, D (1993)

The Prison and the Home Aungles, A (1994)

Women, Male Violence and the Law Stubbs, J (ed) (1994)

Fault in Homicide Yeo, S (1997)

Anatomy of a French Murder Case McKillop, B (1997)

Gender, Race & International Relations Cunneen, C & Stubbs, J (1997)

Reform in Policing Bolen, J (1997)

A Culture of Corruption Dixon, D (ed) (1999)

Defining Madness Shea, P (1999)

Developing Cultural Criminology Banks, C (ed) (2000)

Indigenous Human Rights Garkawe, S, Kelly, L & Fisher, W (eds) (2001)

When Police Unionise Finnane, M (2002)

Regulating Racism McNamara, L (2002)

A History of Criminal Law in New South Wales Woods, G (2002)

Bin Laden in the Suburbs Poynting, S, Noble, G, Tabar, P & Collins, J (2004)

Global Issues, Women and Justice Pickering, S & Lambert, C (eds) (2004)

Aboriginal Childhood Separations and Guardianship Law Buti, A (2004)

Refugees and State Crime Pickering, S (2005)

Reshaping Juvenile Justice Chan, J (ed) (2005)

Interrogating Images Dixon, D (2007)

Imprisoning Resistance Carlton, B (2007)

Recapturing Freedom Goulding, D (2007)

Conflict of Interest in Policing

Problems, Practices, and Principles

Published by
> Institute of Criminology Press
> Sydney Institute of Criminology
> University of Sydney Law School
> 173-175 Phillip Street Sydney 2000
> www.criminology.law.usyd.edu.au

Distributed by
> The Federation Press
> PO Box 45 Annandale 2038
> www.federationpress.com.au

National Library of Australia Cataloguing-in-Publication

Author:	Davids, Cindy.
Title:	Conflict of interest in policing : problems, practices, and principles / author, Cindy Davids.
Publisher:	Sydney : Institute of Criminology Press, 2008.
ISBN:	9780975196762 (pbk.)
Series:	Sydney Institute of Criminology monograph series
Notes:	Includes index.
	Bibliography.
Subjects:	Victoria Police.
	Conflict of interests--Victoria.
	Police--Victoria.
	Police ethics--Victoria.
	Police administration--Victoria.
Dewey Number:	174.93632

Cover design by Cameron Emerson-Elliott
Typeset by The Institute of Criminology
Printed by Ligare Book Printer

DEDICATION

To Gordon and Riley
Love and special thanks;

and to Jewelene
because so much is owed.

Table of Contents

Acknowledgements

It is inevitable that one can not thank all those who have provided assistance, support or encouragement in a project such as this. Nevertheless ...

The research would not have been possible had it not been for the preparedness of Victoria Police to open their files to external scrutiny and I am grateful to senior management of Victoria Police who showed great courage in so doing. In particular, I wish to thank a number of serving and non-serving personnel with whom I engaged during the life of my research including Stuart MacIntyre, Christine Howlett, Graeme Cruise, Michael Gill, Gary McColl, Sean Carroll, and Assistant Commissioner Gary Jamieson. A special thanks to the current Chief Commissioner Christine Nixon whose period of service commenced after the completion of this research work, but whose belief in integrity and openness made this book possible. I thank her for the very kind words in her Preface to this book. In addition, the Victorian Ombudsman's office showed considerable trust and, again, a belief in the practice—not just the rhetoric—of openness and accountability. I wish to particularly thank Brian Hardiman, Senior Assistant Ombudsman at the time. I also wish to than the current Deputy Ombudsman, John Taylor, for his support of this research program and for his review of the research on which some sections of this book are based.

I note that this work is based on my PhD thesis which was undertaken through the Faculty of Law at the University of New South Wales. My particular thanks to Professor David Dixon, my supervisor from the University of New South Wales, for his forbearance, persistence, and intellectual guidance. David was an important source of support throughout my research, and I am also very grateful for the sentiments he expresses in his Foreword. Also, thanks to Professor Janet Chan at UNSW for her invaluable knowledge and advice, and to Professor Linda Hancock of Deakin University for her support and encouragement in the early stages of this work. I am also very grateful to Professors David Brereton, Mark Findlay, and Andrew Goldsmith, who examined the original thesis and provided valuable signposts around which to navigate in producing this work.

The team at the Sydney Institute of Criminology have done an excellent job in producing the book and it was a pleasure to work with Nina Ralph (initially) and Dawn Koester, both of whom were always professional and efficient. I particularly thank Dawn for her input.

A special thanks to my very dear friend and colleague Marilyn McMahon for her support, intellectual input, and advice, particularly with the quantitative aspects of the study. I also thank Carol Floyd for her editing skill in the task of reducing the original 670 pages to a more manageable size, Julia Miller for her editing and proofreading, and Jo Smith for her assistance with transcribing interview material. I am very grateful for the support of my colleagues at Macquarie University and especially to Professor Chris Patel, Head of the Department of Accounting and Finance.

To my long-suffering friends and family, who carried the monkey for as long as I did, sorry but thanks for sticking with me. Special thanks to my friends on Scotland Island, and in Melbourne and Geelong, Ireland, and New York (they know who they are).

Finally, to my husband and colleague, Gordon Boyce, there are no words that can adequately express the thanks that are owed, on both the professional and family fronts, or that would do justice to his contribution. This is definitely a case where thanks seem inadequate (but will have to do).

For my beautiful son, Riley, born during the life of this long research, this is dedicated to you!

List of Tables

List of Figures

Foreword by Christine Nixon

This is an important, well-researched contribution to the public store of knowledge about good and bad policing and how best to encourage the former and minimise the latter. Dr Davids' doctoral study of conflicts of interest in policing was based on the unfettered access given to her by Victoria Police to all the relevant complaints files over a ten year period between 1988 and 1998.

During that period policing across Australia attracted increased levels of public concern about its good standing. In some states the police were subjected to intensive and highly publicised judicial reviews and subsequent one-off and externally imposed programs of reform. In Victoria, reform has been a continuous and unrelenting process, not just during the period of Dr Davids' research but right up to now and it has emanated both from external review and an internally embraced program led by myself.

In the book Dr Davids provides useful and rigorous definitions of the wide range of conflicts of interest that lie in wait to ethically undo the unaware or ignorant police officer in the ordinary course of his and her public duties. She explores in great and useful detail the dimensions of the problem, the different types of cases, and, importantly, how through the complaints system those that are reported are internally investigated and resolved. She also reports on the great strengthening of the system of external review and investigation in Victoria as progressed through the creation of the Office of Police Integrity.

Worryingly, Dr Davids' research uncovered the significant extent to which, only a few years ago, senior police and police management failed fully enough to understand conflicts of interest or downplayed their significance as threats to the public trust in the police. Fortunately, her research has put the current internal and external arrangements for the regulation of conflicts of interest under a strenuous test, and found significant improvement.

External oversight here in Victoria now matches best practice elsewhere. Her searching analysis of causation in these cases of police misconduct also identifies the crucial importance of strong education and training and an engaged, open and trusting organisational culture to minimise the occurrence of conflict of interest cases in the first place.

Victoria Police has greatly strengthened the effectiveness of its internal systems of accountability and supervision. We have also embarked on a pathway of police education reform that will ensure all our officers have the training they need to recognise conflicts of interest when they come across them and the skills and sensibilities to avoid breaches of them. This book will make a significant contribution to the education of future generations of police officers. I commend it to you.

Christine Nixon, APM, Chief Commissioner, Victoria Police
October 2007

Foreword by David Dixon

Quality empirical research on policing in Australia is still regrettably rare. The production of such work depends upon: academics who are prepared to get out from behind their desks; police departments which are willing to open themselves to external scrutiny; funding agencies which value such research; and publishers who are committed to increasing public knowledge and understanding. This excellent book by Cindy Davids makes a significant contribution to the international, as well as the Australian, policing literature. Chief Commissioner Nixon and her colleagues in Victoria Police deserve great credit for allowing a researcher to have unrestricted access to such sensitive material as complaints files. This is an example of Victoria Police's remarkable continuing commitment to engagement with academic research: it would be good to see other state police commissioners following this example.

Dr Davids' book originated in a PhD thesis at the University of New South Wales, which I supervised in collaboration with my colleague, Professor Janet Chan. The thesis defines and explains conflict of interest in policing in ways which add to understanding of both conflict of interest and policing. Distilled into this book, Cindy's research provides insights into complaints and complaints procedures which are unique in the policing literature. She organises, analyses and theorises her data with skill, drawing conclusions which are of interest not just to policing scholars, but to those more generally concerned with conflicts of interest in the broader fields of ethics and regulation. The conceptual framework of trust and confidence makes a valuable contribution to broader considerations of control and accountability. The Institute of Criminology deserves great credit for providing a publishing outlet for research monographs in criminology at a time when other Australian publishers dismiss them as uneconomical. This book is a great credit to the Institute's publishing program.

Professor David Dixon, Dean, Law Faculty, University of NSW
October 2007

CHAPTER ONE

Introduction

A conflict of interest arises whenever the private interests of someone in a position of public authority do not coincide with their official duties such that private interests may impinge on the performance of official duty. Conflicts of interest may be manifested in the use of an official position for pecuniary or non-pecuniary private gain or for the benefit of family, friends, or associates, or may result in dereliction or neglect of public duty. The concept of conflict of interest is applicable whether or not the person acts on their own interests at the expense of official duties, whether or not they are aware of the conflict, or whether they perceive there to be a conflict. In addition to the potential to impinge on the performance of official duties, in the public sector a central problem that arises in relation to conflict of interest is the negative effect on public perceptions, particularly the public's trust in the integrity of public sector organisations, or in the public sector as a whole.

The focus of this study is the problem of conflict of interest in a particular police jurisdiction: the Australian state of Victoria, where police have been the subject of sustained public criticism in relation to misconduct. In contrast to other Australian jurisdictions in the states of Queensland, New South Wales, and Western Australia, revelations of misconduct and the associated campaigns for police reform have not resulted in the attention of a Royal Commission or official Inquiry. Instead, Victoria Police undertook a significant program of reform from within, including an overhaul of internal investigations and the creation of the Ethical Standards Department (ESD) in 1996. However there was sustained public criticism of police and a number of prominent cases of police misconduct damaged public confidence in the integrity of police. Amidst growing media calls for a Royal Commission, in 2004 the Victorian Government created an Office of Police Integrity (OPI) with enhanced powers both for oversight of internal police processes and significant independent investigatory capacities. The OPI's mandate is to ensure the maintenance of ethical and professional standards within Victoria Police, and to investigate serious misconduct and police corruption.

1

This study examines conflicts of interest within Victoria Police for a ten year period preceding the dramatically increased public scrutiny and pressure that led to the creation of the OPI. The period researched for this book (1988–1998) was one of significant disquiet in relation to evident conflicts of interest in policing and in other areas of the public sector (notably in Australian Federal politics). Although there is no prima facie evidence that conflict of interest problems were numerically any greater in policing during the 1980s and 1990s than at previous historical moments, the period witnessed an explosion in concern about the ethical conduct of public sector officials and those who hold the public trust. There was also growing academic interest and comment on these matters and a sustained campaign of criticism directed against Victoria Police (e.g. The Age 1997; Ryle *et al.* 1996; Adams 1996). Major incidents resulting in negative publicity for Victoria Police included a number of controversial police shootings (McCulloch 1997; Lyall and Walker 1998; Task Force Victor 1994), the use of excessive force against protesters (The Ombudsman 1994), the perceived targeting of certain communities (Conroy 1996; The Ombudsman 1994), incidents involving sexual misconduct (The Ombudsman 1997b), and a major kickbacks scheme whereby large numbers of police officers received kickbacks for "tipping off" repairers about "broken windows" (Silvester 1995b, 1995a; Ryle 1997; The Ombudsman 2003: 72). These and other complaints were 'early warnings' that a more fundamental problem existed.

Notwithstanding a renewed concern with the problem of conflict of interest in policing, few prior studies of the problem have been reported in the literature, although research in relation to police corruption and police ethics has addressed questions that relate to scenarios commonly regarded as examples of conflict of interest in policing. In addition to its in-depth analysis of conflict of interest, a key contribution of this book is to lay bare many matters in relation to the internal governance of police that would otherwise remain hidden. The array of behaviours examined in this work traverse the entire policing role and include many interactions between police and the public which are outside the domain of standard operational policing but which are central to the delivery of a 'just' police service. The book situates issues of accountability and control of police misconduct within a framework of notions of trust and confidence in policing. As such, it includes consideration of police ethics, police integrity, police deviance, and police misconduct—terms that are often conflated and dealt with simplistically in media, academic and government commentary.

The perennial nature of many conflicts of interest in policing as outlined in this book offer a fruitful terrain for future work by the ESD within Victoria Police and the OPI as an independent investigation and oversight agency. The OPI's ability to take a proactive stance on intelligence received through the complaints system means that many of the conflict of interest problems identified in this book may be addressed in a more systematic manner than their hitherto ad hoc treatment as complaint cases against individuals (outlined later in the book). Some of the types of conflict of interest have now been flagged as priority areas for future investigation by OPI.

I   Conflict of Interest and Police Corruption

The breach of public trust entailed in conflicts of interest damages confidence in the integrity and impartiality of those in official positions. The undermining of public trust in government, in general, and in policing in particular, is so problematic that conflict of interest has become a form of unethical conduct that raises particular concern and controversy (see Kernaghan and Langford 1990: 139–140). In the United States, it has been argued that "conflict of interest (a relatively subtle form of transgression) has replaced bribery, kickback, office-buying, and other gross forms of corruption as the principal malfeasance in ... public life" (Stark 2000: 36). Indeed, it has been argued that increased concern over conflict of interest in Western countries is associated with a more general cleaning up of the worst forms of corruption, reducing the "grosser larcenies in government ... to tolerable limits" (Kernaghan and Langford 1990: 138–139). Kernaghan and Langford suggest that conflict of interest as a particular public problem may come to public attention when other major forms of public corruption have been largely eliminated through laws, regulations and guidelines that attempt to deal with the use of public office for private gain.

However, whilst it is certainly the case that conflict of interest has become a topic of debate in many areas of the polity and in society generally (Davids 1998), there is little evidence that this coincides with a decline in general concern with official misconduct and corruption. Indeed, the opposite seems to be the case, as increasing public concern over conflict of interest has coincided with a general decline in public confidence in official conduct in public life more generally (Nolan *et al.* 1995; Nolan 1996; Graham 2006), and policing in particular, where corruption seems to be a relatively constant phenomenon (Miller 2003; HM Inspectorate of Constabulary 1999; Newburn 1999; Finnane 1994). The particular concern with conflict of interest in policing in Australia has followed a series of major police corruption scandals (as reported in Fitzgerald 1989; Wood 1997a, 1997b, 1997c; Kennedy 2004a, 2004b). In Victoria, the rise in concern with conflict of interest followed a series of scandals and public debate over allegations of excessive use of force, use of lethal force, discriminatory policing, sexual impropriety, and kickback scams engaged in by a large number of police officers. This rise in concern is evidenced in a series of reports from the office of the Ombudsman in the 1990s (The Deputy Ombudsman (Police Complaints) 1993, 1994, 1995; The Ombudsman 1994, 1997b, 1998b, 1998a). This evidence suggests that links between conflict of interest and possible corruption are recognised, at least implicitly.

A   Conflict of Interest and Corruption

Conflict of interest is a small but significant part of the wider problem of police ethics and corruption. Traditionally, conflict of interest in the public sector was not conceptually distinguished from corruption, where the general focus was on an official placing private financial interests ahead of public duties (Owen 1997). In many discussions, the problem of conflict of interest is not clearly distinguished from a range of behaviours that are portrayed as part of a continuum of corrupt activities and involvements (e.g. see Wood 1996). Alternatively, conflict of interest may be seen as a distinct category of misconduct (Moss 1996), as part of a 'slippery slope' leading to more serious forms of corruption (see Kleinig 1996: 174; Newburn 1999), or as a potential precursor or catalyst to involvement in corrupt conduct (Comrie 1995).[1]

When various forms of police misconduct are revealed, they may be described under a broad banner of 'corruption', particularly in the media, with little attempt to clearly distinguish variations in types of misconduct.[2] Recent official reviews in the United Kingdom have identified within the broad rubric

---

[1] The "slippery slope" argument suggests that minor acts that create a sense of obligation outside or beyond official police duties may have the potential to lead to other more corrupt forms of behaviour, being the first step in a "moral career" from lesser to greater forms of corruption (Sherman 1985), although this argument is not universally accepted (see Kleinig 1996: 174–181). Indeed, "it is perhaps more important to examine a general atmosphere or culture in which deviance is encouraged than to seek causal connections between types of deviance" (Dixon 1999b: 45).

[2] A wide range of police misconduct may be portrayed as "corruption", although corruption is sometimes distinguished from non-corrupt forms of unethical activity, which may include conduct that "does not involve an exchange with a 'corrupter' or abuse of position" (Miller 2003: 2).

of corruption a number of behaviours that are classified here as conflicts of interest or conflict of interest breaches (Newburn 1999; Miller 2003). For example, unauthorised access to and disclosure or other misuse of police information has been identified as dominating corrupt activity in English and Welsh police forces (Miller 2003).

The Wood Royal Commission in New South Wales acknowledged that corruption was "notoriously difficult to define" however, for the purposes of its inquiry, corruption was initially defined as "deliberate unlawful conduct (whether by act or omission) on the part of a member of the police service, utilising his or her position, whether on or off duty, regardless of its motivation" (Wood 1996: 32; Wood 1997a: 33).

Corruption was clearly seen by Commissioner Wood to be the most serious form of police misconduct, and conduct was "considered to be corrupt, whether motivated by an expectation of financial or personal benefit or not, and whether successful or not" (Wood 1996: 33; Wood 1997a: 25). Commissioner Wood identified and listed well-known forms of corruption, including bribe-taking, protection, stealing, and involvement in various forms of criminal activity. Included in his list were some forms of behaviour consistent with those that this book argues fall within the rubric of conflict of interest breaches. These include the release of confidential information, interference in police processes, and stealing and recycling money or property obtained during the course of otherwise legitimate police operations (Wood 1997a: 33).[3]

The Queensland *Commission of Inquiry into Possible Illegal Activities and Associated Police Misconduct* (Fitzgerald 1989) avoided trying to specifically define police corruption, instead dividing police misconduct into two key areas: "verballing" and "corruption". Commissioner Fitzgerald made reference to activities that could *not* be labelled as corruption but which "involved much more diverse behaviour and degrees of culpability as police take advantage of opportunities which arise in the course of their duties to obtain personal benefits" (Fitzgerald 1989: 207). Much of this latter group Fitzgerald termed "local misconduct" and some of it is the type of police

---

[3] One dimension that may be seen to distinguish conflict of interest from corruption is that the latter may necessarily include the *mala fide* exercise of police powers (Wood 1997a: 25). This aspect is included in the official definition of police corruption adopted by Victoria Police, which is wholly based on Commissioner Wood's report.

misbehaviour that this book categorises as examples of misconduct flowing from conflicts of interest.

For the purposes of the analysis, conflict of interest is categorised as a possible precursor to police misconduct.[4] This recognises that police misconduct, and in the extreme corruption, exists within, and takes its form in part from, "specific environments of opportunity" (Findlay 1993). Such misconduct may involve less serious breaches of disciplinary and regulatory norms, or may involve corruption, manifested in more serious breaches of disciplinary rules and regulations, and of the law.[5] In this sense, conflicts of interest are regarded as leading to (or being associated with) transgressions ranging from minor misconduct through to corrupt behaviour (this may be conceptualised as a continuum). Specifically, conflicts of interest may provide motivation and/or present opportunities for various (but not all) forms of police misconduct. However, the problem with conflict of interest is not necessarily manifested in improper motives, but in failing to recognise conflicts or acting in disregard of them. This may result in the impairment (consciously or not) of an individual's judgment in relation to official duty (see Werhane and Doering 1992).

The discussion of corruption and fraud in police procurement processes by Ayling and Grabosky (2006) showed how conflicts of interest may improperly influence the performance of police administration and management processes. The examples provided by Ayling and Grabosky were based in conflict of interest situations where fraud or alleged fraud in the procurement process may be related to: a) the alleged receipt of private benefits; b) an improper relationship with a tenderer; and, c) a post employment relationship with private providers. The potential for such conflicts to manifest themselves is magnified in an environment where there is greater use of

---

[4] It is recognised that where regulatory provisions prohibit conflicts of interest *per se*, any conflicts of interest is itself *ipso facto* able to be defined as police misconduct.

[5] This analysis avoids the use of the term 'deviance', although it is recognised that 'misconduct' and 'deviance' are often used interchangeably. For example, Kappeler (1998) uses both terms within the same text, seemingly to mean the same thing; Dixon (1999a) uses the term "deviance" to refer to the broad and undifferentiated (between less serious and more serious forms) category of what is here referred to as "misconduct"; while Neyroud and Beckley (2001) use the term "misconduct" to refer to the same thing. It is more generally agreed that corruption is a label appropriately applied to serious forms of deviance/misconduct. Here, "misconduct" is generally used to mean forms of misconduct that do not fall into the more clearly defined categories of corruption (even though such clarity may itself prove elusive) for analytical and discursive convenience.

outsourcing, private provision, and other 'economically rational' processes (see Davids and Hancock 1998).

Concern with the need to regulate the area of conflict of interest may arise from a desire to eliminate various types of police misconduct that flow from or are associated with conflicts of interest. Conflict of interest breaches are generally regarded as being less serious than major forms of corruption such as bribery, although it is recognised that conflicts of interest may give rise to more serious forms of corrupt behaviour. Indeed, to some degree, regulation of conflicts of interest is an attempt to "head off corruption at its source" (Kernaghan and Langford 1990: 139).

Distinguishing the variation in different types of misconduct may prove crucial to understanding motivational and behavioural roots of problem behaviours in policing. This book aims to provide specific definitions and behavioural classification of conflict of interest as a particular type of police misconduct, and its relationship with other forms of police misconduct.

B Relationship with Recognised Causes of Police Misconduct

Policing is characterised by a broad range of tasks, a relative lack of scrutiny, significant authority on the part of individual police officers, inevitable and necessary discretionary components, and significant power. These unique characteristics of policing give rise to an extraordinary array of circumstances and contexts in which police misconduct can occur. This means that opportunities for misconduct can never be completely eliminated—indeed, such opportunities are intimately connected with "approved ways of working" (Dixon 1999b: 68). Many studies testify to the amount of discretion necessarily involved in policing (Goldsmith 1990; Dixon 1999a; Davis 1976; Lipsky 1976; Miller et al. 1997; Miller 1998; Lustgarten 1986). In short, at least some level of police discretion is not only unavoidable—it is also operationally necessary, legally sanctioned, and desirable (Reiner 2000: 169; Dixon 1997).

Within the broad framework of police discretion, a range of causal factors have been identified in the literature as giving rise to police misconduct. These include individual 'bad apple' police officers, organisational factors, and police culture (see Newburn 1999). The 'bad apple' (or 'rotten apple' or 'black sheep') theory of corruption rests on an 'individual pathology' view of human nature. This rests on a belief that a 'bad apple' officer will maximise the opportunities for corruption provided by the varying degrees of unsupervised discretion inherent in the policing role (see Knapp 1972; Finnane 1994). On this view, conflicts of interest would be more likely to be engaged in by errant individuals who seek opportunities for misconduct.

Although the bad apple characterisation has been readily accepted by police forces and some official inquiries (see Dixon 2004), it is widely rejected as a major cause of corruption (see Fitzgerald 1989; Wood 1997a; Mollen 1994). Whilst Commissioners Fitzgerald and Wood did not deny that individual pathologies could and did lead to corrupt behaviours, they were not regarded as the principal cause of corruption. Bad apple theories are regarded as superficial and paying too little attention to the structural and organisational patterns and characteristics that lead to corruption (Palmer 1992), possibly leaving the wider organisational problems undetected or unreasonably dismissed (Wood 1997a: 26–27). This means that explanations of conflict of interest must look beyond individual pathologies as an explanatory factor. Organisational factors, including ingrained patterns of working in day-to-day policing, provide a more powerful explanation of the propensity of police officers to engage in conflict of interest behaviours (see Fitzgerald 1989; Wood 1997a).

Many explanations of corruption link it with the characteristics of police culture and police culture may also provide some explanation for the existence of conflicts of interest. Identifiable forms of police culture may influence the exercise of the discretion afforded police officers in street-level policing, and this discretionary realm is a key area within which conflicts of interest may be manifested. In addressing the causes of police misconduct, Commissioner Fitzgerald noted:

> [T]he lack of any clear definition of what is permissible and ambivalent community attitudes have the general effect of blurring the distinction between proper and improper conduct for police in relation to some activities. Some matters are relatively easy to cloak in self-justification in various circumstances, for example the acceptance of gifts or discounts can be rationalised on bases which in theory, create no obligation upon the recipient police. Other conduct engaged in by police is blatantly improper. Participation is made easier by involvement in more ambiguous activities, the example of colleagues and sometimes the delusion of corruption is acceptable because particular laws lack universal community support or the offences are consensual and victimless. Police are exposed to enormous temptation whilst knowing that they are protected by the police code. The insurance that it provides against detection and punishment is certainly a major factor which causes many who might not otherwise do so to succumb to that

temptation particularly when the alternative might be ostracism or even persecution (Fitzgerald 1989: 208).

Here, Commissioner Fitzgerald had articulated the notion that organisational factors may combine with distinct forms of police culture to produce motivations and opportunities for misconduct. Police culture is significant because whilst police organisations are characterised by a formal structure, a less formal set of guidelines governs actual police behaviour on a day-to-day basis (Chan 1997, 2001).[6] It is these less formal "states of mind" that give police work its meaning (Crank 1998). A significant amount of police activity may be as much determined by police culture as it is by the formal regulatory structure in which police operate (Reiner 2000: Ch. 3). Police culture is "rooted in the constant problems which officers face in carrying out the role they are mandated to perform ..." (Reiner 2000: 87), and it is largely through police socialisation processes that successive generations of police officers learn the assumptions, values, attitudes, and behaviours acceptable to members of the organisation (Chan 2001; Crank 1998; Reiner 2000: 87).

Particular cultural practices may engender questionable ethical practices within policing. For instance, police may use 'bad' means (breaking or 'bending' the law) to achieve a 'right' end—the prevention or detection of crime, particularly in relation to 'hard to police' areas such as drug trafficking, prostitution and gambling (see Dixon 1999b). These police activities can generate an environment or culture of questionable ethical practice although they may produce effective law enforcement outcomes (Palmer 1992; Settle 1995; Kleinig 1996; Miller et al. 1997; Skolnick and Fyfe 1996, 1993). The path to 'good cause' or 'process' corruption can be rationalised throughout the ranks of the police service as actually *facilitating* the policing role (Dixon 1999b: 44; Wood 1997a; Feldberg 1985). Indeed, evidence suggests that police develop a "hierarchy of wrong" where some actions may be seen as "dead wrong, wrong but not bad, wrong but everybody does it" (Baker 1985: 15; see also Skolnick and Fyfe 1996: 240). In this sense, police themselves make distinctions between "acceptable and non-acceptable deviance" (Dixon 1999b: 45). These rationalisations for unethical or corrupt behaviour are based on a notion that ends can justify means; ends which are, of course, partially

---

[6] A range of work has contributed significantly to the understanding of police culture (e.g. Chan 1997, 2001, 1999a, 2000, 1996; Fitzgerald 1989; Wood 1997a, 1997b, 1997c; Skolnick 1994; Reiner 1992; Sherman 1985; Shearing and Ericson 1991; Coady et al. 2000; Bellingham 2000; Bolen 1990; Dixon 1999a; Gould 1997; Goldsmith 1990; Kappeler et al. 1998; Crank 1998).

constitutive of the police role (Miller *et al.* 1997: 103), even though this ignores the centrality of legal *means* that are equally constitutive of the police role. However, when questionable ethical practices are ingrained in police culture, this inhibits public trust in policing:

> The organizational culture of the police service—the shared assumptions, beliefs, and most important, behaviour of individual officers and the service as a whole—is critical if the public is to trust the police to do their job in an honest, fair, efficient and lawful manner. And if that trust is there the public is far more likely to co-operate fully with the police ... (Graham 2006: 4).

These insights about police culture are particularly relevant to the problem of conflict of interest for two key reasons. First, consistent with the notion of 'process corruption', police officers may perceive the furthering of relationships and contacts gained in the course of their work, through the granting of favours or acceptance of gifts, to be consistent with the ends of policing, and therefore not giving rise to an ethical problem. Secondly, many types of conflict of interest may be culturally ingrained within street-level police practice and therefore be perceived by police officers as being relatively low on the hierarchy of wrong. Police officers may perceive such 'minor' conflicts of interest as presenting less of an ethical dilemma than more obvious forms of corrupt activity.[7]

II   This Study

The term *conflict of interest* covers a wide variety of behaviours. This study identifies 25 separate types of transgressions. Each type of behaviour is explored in detail, examining the nature of the conflicts and types of interests involved and providing an explanation of why these behaviours are problematic for both the police force and the public. Overall, this book addresses five core areas:

♦   An appropriate definition for conflict of interest;

---

[7] The window-shutter kickback scam provides an excellent example of a form of misconduct that may be regarded as "low-level corruption" where many officers failed to see that their conduct was unethical—as concluded by the Victorian Ombudsman (1998b).

- An examination of the dimensions of the problem of conflict of interest in policing and how conflicts of interest may impact on police officer performance of duty;

- Consideration of how the problem of conflict of interest relates to the ethical conduct of police officers, and to broader questions of police accountability;

- Studying how the problem of conflict of interest is governed in practice; and

- Analysis of how the problem of conflict of interest should be appropriately governed.

At a micro level the book identifies and describes the policing scenarios that give rise to complaints of conflict of interest, and categorises these into types of conflict of interest, exploring the circumstances, relationships and pressures that may give rise to conflict of interest breaches. In addition to the collection of information relating to situational and organisational factors, the study also assembles an array of data relating to individual officers' involvement, examining profiles and motivations. Outcomes and sanctions are documented along with the various processes that police officers employ to avoid sanctions and responsibility, and police management attempts to discipline officers. In addition, the study offers insights into:

- The way complaints proceed through the police discipline system, particularly in relation to initial investigation and internal review;

- The way in which the oversighting role of the office of the Ombudsman works in practice;

- The way in which police management responds to the public (complainants), the office of the Ombudsman, police members, and (to a lesser extent) the Victoria Police Association; and

- The manner in which contemporary police policy in relation to conflict of interest is created.

The empirical research for the book is based on conflict of interest complaints case files containing original, uncensored, first hand, documentary evidence. These files represent a hitherto unexamined profile of the various regulatory processes undertaken by Victoria Police involved in dealing with complaints about particular forms of police behaviour. They provide details of the inner workings and actual practice of the Ombudsman's oversight and monitoring role of complaints against police in the arena of conflict of interest.

A   Complaint Cases

This book draws on a study of 377 conflict of interest complaint cases for the ten-year period commencing in May 1988, when the position of Deputy Ombudsman (Police Complaints) was established with responsibility for reviewing complaints against police. The cases examined were identified by the Victorian Ombudsman's office as constituting *all* complaints against police for the ten-year period where conflict of interest was the primary element of complaint.[8] A total of 539 police officers were involved in these complaints.[9]

Figure 1.1 shows the pattern of complaints over this ten-year period. The *year* in this breakdown relates to the time the case file was established—that is, the year the complaint was lodged and acted upon, not the year the case was finalised. (Most cases are lodged, investigated and finalised within the same year, but some cases take longer from file initiation to completion.)

Whilst the number of complaints varied from year to year, most notable is the increase in the number of complaints lodged in the years 1994–1996. The increase across this period occurred against a backdrop of an across-the-board *decrease* in complaints against police more generally, at least according to Victoria Police annual statistics (Victoria Police 1995, 1994, 1996a). This rise in conflict of interest complaints during 1994–1996 suggests that there may have been greater attention to the problem of conflict of interest during this period.

---

[8] The sample is not likely to include *all* examples of complaints against police for conflict of interest breaches over the ten-year period, due to several factors. These include: a complainant did not proceed with a complaint; complaints may have been resolved via an apology or remediation at a local station level and therefore not progress to an Internal Investigations Department or Ethical Standards Department complaint file; some complaints may have involved conflict of interest as a secondary element of a complaint where the primary focus was on another allegation (such as assault); and a small number of case files were unavailable for examination because they had not progressed through to finalisation in internal Victoria Police disciplinary processes.

[9] Although 377 cases and 539 police officers are included in this study, case and officer numbers referenced in the qualitative discussion later in the book range from 1-394 for cases and 1-562 for police officers. These numbers were assigned in the initial stages of analysis, but several cases and police officers were deleted from the data set during the detailed data checking processes undertaken – mostly due to repetition within the data set (see Davids 2005: Ch 2).

Figure 1.1: Ten Years of Conflict of Interest Complaints[10]

Number of Complaint Cases per Year

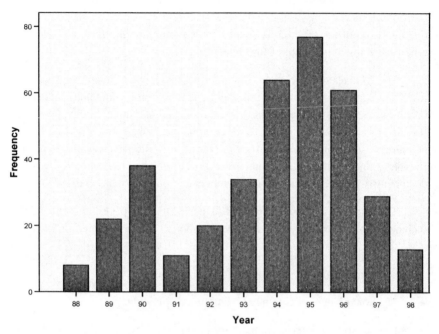

(Total of 377 cases in the ten year period)

(These cases involved complaints against a total of 539 police officers)

The period does approximately coincide with the operation of the Conflict of Interest Working Party (1995–1997), which represented an official recognition within Victoria Police management of the magnitude of the problem. It is perhaps not surprising, therefore, that a greater number of complaints against police officers were formally classified as involving

---

[10] The 1988 and 1998 years include less than twelve months, as the sample commenced in May 1988 and finished in mid 1998. In addition, figures from 1996–1998 are slightly understated due to 20 per cent of the files for these years being unavailable, mainly due to their not having progressed to finalisation.

13

conflicts of interest during this period,[11] although there was no apparent policy change in recording or complaint categorisation that would otherwise account for this increase. In addition, some commentators have noted that in periods characterised by greater publicity of police misconduct, people are less inclined to accept in silence what is unacceptable to them (Stubbs 1992). The period 1994–1996 was recognised by Victoria Police itself as being a testing time for the organisation. Thus it might be the case that the increase in complaints relating to conflict of interest relates to a reduction in the rate of *under-reporting* of this type of police misconduct.

The complaint case files contained a diversity of complaint sources including aggrieved members of the public acting alone, complaints lodged on behalf of members of the public by solicitors, other public service agencies, friends, or private businesses, and complaints lodged by Victoria Police members against other police officers. Due to their largely *formal* nature, the files examined were in the main composed of detailed and well-written documents written by senior police members and other professionals.

The files varied in size from 100 pages to 400 pages or more. They included information relating to the investigation of the case, including:

♦ The allegation against a police officer or police officers and supporting statement from the complainant;

♦ Personal letters of complaint from the complainant;

♦ Transcripts of interviews by the investigating officer of the complainant, officer(s), witnesses;

♦ Reports and photographs from medical personnel, if appropriate;

♦ The personal details of the police officer(s) involved;

♦ A full description of the case;

♦ A summary and recommendations by the investigating officer;

♦ Comments and recommendations from senior or oversighting officers (usually of the rank of superintendent) within Victoria Police;

---

[11] The Deputy Ombudsman and Victoria Police operate a dual entry, cross-notification classification coding system for complaints.

◆ Records of scrutiny of the recommendations by the Internal Investigations or Ethical Standards Department (if they had not conducted the initial investigation); and

◆ Comments from the Deputy Ombudsman (Police Complaints), in oversighting the investigation and outcomes;

◆ Documents outlining the charges and associated Briefs if the police officer chose to have the matter determined by the Chief Commissioner;

◆ Documents relating to the resolution of each complaint, such as letters from Victoria Police to the complainant and the officer(s) advising them of the outcome of the investigation, letters from the Police Association, or if the matter was a minor one but the police officer concerned still contested the outcome, letters from the police officer's welfare officer or other key supporters within Victoria Police;

◆ Comments from the Assistant Commissioner, Internal Investigations, when relevant, and if a case had sparked debate either as to the quality of the investigation and its outcome, or the policy ramifications of the particular type of complaint, relevant correspondence between Victoria Police and the Deputy Ombudsman and documents relating to legal opinion as to whether a charge was likely to be successful, and what the overall policy ramifications might be.[12]

The complaints history of police officers was not included in each complaint file, and was therefore not available for the research. Unlike the standard practice in some other police jurisdictions, at the time of this study Victoria Police complaint files did not, as a matter of procedure, include a summation of the police officer's complaint and disciplinary record. However, there were occasional references to an individual's record, and if a complaint proceeded to a Disciplinary Hearing, then the police officer's complaints and discipline history was often requested and may have been included in the relevant Brief.

Two-thirds of complaints during the period under examination were against a single police officer; a further 16.7 per cent of cases involved two

---

[12] It should be noted that material contained within the complaint case files is drawn upon throughout the book, but unless the specific name or type of document or author is relevant to the analysis, these details are not included in order to ensure that maximum confidentiality is maintained.

officers, and 7.2 per cent of cases involved three officers. In 4.8 per cent of cases there were 4–7 officers involved. The remaining cases were not directed against a specific officer or officers—these were complaints against police in general, or against all police at a nominated station, for example (18 cases—4.8 per cent of the total sample).

In summary, the nature of the empirical materials provides the opportunity to map the following key features:

♦   Types of behaviour regarded as constituting conflict of interest;

♦   Responses by the police force to conflict of interest complaints;

♦   Policies and procedures adopted by the various parties; and

♦   Outcomes and sanctions applied to police officers.

The research for this book did not in any way set out to duplicate official investigations of conflict of interest complaints. Attempts were not made to 'judge' whether investigators 'got it right'. In short, the focus is on qualitative and quantitative description, analysis, explanation, and evaluation of conflict of interest complaint cases. The files represent the 'stories' of multiple 'tellers' and reflect, to a significant degree, their lived experiences and own (often competing) values and interests (see Manning and Cullum-Swan 1994).

The use of original documentation from within the files means that the empirical materials are *non-reactive*, that is, they were constructed for purposes other than study or research. The various contributors to the totality of each individual file did not envisage or anticipate being studied, thus each contributor is unlikely to have felt or been bothered by the 'guinea-pig' effect. This does not mean that the contents of the files, or indeed the research, are free of bias but rather that this form of data collection itself has not changed the data being collected (see Bailey 1994: 295).

Chapters Four to Seven provide detailed analyses encapsulating most of the individual cases included in the study. For these chapters, individual case scenarios were chosen for their ability to illustrate wider points that emerged from the full set of cases, illustrating the breadth and range of the issue of conflict of interest, giving an overview of the types of activities that can undermine the public's trust in a police force.

CHAPTER TWO

Conflict of Interest:
Defining the Problem and its Dimensions

I   Introduction

This chapter defines the problem of conflict of interest and its various dimensions, and considers the relationship between conflict of interest, police misconduct and police corruption. The chapter has three major aims. First, an extensive critical examination of the literature on conflict of interest is undertaken, drawing both on the limited literature relating to conflict of interest in policing and more general literature from other public sector and professional domains. The second major aim is to develop an outline of the various types of conflict of interest that may be manifested in policing. This draws on an examination of the different types of conflict of interest evidenced in the ten years of complaint case files, which are used to develop a topographic picture of the various manifestations of conflict of interest. The third major aim of the chapter is to consider how conflict of interest relates to the broader questions of police ethics, police misconduct and corruption. The chapter also briefly considers the regulatory realm within which conflict of interest is dealt with at an official level.

II   What is Conflict of Interest?

A   *Conflict of Interest*

Conflicts of interest involve clashes between two key factors: private interests and official or public duty. Some studies have distinguished *three* types of interests when discussing conflict of interest: (1) the personal interests of an actor; (2) the interests of the actor's organisation; and (3) the interests of society or the public (e.g. Macklin 1983; see Rodwin 1993: 253–255). In the present study, due to the public role of policing as the domain of interest, the latter two categories are conflated within the general notion of the official/public duty of a police officer. Thus, conflict of interest in policing may be characterised as a disjunction between private interests and the public interest, because police, like other public officials, are regarded as having served the public interest when they "faithfully perform their official duties" (Integrity Commissioner 2002a: 2).[1]

In recent times, the Victoria Police Code of Conduct has characterised conflict of interest as arising for a police officer "if you allow your personal beliefs, associations or financial interests to interfere with the impartial performance of your duties" (Victoria Police 1998b: 15). Although recognised as a particular type of problem, conflicts of interest are dealt with within a general framework of otherwise undifferentiated discipline processes and procedures of Victoria Police.[2]

1   *Public Duty*

A *conflict of interest* is possible where there is a divergence between any part of a police officer's private interests and their work or public duties, such that the police officer may neglect his or her official duties in the pursuit of private interest. Therefore, a conflict of interest can be manifested at any point where an officer must make a choice between taking an action that furthers private or personal benefit, and the 'disinterested' performance of official work duty. Official duty is necessarily broadly defined in order to encompass not only clearly enunciated and specific work roles, but also other factors such as the good management, public perception of the police force as a whole, and the maintenance of public trust in policing.

Conflicts of interest are particularly important because they represent a key threat to at least four of the seven core principles of public life, as

---

[1] Conflicts of interest have also been distinguished from conflicts of *commitment*. In the latter, the conflict is between two or more sets of professional commitment (arising within the same role or from competing professional roles) (e.g. Werhane and Doering 1992).

[2] In 2006, Victoria Police produced a conflict of interest training package as part of an "ethical best practice" series. The package includes a DVD depicting a series of ethical breaches and showing Victoria Police employees in conflict of interest situations. The training program which utilised the DVD package is expected to take approximately 90 minutes to complete. It is regarded as an important means of tackling the problem of conflict of interest through ongoing training and awareness-raising.

enunciated in the United Kingdom by the Committee on Standards in Public Life:

Selflessness

Holders of public office should take decisions solely in terms of the public interest. They should not do so in order to gain financial or other material benefits for themselves, their family, or their friends.

Integrity

Holders of public office should not place themselves under any financial or other obligation to outside individuals or organisations that might influence them in the performance of their official duties.

Objectivity

In carrying out public business ... holders of public office should make choices on merit ...

Honesty

Holders of public office have a duty to declare any private interests relating to their public duties and to take steps to resolve any conflicts arising in a way that protects the public interest ... (Nolan *et al.* 1995: 14).

Of these values, integrity, in particular, occupies a central place in the Victoria Police discipline system, where it has been defined as "demonstrated uprightness, trustworthiness, honesty and moral soundness in actions and decisions. Its basic manifestations are personal values and beliefs, organisational aims, and individual behaviour" (Victoria Police 1996d: 23).

This focus reflects a wider contemporary emphasis on integrity as a key value of public life. The OECD (2000) has identified integrity as the key to forging strong links between expected ideals and formal behaviour. The Committee on Standards in Public Life recognised that a series of well-publicised cases of misconduct by various public officials had led to conflict of interest becoming a major issue in damaging public perceptions of integrity in the United Kingdom and other Western countries. Conflicts of interest were found to contribute to an erosion of the "principles and values of public life", bringing public institutions into disrepute (Nolan 1996).

Integrity, and the trust that flows from it, may thus be regarded as the key value under threat from conflicts of interest (Werhane and Doering 1992; Siemensma 2000; Graham 2006).

2 Two Components

Mere differences in interests between two parties are not sufficient to constitute a conflict of interest from an organisational or professional perspective. It is the capacity of a particular interest or particular kind of interest to conflict with the discharge of occupational or professional duty that gives rise to a problem (Carson 1994). The *conflict* in conflict of interest takes place *in the mind*. It is the impaired or undermined judgment that may flow from a conflict, rather than a role conflict *per se*, that is problematic (Davis 1982). The types of *interests* that may conflict with official duty may include a range of financial and non-financial interests.

Conflicts of interest are pervasive in many aspects of social, organisational and political life, and it has been said that they give rise to one of the most common forms of unethical conduct in the public service (Kernaghan and Langford 1990: 133). In his study of conflict of interest in American public life, Stark (2000) argues that the debate about conflict of interest in the United States, and the treatment of it, particularly in relation to the behaviour of politicians and other public officials, has transformed over the last thirty years. In the United States a distinctly *objective* approach has been taken to the concept of 'conflict' whilst a deeply *subjective* understanding of 'interest' has emerged.

(a) Interests

Conflicts of interest are not in themselves unethical because the existence of multiple interests is to be expected as a "part of the human condition" that is common for any "socialized, passionate, interested human being functioning in a complex world" (Werhane and Doering 1992: 51, 50; Preston *et al.* 2002: 83–85). Therefore, it would be expected that individuals would have some interests that may conflict with official duties at some time. The ethical challenge lies in the recognition and management of conflicts of interest in a way that keeps interests that are extraneous to official duty from directly or indirectly influencing the exercise of that duty. The key element of interests that distinguishes conflict of interest from other forms of official wrongdoing is, indeed, that they have the *capacity* to affect the performance of public duties, *whether or not* this capacity is actualised (see Owen 1997: 41).

The *interests* of concern in conflict of interest are encumbrances on an official in the performance of official duties (Stark 2000: 9). In this context, the term 'interest' may be taken as shorthand for "any influence, loyalty, or other concern capable of compromising ..." the performance of a duty specific to a role (Davis 1982: 18). In situations where a police officer's private interests may *coincide* with his or her public duty, and the performance of that duty may further his or her private interests, a conflict still exists because of the police officer's general duty to perform official functions in a disinterested manner. The private interests that exist in such circumstances cannot be objectively removed from the situation, and thus it is not possible to clearly determine whether such interests have influenced the performance of official duty. Therefore, conflicts of interest may appear even where there is a *coincidence* between the private interests and public duty of a police officer. For example, an officer may be in a position where he or she must decide whether or not to arrest someone he or she knows. Solely on the facts of the matter as known to the police officer, it may be decided to not make an arrest. Even though this decision may be regarded as appropriate in the circumstances, it is nevertheless tainted by the police officer's personal interest in the matter. The police officer's state of mind may not subjectively be tainted, but a reasonable observer would not necessarily conclude that the police officer had the necessary degree of disinterest in the matter. Although such a situation may not involve a breach of the duty of the police officer in relation to the powers of arrest, it falls within the rubric of conflict of interest because it involves a breach of the police officer's general duty not to become officially involved in, or take action in relation to, matters in which he or she has a personal interest.

Traditionally the types of interests included within the concept of conflict of interest were exclusively financial or pecuniary (Owen 1997: 41). *Black's Law Dictionary* defines a conflict of interest as relating to the "private pecuniary interest of the individual" (cited in Carson 1994: 390). A number of authoritative sources continue to restrict conflict of interest to its narrow pecuniary sense, where the individual stands to gain in money (or equivalent) terms (see Rodwin 1993: 9, 274; Kernaghan and Langford 1990: 136–137; Nolan *et al.* 1995). This is of limited use because it ignores the fact that a range of non-financial interests, including 'subjective' or 'ideological' biases, can encumber an official in much the same way as financial interests can, having similar effects. It is also misleading because the financial sense only brings out a narrow range of concerns that relate to conflict of interest.

Thus, in its most contemporary use, the concept of *interests* has been expanded to include "various associational and partisan attachments and diverse other influences, loyalties, concerns, emotions, predispositions, prejudgments, even moral beliefs and aesthetic judgments"—all of which can arguably encumber an official's judgment every bit as much as financial holdings (Stark 2000: 4–5, and Ch. 10; Preston *et al.* 2002).

With the expansion of the notion of interests, the key problematic within conflict of interest has moved from a "diversion of the state's resources to [a] private official" (centred on pecuniary interests) to interference with the effective performance of official duties (dealing with a range of interests) (Langford, cited by Owen 1997: 42). Even objective pecuniary interests have come to be regarded as problematic *because* they can be taken to represent an underlying *ideological impairment* or prejudice, in a similar manner to these other broader interests. Concomitantly, the central concern with conflicts of interest has moved towards the broad issues of integrity of officials, public confidence in the public sector, and the legitimacy of the public sector itself (Owen 1997).

For conflict of interest regulation, the key distinction is between interests that are encumbering and those that are not (Stark 2000: Ch. 10), although a more distant *potential* or *possibility* that interests may interfere with proper action in an official capacity is also regarded as problematic (see Davis 1982: 18–21). Encumbrances may be internal or external. *Internal* encumbrances act from *within* the person, being based in personal pecuniary interest, predispositions, preferences, beliefs, prejudgments and the like. A desire to enhance one's professional or personal reputation could also give rise to a conflict of interest if this desire became so significant that it influenced an individual to neglect official duty in pursuit of an action or outcome that might enhance personal reputation (see Werhane and Doering 1992). These may be regarded as *direct* conflicts of interest. *External* encumbrances are imposed or initiated by others who act *on* the person. These include familial, friendship, professional, and associational relationships, where the interests of the *other* person may have the capacity to affect the performance of official duties (see Carson 1994; Macklin 1983; Boatright 2000: 144–145). Such interests may be regarded as relating to *indirect* conflicts of interest.

Interests of concern relate not only to the positive interests of self, family, friends, or associates, but also include an interest in action that thwarts the interests of 'enemies', or parties in opposition to the self (see Carson 1994: 388). Thus conflict of interest may be manifested in the *opposite* of preferential treatment for enemies of the actor. In policing, this could involve discriminatory enforcement of the law against particular individuals (or groups) (Royal Canadian Mounted Police External Review Committee 1991: 69). That is to say, it could be *in* the interests of a person to act *against* the interests of a party opposed to that person. Where such a situation exists and there is a potential neglect of official duty, it is regarded as a conflict of interest.

(b) *Conflicts*

Problematic interests are those that conflict with official duties, and the *conflict* in conflict of interest "is a collision between competent judgment and something that might make that judgment unable to function as the ... role requires" (Davis 1982: 19). Conflict arises when a personal interest does not coincide with an obligation to serve the interests of another (Boatright 2000; Werhane and Doering 1992). The element of obligation to another is important because it is the potential for breach of this obligation in the pursuit of personal interests that makes conflict of interest problematic. The conflict is relative to the exercise of competent judgment that is required within a particular role, where there is a discretionary element in the judgment to be made (Davis 1982: 22–25).

Although the *conflict* in conflict of interest takes place *in the mind*, affecting an official's capacity for judgment, it is extremely difficult to peer into the mind in order to determine whether an official actually *was* affected by his or her own interests in judgment, decision-making, and action (Stark 2000). Conflict is therefore regarded as present when there is the *capacity* for a private interest to affect the performance of public duties (see Owen 1997: 40–42).

Conflict of interest regulation deals with acts or situations that are *anterior* to states of mind that might impair judgments. Because the mental disposition of an official would be highly contestable legally, and is "insufficiently factually accessible to constitute the object of regulation and sanction" (Stark 2000: 22), regulation does not focus on the subjective state of mind of an official, but on situations that can be objectively perceived to give rise to conflicts of interest. For example, since it would be practically impossible to legislate or regulate in order to prevent officials becoming judgmentally impaired by their own interests (the real concern), conflict of interest regulation tends to prohibit the holding of certain kinds of interests altogether, and specific conflicts of interest are dealt with when they arise. Because it would be impossible to enforce a law or regulation that prohibited officials from becoming psychologically beholden to others who give gifts to officials, conflict of interest rules tend to prohibit the very act of receiving gifts under an array of circumstances.

Regulatory regimes have therefore moved from "hortatory [exhortive] strictures requiring certain inner states-of-mind toward prophylactic [preventive] laws that prohibit external circumstances or actions that *might lead* to impaired mental states, to conflicted judgment" (Stark 2000: 4, original emphasis). The contestability associated with a subjective definition of conflicts based on states of mind, where in the final analysis adjudication relies on personal judgment, is obviated with the move towards prophylaxis such that regulation and enforcement of conflicts deals with directly observable states, rather than interpretation of perceived mental states. The observable states of concern are those that are thought to give rise to encumbered states of mind, rather than the subsequent acts (breaches of duty) that may flow from such states of mind.

(c)   *Practical Difficulties*

Difficulties remain in relation to the identification and regulation of a broad range of interests and motivations, and with monitoring appropriate boundaries between the personal interests of the employee/official and the proper and impartial execution of their duties and responsibilities. If conflicts of interest cannot be eliminated entirely, decisions must be made about where to draw the line (see Young 2002; Rodwin 1993: 10). For an interest to be regarded as problematic, does it have to be a direct, internal interest or is an indirect, external interest sufficient to require scrutiny? As noted above, an indirect, external interest might be a situation where a benefit is provided to some other person with whom the official has a relationship as a friend, family, colleague, neighbour, or club affiliate, amongst a range of possible problematic relationships. In such situations, a test of remoteness may be used to assess whether a personal interest cannot reasonably be regarded as exercising influence on an individual, and therefore not considered to be conflicting (Royal Canadian Mounted Police External Review Committee 1991: 4–8).

A further test of triviality may be required to determine whether an interest is so minimal so as not to pose a *conflict* at all. Such considerations demonstrate that elements of judgment remain in determination of conflict of interest problems, notwithstanding the move to more objective notions of conflict. Siemensma (2000) describes conflicts of interest as "blind spots" that arise from clashes between different aspects of the lives of individuals. She suggests that recognition of problems of conflict of interest require individuals to "shift position" in order to see the connections and influences between different aspects of their lives.

3   *Financial and Non-financial Interests*

In light of the discussion and distinctions in the above subsection, the nature of the interests involved in conflict of interest complaints was examined. Complaint cases were coded as to the broad type of interest involved, with the breakdown as follows:

1.   Conflict relating to the private financial interests of the police officer (21.2 per cent);

2.   Conflict relating to the private non-financial interests of the police officer (54.6 per cent);

3.   Conflict relating to the private financial interests of a friend, family member, or acquaintance of the police officer (4.6 per cent);

4.   Conflict relating to the private non-financial interests of a friend, family member, or acquaintance of the police officer, or both (19.5 per cent).[3]

This illustrates two key factors. First, the significance of non-financial interests, with almost three-quarters of cases examined involving non-financial interests, either in relation to the direct interests of the police officer or those of family, friends, or acquaintances of the police officer. This finding underlines the importance of extending the definition of interests to incorporate a range of non-financial encumbrances. The second key point relates to the proportion of cases where there was not an internal or direct interest of the police officer involved, but an external interest—that is, the interests of family, friends, or acquaintance of the police officer. Almost one-quarter of all cases involved such external interests, illustrating that although direct interests constitute the

---

[3] The intention here is to examine the *range* of interest involved. Therefore the complex mix of internal/external, financial/non-financial conflicts was simplified as follows. Wherever the police officer concerned had a direct/internal conflict of interest in the matter, the coding was based on the police officer's interest. If the conflict of interest was indirect/external—the interest of a friend, family member, or acquaintance of the police officer only—the matter was coded according to that external interest. A number of specific financial and non-financial encumbrances relating to the private lives of police officers were identified from the complaint case files; these are discussed later in the book.

greater proportion of cases, indirect and external interests are also an important part of the problem.

The breakdown of type of interest each year over the 10-year period of the study is illustrated in Figure 2.1. There is no discernible change in pattern during the period. Non-financial interests constitute the majority of complaints in each year. For almost all years, the complaints included a mix of direct/internal and indirect/external conflicts of interest, again underlining the general importance of a broad notion of conflict of interest.

Figure 2.1: Financial and Non-financial Interests (Year-by-year)

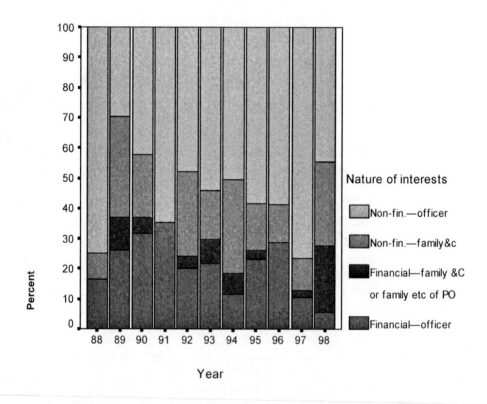

Where financial conflicts were involved—for the police officer or relating to a friend, family or acquaintance of the police officer (matters relating to 143 police officers; almost 27 per cent of the total)—the type of financial interest concerned was examined, in order to provide insight into the various *types* of financial interests that may be involved. The principal types of financial gain found are summarised in Table 2.1. As the table shows, financial gains in terms of money or money equivalents represented almost half of matters alleged against police officers (48.3 per cent), with free or reduced price goods or services or better quality goods or services being the gain in relation to an additional 19.6 per cent of police officers. For almost 10 per cent of police officers, the gain related to the private use of police resources without fully paying for their use. Some form of business advantage was alleged in relation to almost 10 per cent of police officers, and for a further 12.6 per cent the gain related to secondary employment arrangements (including the holding of a second job, self-employment, or undertaking private business).

Table 2.1: Types of Financial Gain

Principal financial gain attained or alleged	N	%
Free or reduced price good	19	13.3
Free or reduced price service	7	4.9
Money or money equivalents	69	48.3
Employment (incl. self-employment; private business)	18	12.6
Police resources used (private use; not fully paid for)	14	9.8
Business advantage	14	9.8
Better quality good or service, or guaranteed completion or delivery	2	1.4
Total number of cases	**143**	**100.0**

These financial gains are grouped into four major categories as shown in Figure 2.2. Gains related to money and money equivalents dominate the financial gains during the period of this study, but other areas of gaining of price or similar advantages, and secondary employment arrangements are significantly represented. This finding shows the need to consider a wide range of financial interests within the concept of conflict of interest.

Figure 2.2: Types of Financial Gain
(grouped by type of gain for police officers)

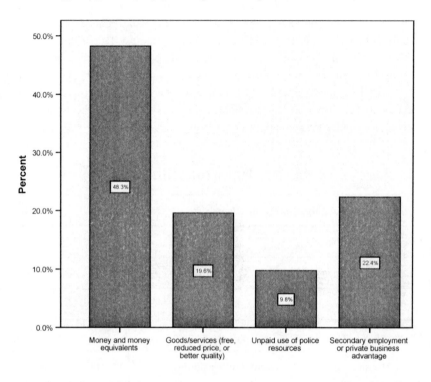

Together, the findings in this subsection are particularly important in light of the earlier discussion about the changing concept of interests within conflict of interest. It is clear that the expansion of the concept to include non-financial interests is in accord with the pattern of public complaints about conflicts of interest in policing. These findings also clearly demonstrate that, in addition to the inclusion of non-financial interests within the concept of conflict of interest, a variety of *financial* interests must also be clearly identified and considered in any attempt to deal with the problem. Further, the inclusion of external interests, that is, those of family, friends, or acquaintances of a police officer, in addition to direct and internal interests, is important. It can therefore be concluded on the basis of this evidence that the broader concept of interests is in accord with public expectations, in so far as these expectations are reflected in complaints received about conflicts of interest in policing.

4   *Real, Potential, and Apparent Conflicts of Interest*

In a widely used definition of conflict of interest, it has been argued that a conflict of interest can be found in three different forms:

1.   A *real* conflict of interest is when a person allows a private interest to influence the exercise of their public duties;

2.   A *potential* conflict of interest is when a person can foresee that a private interest may one day create a conflict of interest but at present it has not;

3.   An *apparent* conflict of interest is when a reasonably well informed person should properly conclude that a conflict of interest could be seen to exist (Parker 1987).

The model of Commissioner Parker has proven popular and has become a basis for discussion about the problem of conflict of interest in a range of contexts (see Kernaghan and Langford 1990; Young 1998, 2002; Royal Canadian Mounted Police External Review Committee 1991; Boatright 2000). The tripartite model of conflict of interest has been formally adopted in the ethical codes of some public service jurisdictions, including police jurisdictions. For example, the Queensland Police *Code of Conduct* specifically singles out conflict of interest as an area of concern. Section Six of the Code instructs officers to arrange their private affairs in a manner that will "prevent any real, potential or apparent conflicts of interest from arising. Ensure there is no incompatibility between their personal interests and the impartial fulfilment of their official duties and responsibilities" (Queensland Police Service undated). When a conflict does arise the officer is instructed to resolve it in favour of the "public interest" and the Queensland Police Force (s 6.1.1).

However, despite its seeming appeal, there are problems with Commissioner Parker's schema in relation to all three forms of conflict of interest outlined. The first set of problems flows from the relatively narrow conception of *real* conflict of interest as requiring *actual acts* at variance with public duty. That is, for a conflict of interest to be regarded as *real*, it must go beyond the conflict itself to a situation where the performance of official duties is *actually* influenced or affected. Anything less is regarded as something that is not 'real'. This obviates the conception of conflict of interest as an encumbrance on an official that may *lead to* a neglect of duty.

Where the term conflict of interest is reserved for *actual* acts at variance with duty, and the lesser expression *potential conflict of interest* is used if the potential for wrongdoing is merely possible, the latter terminology understates the very real risk for harm to be caused (Rodwin 1993: 9–10).[4] Drawing a distinction between actual and potential conflict of interest in this way easily leads to the conclusion that potential conflicts of interest are less problematic than actual conflicts of interest (e.g. Boatright 2000: 143–144). Standard legal usage recognises that conflict of interest situations may cause harm, whether or not the harm has yet occurred (Rodwin 1993: 9).

Parker sees a *potential* conflict of interest as a situation where it could be foreseen that a current interest may have such a deleterious effect, although it has not yet done so. Under this approach, the category of real conflict of interest is reserved for the situation where duty or obligation is actually neglected. It follows that a situation where a person holds private interests that *do* clash with official duties is not recognised as a real conflict of interest, but the less serious situation of a 'potential' conflict of interest. Thus, for example, where a news reporter has private interests that could be affected by the way the reporter writes certain stories, there would only be a *potential* conflict of interest. Only if the reporter actually writes about events that could affect those personal interests could there be an *actual* conflict of interest, and then only once a judgment was made about the reporter's 'objectivity' (this example is used by Boatright 2000: 144). Clearly, this construction narrows the definition of 'actual' conflict of interest considerably.

Drawing on the American Bar Association's Code of Professional Responsibility, Davis (1982: 19) argues that an *actual* conflict occurs when an interest is "certain to affect adversely" the performance of an official duty. But the effect to which Davis refers in subsequent discussion is a *conflict*, not necessarily neglectful or wrong action. Conflicts of interest are situations where the judgments or actions in relation to the official obligations of a person are *compromised* by private interests. Where official obligations are breached, something more than a conflict of interest is evidenced, and calling such *breaches* of duty or obligation 'conflicts of interest' actually obscures the violation of obligations, which goes beyond the problem of conflict of interest itself (Rodwin 1993). Strictly, conflicts of interest are *not* acts; they are situations that increase the risk of deleterious acts (or, of acts that violate

---

[4] Some argue for an even more constrained view of conflict of interest. Kernaghan and Langford (1990: 137–138) relate (and argue against) arguments that seek to define conflict of interest more narrowly than Parker, such that a real conflict of interest would be deemed to exist only where a person actually obtains a private benefit as a result of an official decision or act.

obligations). The key distinction here is between the conflict of interest and the neglects of duty (or other conflictual influences on the performance of official duty) that may flow from such conflicts. Parker's notion of "real conflict of interest" conflates the two. A more appropriate distinction would therefore acknowledge that a conflict of interest (in any form) gives rise to a *potential* breach of duty or obligation.

The second set of problems relates to difficulties with the notion of potential conflict of interest. These problems arise whether real conflict of interest is defined narrowly (as done by Parker) or more broadly. Preston, Sampford and Connors (2002: Ch. 5) define an actual conflict of interest more broadly than Parker—as arising when public and private interests clash, whether or not an official (wrongly) prioritises private interests. Consistent with this broader definition of real/actual conflict of interest, Preston *et al.* (2002: Ch. 5) also discuss what they term *potential* conflicts of interest, using a different notion to Parker's. A public servant is said to be in a potential conflict of interest if a private interest has the potential to interfere with the *future performance* of official duties. The conflict of interest is only 'actualised' if official duties *come into conflict* at some future time. Similarly, Davis (1982) notes that a *potential* conflict of interest may be recognised to be one where it can be *reasonably foreseen* that a future *actual* conflict of interest may arise *if and when* present circumstances change. Such a conflict is regarded as a potential conflict of interest because circumstances must change to make the conflict an actual or real conflict. The key focus of potential conflict of interest here is not a future act in breach of duty, but a future development in official duties that brings them into conflict with private duties. The example provided by Preston *et al.* is of a public official who is appointed to a Statutory Board which may at some future time make decisions regarding a company of which he is a director. They argue:

> The conflict of interest is actualised when matters regarding his company are on the Board's agenda. Recognition of the conflict at its 'potential' stage minimises the prospects of an 'actual' conflict damaging public confidence either through perception or, at worst, some criminal corruption (p 86).

This formulation does not require a possible future *actual* neglect of duty, but a possible future actual clash in private and official interests. A potential conflict of interest for Preston *et al.* is where one might envisage that such a clash *could* emerge in the future. But in this version, where conflict of interest is broadly defined, the category of 'potential conflict of interest' remains problematic for two main reasons. First, it would be nearly impossible to draw the boundaries of the category: by definition *all* interests could be regarded as potential conflicts of interest, since they could come into future conflict with official duties (particularly as the duties themselves evolve).[5] Therefore the category is of limited analytical utility. Secondly, this particular formulation, with its emphasis on perceptions, adds little to the notion of *apparent* conflict of interest, and its attendant problems, to be discussed below.

A more useful distinction may be drawn between conflicts of interest that are *latent* and *actual* (Davis 1982, drawing on the American Bar Association's Code of Professional Responsibility). An *actual* conflict of interest is one where present actions or decisions must be taken in a situation of conflicting interests. A *latent* conflict of interest is where there is no such present action or decision to be taken, but such actions or decisions are within the realm of present duties. Thus a conflict of interest is regarded as *latent* where it has not yet come into *actual* conflict in terms of a specific action to be taken or a decision to be made, but where the particular official responsibilities of the individual are such that there is a 'reasonable probability' that such a conflict will arise in the normal course of those present duties.[6] In either instance— latent or actual—a conflict of interest still exists and is problematic in this particular formulation.

Although the distinction between actual and latent conflicts identified by Davis is somewhat useful, it does not deal with the difficulty implicit in the notion of *potential* conflict of interest. Either an interest can be regarded as conflicting with duties, in the present, or it cannot be regarded to conflict in this way. It is true that as and when official duties evolve and change, conflicts of interest may *emerge*, but the recognition of the problem of conflict of interest *per se* is adequate to deal with such a situation as and when it arises. The notion of potential conflicts of interest adds little of substance to the analysis because

---

[5] Parker's inclusion of a foreseeability factor attenuates this particular problem to a degree, and Davis (1982) notes that a *potential* conflict of interest may be recognised to be one where it can be *reasonably foreseen* that a future actual conflict of interest may arise *if and when* present circumstances change. But, as Davis notes, potential conflicts of interest are regarded as less problematic than actual conflicts of interest (Davis 1982: 20).

[6] Davis describes this as a reasonable probability of "adverse affects" (as opposed to "certainty"). In further discussion, this is related to the likelihood that a conflict will come to fruition (become actual) in relation to a *specific* action that is likely to be taken or decision to be made (but not presently to be taken or made). As noted in earlier discussion, Davis defines a *potential* conflict of interest as requiring a change either in duty or the conflicting interests to make the conflict latent or actual. The American Bar Association's Code of Professional Responsibility condemns both actual and latent conflicts, but potential conflicts of interest are regarded as less problematic.

potential conflicts of interest are not necessarily to be regarded as a separate problem from the general problem of conflict of interest. A separate category of 'potential conflict of interest' is not required to explicitly recognise that any private interest could potentially conflict with public duty. The only interests of real concern from a public policy perspective are those that are real (actual *or* latent) in the present tense, as it is these interests that have the capacity to deleteriously impact on the actual performance of official duties.

The third set of problems with Commissioner Parker's formulation of conflict of interest is associated with the notion of *apparent* conflict of interest (these problems exist whether a broad or narrow conception of conflict of interest, as discussed above, is used). A key difficulty lies in determining whether the test for an *apparent* conflict of interest should be a subjective or an objective one. A subjective test would rest with the judgment and perceptions of a particular individual person (such as an employer or manager, or a member of the public), assuming them to be in the best position to decide. Because such a subjective test rests on individual perceptions, it is not open to independent or outside determination. By contrast, an objective test would rest on a variation of the 'reasonable person' notion, turning on whether a person with average sensibilities would determine that a conflict of interest existed, or at least appeared to exist (whether or not subsequent investigation or the possession of additional information confirmed this appearance). Commissioner Parker clearly felt the reasonable person test should be applied to appearances, with his notion that an apparent conflict of interest occurs when a reasonably well informed person should properly conclude that a conflict of interest *could be seen to* exist (Parker 1987).[7]

In relation to appearances, it is arguable that police officers should be guided by a preparedness to question the way in which their own behaviour may appear to the public. Indeed, in many police codes of conduct around Australia, police officers are now being asked to consider whether their behaviour may have the *appearance of impropriety*. This would seem to involve an attempt to prohibit *apparent* ethical breaches, representing

---

[7] There are different ways that the "reasonable person" test could be applied to appearances or facts (to be determined upon investigation). Should the test be applied to the question of whether a reasonable person, in possession of knowledge about appearances, would determine that it *appeared* there was a conflict of interest (as in the Parker formulation)? Alternatively, is the test to be applied at a later stage in the reasoning process, to the question of whether a reasonable person could conclude that a *prima facie* appearance was sufficiently backed by facts such that *a reasonable person* would conclude there was an *actual* conflict of interest?

application of a higher ethical test than the question of whether the officer has violated a particular law, instruction or rule—a *real* breach. Justification for this higher standard of behaviour for police officers rests with the notion of public interest. It is accepted that police forces "can legitimately demand the highest standard of ethical conduct from their members because of the exigencies of law enforcement" (Royal Canadian Mounted Police External Review Committee 1991: 15). The public interest rests in part with the need for police to carry out their duty with impartiality, along with aspirations by police services to elevate the status of the policing occupation to that of a profession, requiring a higher standard of integrity (Goldstein 1990; Kleinig 1996; Glare 1988, in Victoria Police undated: 4). In dealing with conflict of interest, the application of higher standards than would otherwise prevail is important if a professional group is to gain public respect (Davis 1992: 189).

Critics of this approach, however, question whether police or other officials should be held to account for improper *appearances* even though they may not be in any *real* conflict of interest (Stark 2000: 9–10, 207–212). Stark outlines objections to prohibition of the appearance of conflict of interest in relation to the premise that the appearance standard violates two important legal principles. First, it involves an element of factual pre-judgment in so far as the individual is penalised in advance of or regardless of, any legal determination as to whether an act of impropriety has *actually* been committed prior to an examination of the facts of a particular case. Secondly, the appearance standard involves an element of retroactivity. If the conduct complained about is only one of an appearance of conflict of interest rather than an actual breach of a provision then it is not a violation of a rule or law that can be (specifically) known in advance of the act *per se*. The substance of what is prohibited can only be gauged after the situation has arisen, contingent as it is on whether the behaviour complained about was objectionable to the member of the public or other complainant. Thus, it is argued, conflict of interest appearance standards may be at variance with a fundamental tenet of law that an individual be punished only after a breach of law has been proven, and the substance of that offence be defined before the fact such that an individual can know in advance what is prohibited (Stark 2000: 10).[8]

---

[8] Although it must be recognised that judicial specification of law is commonplace, and thus the "reasonable person" test moves such specification from a subjective to an objective notion of appearances. As with other laws of an open textured nature, over time judicial specification in case law would provide clear indication as to the application of the objective test.

Because it would not be possible to construe conflict of interest regulation so as to prevent the *appearance* of a conflict of interest (at least in a subjective sense), the appearance standard is not prophylactic law, but is hortatory (Stark 2000: 26–27).[9] Mere appearances (to an observer) are not sufficient to impair one's state of mind or to deleteriously impact on one's actions (at variance with official duty). However, if apparent conflicts of interest are prohibited by regulation or law, such a prohibition may *ipso facto* be regarded as prophylactic in terms of preventing diminution of public trust and confidence, but not prophylactic in the sense of preventing impaired judgment or breaches of duty (other than the duty not to *appear* to be in a conflict of interest, where, again, the standard is hortatory).

Once again, a key issue is whether the standard of judgment should be subjective or objective. In the former case, any appearance of a conflict of interest would be prohibited and the exact nature of the relevant perception would be undefinable in advance. But an objective test would be based in the legal notion of the reasonable person—whether a reasonable person would conclude that a conflict of interest appeared to exist (the 'reasonable person' test can thus be applied to both real and apparent conflicts of interest).

In line with these considerations, the definition of conflict of interest produced by Preston *et al.* (2002: 86) is "a potential or actual conflict between [private interest and public duty] sufficient to appear to influence the exercise of one's duty as a public official". This formulation envisages an objective test of appearances: "a conflict of interest involves any situation in which those officials have (or appear, to a reasonable person in possession of the facts, to have) the opportunity to obtain improper advantage for a private interest ..." (Preston *et al.* 2002: 86).

Even if an objective test of appearances is applied, prohibitions of *apparent* conflicts of interest where there is no underlying *real* conflict represent a problematic area for ethical enforcement in so far as appearances are prioritised over actual ethical lapses. But even when no wrong *is* done, in terms of breach of duty, *appearances* of a conflict of interest may still be regarded as problematic due to their capacity to affect public perceptions (Preston *et al.* 2002) or the credibility of police officers (Devery and Trevallion

---

[9] A prophylactic rule or law can be breached without *necessarily* violating the obligations or otherwise neglecting duty, such violation as the rule or law is designed to prevent (see Grano 1985; Stark 2000: 25–27).

2001). The mere appearance (or perception) of conflict of interest can erode public confidence and trust in the individuals concerned and the organisation as a whole. This capacity for *apparent* conflicts of interest to subjectively affect *observer* (public) perceptions can become so important in the management of ethical confidence in the public sector that it assumes centre-stage. Community satisfaction with the police may depend as much on public perceptions, such as may be determined by the quality of interactions between members of the public and individual police officers, as it does on the successful investigation of crime *per se* (Tyler 1990; Loveday 1994; Tyler 2004; Sunshine and Tyler 2003). Indeed, the impact of appearances of conflict of interest on public trust may well be a primary reason for concern about conflict of interest (Graham 2006), which might otherwise be regarded as a minor matter (see Kernaghan and Langford 1990: 139–140). In general, the overriding goal of conflict of interest regulation is to "enhance confidence in public institutions" (Young 1998: 2), and this imperative may justify the appearance standard if it is believed that departures from apparent impartiality negatively affect levels of public confidence and trust in police and policing (Royal Canadian Mounted Police External Review Committee 1991: 9). Indeed, it is widely regarded that "perceptions of conflict of interest can be just as damaging as actual conflicts because they undermine public confidence in government" (Crime and Misconduct Commission undated).

Police officers do place themselves in situations that *may* affect their impartiality, judgment, or fairness, and members of the public may construe such behaviour as problematic. That members of the public do so is evidenced by the lodgement of complaints. The regulatory aim to ensure integrity in both appearance and fact is related to the need to gain and retain public trust in policing. This underlies the requirement that police officers remain disinterested in relation to performance of duty, and thus not to become officially involved in matters even where there is a coincidence between private interests and public duty (as discussed earlier), since public confidence that official duties have been performed in a disinterested manner is likely to be diminished in such circumstances.

As Stark notes, prohibition and penalisation of apparent conflicts of interest, whilst going against legal norms, serves an overriding *political* purpose in terms of the maintenance of public trust. It is this concept of public trust that underlies conflict of interest regulation, both in its aim to promote impartiality and integrity in public life and the desire to prevent abuses of official positions (Young 1998). Consequently, regulators and public oversight bodies may take the view that the impact on "public confidence in the integrity of the public sector" makes appearances of conflict of interest as serious as actual conflicts (e.g. Integrity Commissioner 2002a). On this view, it is considered legally and morally appropriate to penalise public officials for "mishandling political optics as well as political realities ... for neglecting to consider 'how things look.'" (Stark 2000: 17).

Nevertheless, different responses to different kinds of conflict of interest may be deemed appropriate: disciplinary responses for real conflicts of interest and non-disciplinary responses for apparent (or potential) conflicts of interest (Royal Canadian Mounted Police External Review Committee 1991: 35).

B   *Clarifying the Definition*

Drawing on the discussion and critique in the preceding subsection, this book will use three definitions to clarify the various elements of conflict of interest and to distinguish between problematic *situations* (or potentially problematic ones) and problematic *actions* (breaches or neglects of duty): conflict of interest, conflict of interest breach, and apparent conflict of interest.

A *conflict of interest* is present when a person's private interests conflict with their official duties, including the general duty to perform official functions in a disinterested manner. Private interests may be direct or indirect and include those of an *associate* of a police officer, such as a family member, business colleague, or friend. This range of interests is significant because a police officer may act in furtherance of them.

This definition is similar to the definition of Commissioner Parker (1987) of a *potential* conflict of interest, although it is not necessary under this formulation for the person with the conflict to be aware of or foresee the conflict of interest. This definition is distinguished from Parker's *real* conflict of interest, as a conflict of interest is regarded as existing *whether or not* a person acts on it by taking any action or decision (or failing to do so) at variance with official duties, or otherwise allows a private interest to influence the exercise of public duties. The definition here is consistent with the approach of Rodwin (1993) and Preston *et al.* (2002), and encompasses both *actual* and *latent* conflicts of interest, as discussed by Davis (1982). The mere existence of a conflict of interest, with or without an attendant breach of duty (discussed below), may require resolution without waiting to see if the conflict does actually produce culpable conduct (Royal Canadian Mounted Police External Review Committee 1991: 36).

A *conflict of interest breach* is a neglect of duty that results from a conflict of interest, including the duty to remain impartial in relation to the performance of the policing role. This is similar to the earlier definition by Commissioner Parker of a *real* conflict of interest. Conflict of interest breaches could be manifested in a number of behaviours and outcomes, including situations where a police officer takes an action or decision in the furtherance of private interests, or fails to take certain actions or decisions in matters in which the officer has a private interest.

The range of possible manifestations of conflict of interest will be considered further below, and in more detail in relation to policing later in the book.

An *apparent conflict of interest* is a situation where it is possible to *prima facie* perceive that a conflict of interest exists, although there is insufficient immediate evidence to conclude as to whether such a conflict actually does exist. The attainment of further information or evidence in relation to the nature of the private interests of the police officer would permit a conclusion as to whether the conflict of interest did exist or not. This definition is at variance with the earlier definition by Commissioner Parker of an *apparent* conflict of interest, taking into account the differences in real conflict of interest, discussed above (that is, a consequent breach of duty is not a necessary component).

Apparent conflicts of interest may be problematic in themselves in so far as they are damaging to the public trust, and/or they may be regarded as a cause for further investigation to determine whether a (real) *conflict of interest* is evidenced.

The pervasiveness of conflict of interest has been highlighted by the Royal Canadian Mounted Police External Review Committee (1991) who argued that almost any complaint against a police officer could conceivably involve a conflict of interest. For example if a police officer failed to properly and thoroughly investigate an offence, this would represent a neglect of duty; however if the police officer had failed to properly investigate an offence of a person whom they knew socially, then it would be both a neglect of duty and a conflict of interest. Indeed, the neglect of duty would be compounded by the conflict of interest and there may be a causal relation between the two (although this particular distinction is not directly made by the Royal Canadian Mounted Police External Review Committee 1991). It is the fact that the neglect flows from the conflict of interest that makes the conflict of interest itself problematic. In a further example, if a member disclosed confidential information they could be charged with a disciplinary offence, however if the member did the same thing but the information was for a family member or relative then it would also be a conflict of interest. Again, the disciplinary offence and the conflict of interest would be related.

Thus, whenever a police officer makes an official choice or takes an official action that puts their private interests ahead of those of the police force, a conflict of interest could be manifested in a neglect of duty or other disciplinary matter. This situation would represent a *conflict of interest breach* in the terms outlined above. Apparent conflicts of interest (or conflict of interest breaches) would be present in situations where another party, on the basis of *limited* or partial information or perceptions, preliminarily concluded (and, for the present purposes, alleged) that there was (or appeared to be) a conflict of interest or a conflict of interest breach, in the terms outlined above. Such an appearance could be confirmed or refuted on further investigation. Nevertheless, appearances of conflict of interest may be regarded as problematic in themselves, and conclusions may be drawn through the application of an objective standard in the terms outlined previously.

By clarifying the distinction between conflict of interest, perceptions of conflict of interest, and neglects of duty or obligation that may arise, it is possible to avoid the potential confusion between conflicts of interest *per se* and wrongful conduct that flows from such a conflict (in the terms provided above, a 'conflict of interest breach'). The distinctions are important because it is possible that dealing with conflict of interest presents a way to eliminate the potential for (and therefore the actuality of) many associated neglects of duty. Understanding the place of conflict of interest within the wider police ethics and police corruption debates becomes important, therefore, in understanding what conflict of interest regulation should be attempting to do. Confusion may be manifested in official ethical pronouncements, making them less effective. For example, the Queensland Government Integrity Commissioner argues that:

> In many instances there will be the perception of a conflict rather than a direct conflict of interest. For example, if a public official has the responsibility of preparing a report on a particular development project and is paid $10,000 by the person developing the project, there is a direct conflict of interest. The developer has bought a favourable report by paying a bribe. On the other hand, if the developer offers to take the official and partner for a weekend cruise on a yacht to inspect the site of the development, the acceptance of such an offer would make it appear that the official is receiving a benefit that will conflict with the duty to prepare an impartial report (Integrity Commissioner 2002b).

The construction of the issues in this example marginalises the *conflict* (impairment) by focussing on different (direct or indirect) *interests*. Whilst it would seem that there is room for interpretation as to whether the cruise (note: in the particular example, with a "partner" on a weekend and more than mere "transportation" to a development site!) represented a conflict of interest *breach* (that is, in a judgmental sense, the facts are not clear-cut) that there is a *prima facie* conflict of interest seems clear. There is a failure to recognise that the second part of the example may well represent a 'direct' conflict of interest *breach* if the receipt of yacht cruise had an impact on the performance of official duty (writing the report). In brief, in the example used, there *is* a conflict of interest under the definitions provided here, it is likely that the public would also *perceive* there to be conflict of interest and a breach of duty. Whether an actual breach was evidenced would be a matter for further investigation and judgment.

III   Manifestations of Conflict of Interest

One of the earliest Australian governmental attempts to specifically identify key aspects of the problem of conflict of interest was presented in a June 1997 special report to Parliament of the then New South Wales Ombudsman, Irene Moss (Moss 1997b). The Ombudsman identified five common areas where conflict of interest complaints continued to be made to her office:

1.   Separating duty and friends;

2.   Separating duty and family;

3.   Separating duty and relationships;

4.   Separating duty and employment; and

5.   Computer accessing.

These areas provide an indication of the types of situations where conflicts of interest may arise in policing, and it is clear that particular kinds of relationships may be problematic. The emphasis on friends, family and other personal relationships underlines the ubiquity of potential conflict of interest situations. It is clearly not possible for a police officer to avoid friendships or familial and other relationships, thus further understanding of the specific types of conflicts that may flow from such relationships is needed.

Stark's "topography of conflict" (Stark 2000: Ch. 2) starts from the "prototypical" offence of self-dealing, and builds four other categories. Kernaghan and Langford (1990: Ch. 6) include eight categories of conflict of interest, many of which are similar to those of Stark. Drawing principally on these two works, along with Moss (1997b; 1997a; 1995), and the Royal Canadian Mounted Police External Review Committee that considered conflict of interest (1991), this section develops a topography of conflict of interest in policing based on the extant literature. The problem is outlined here in terms of two broad domains: the *private* life and *private* involvements of a police officer; and the *public* life and *official* involvements of a police officer (in the capacity of a police officer), reflecting the key problematic in conflict of interest.

The analytical distinction between the private and public domains recognises that involvements, activities, and relationships in either domain can give rise to problems of conflict of interest, but that conflict of interest *breaches* occur in the latter. That is, conflict of interest breaches, by definition, occur in the realm of the public (or official) involvements, activities, and relationships, as this is the context within which neglects of duty may occur, most often within the discretionary realm of policing. Yet the nature of conflict of interest means that the underlying roots of such breaches, in terms of motivations acting on a police officer, are most often to be found in the private life of a police officer.

A   Types of Conflict of Interest

Several different types of conflict of interest relating to elected and other public officials in the administrative and policy-forming organs of government are identified in the literature. Although they will not necessarily directly apply in the domain of policing, they are used in this study as a starting point to build a typology of conflict of interest directly relevant to policing. The typology is developed on the basis of empirical evidence of actual complaints against police.

1   *Private Relationships and Involvements*

Conflict of interest problems arising from the private life of a police officer come about when the relationships and involvements of the police officer *as a private citizen* come into conflict with official duties and obligations. More specifically, private relationships and involvements may provide a source of *motivation* that leads to a neglect of duty in pursuit of the furtherance of a police officer's private interests.

Six broad areas of conflict of interest in this group are identified in the literature. None of these conflicts of interest *necessarily* result in a neglect of duty, and thus a conflict of interest *breach*, but they all elevate the chances of such a breach occurring by providing a possible source of motivation that could lead a police officer to act in such a way as to favour their private concerns and neglect official duties or obligations.

(a)   *Moonlighting and Post Employment*

In policing, neglects of duty may arise if a police officer takes action in their official capacity to favour the interests of an outside employer, or their own interests as an employee, or if the police officer uses their official position to solicit or otherwise gain private business for themselves or their employers. This is an area that has historically produced a large number of complaints, according to both the New South Wales Independent Commission Against Corruption (1997) and the New South Wales Ombudsman (Moss 1997b). The practice of police officers 'moonlighting' in other jobs has been widely recognised by research into police practice (Finnane 1994; Haldane 1986; Shearing and Stenning 1987).

The performance of outside work may clash with the performance of official duties, particularly if the outside employer is in competition with the official employer, if one's work performance is affected, if official property or confidential information is used in the furtherance of outside employment, or if the official uses his or her official position to solicit private business (Kernaghan and Langford 1990: 147). Problems of *appearance* may be particularly significant in this category.

Post employment involves a person, upon ceasing official employment, taking up employment with a private party with whom official dealings had been held, or whose private interests the official had the capacity to influence whilst in official employment. Post-employment can be problematic if a police officer uses his or her official position to cultivate future employment prospects because, in seeking to favour the interests of a potential future employer, the officer may neglect their official duty. A conflict of interest may also arise in such circumstances in so far as the official's performance of duties prior to ceasing official employment is affected by post-employment prospects. Conflicts may also arise if a former police officer is seen to be taking improper advantage of their previous office, such as through the use of confidential information or seeking or gaining privileged access or preferential treatment from former colleagues (Kernaghan and Langford 1990: 149–151; Royal Canadian Mounted Police External Review Committee 1991: 66 and Ch. VIII).

(b) *Political Involvement*

Political involvement may have a negative impact on the impartiality, or appearance of impartiality, of a police officer in the performance of official duties (Royal Canadian Mounted Police External Review Committee 1991: 52–59). This can give rise to a conflict of interest because a police officer may use the prestige and power of their position to further or advance their participation in political activities, or other political objectives.

(c) *Other Associational Involvement*

Involvement in a range of associations may influence or otherwise constrain an officer in the performance of official duties (Royal Canadian Mounted Police External Review Committee 1991: 69–71). For instance, involvements in civic, social, sporting and other community groups may give rise to a conflict of interest in so far as a police officer may use their position to further their participation in such activities.

(d) *Personal Conduct and Relationships*

Where improper personal or private conduct may deleteriously impact on the proper performance of official duties, a conflict of interest may become evident. Private conduct, such as drug addiction, may make one vulnerable to outside pressure, or may bring discredit to the police force as a whole, undermining public trust (Kernaghan and Langford 1990: 152–153). Clearly, a range of private activities could put an individual police officer in a difficult position in relation to their official duties. These include family law related problems, involvement in illicit or illegal activity including drug-taking, potentially problematic sexual relationships, or personal associations with persons of ill repute. For a police officer, particular personal relationships, such as close involvement with a victim of crime, a witness, or an offender, may make it difficult to remain objective in the performance of official duties involving these other parties (Devery and Trevallion 2001).

In brief, personal conduct associated with otherwise private involvements may impinge on the performance of public duty, thus giving rise to a conflict of interest, if it provides a motivation to use an official police position to favour one person or another, or to overlook or otherwise inadequately police particular types of illicit or criminal conduct such as drug-taking, gambling or prostitution.

(e)   *Public Comment*

Public comment on particular areas of interest may flow from an official's private relationships and involvements. Public comment may be detrimental to a police force, particularly where it involves public *criticism*. This may constitute a conflict of interest if it impinges on the confidence of the employer in the police officer to impartially discharge official duties. Even where public comment is explicitly made in one's capacity as a private citizen, if it includes or implies criticism of the police force a conflict of interest may be involved.

On the other hand, 'whistleblowing', the disclosure of *wrongdoing* within an organisation, may constitute a legitimate exception to the general position on public comment (Royal Canadian Mounted Police External Review Committee 1991: 71–73), although it is difficult to distinguish what might be called legitimate and illegitimate public comment.

Where public comment involves the disclosure of official information, this is incorporated within the broad category of *use of confidential information*, discussed in the section on public activities and actions, below.

(f)   *Private Gain from Public Office*

In situations where an official draws on the prestige of their position to reap private gain (which may, for example, be in the form of board membership, fee-for-service transactions, and expenses-paid trips), a conflict of interest may be involved. The official may not become beholden to the external party, and may not be in a position to advance the specific interests of the external party, but the problem arises because they may use their official position to gain private benefit (Stark 2000). This type of conflict of interest is included here as a *private* involvement as it involves a police officer drawing on the prestige of their official position, but not within the realm of their official duties (in board memberships, for example). Thus the conflict of interest flows from the private involvements of the police officer. A conflict of interest arises because the prestige of a police officer's official position has been drawn upon in a private capacity and this may have a subsequent influence on their performance of official duty, particularly in relation to the source of the private gain.

2   *Public (or Official) Actions and Activities*

The public (or official) actions and activities of a police officer provide the context where conflict of interest breaches, as neglects of duty, occur (by definition). While many conflicts of interest arise from the private life of a police officer, as described above, such conflicts may also arise during the course of actions and activities undertaken in the course of the *public* life of a police officer. That is, these actions and activities undertaken *in the course of work as a police officer* may give rise to conflicts with official duties and obligations.

This broad group of problems includes at least seven types of conflict of interest identified in the literature. These conflicts of interest are often played out in the public actions and activities of a police officer, resulting in a range of neglects of official duty (thus conflict of interest *breaches*).

(a)   *Self-dealing*

Where an official has a straightforward capacity to use their official position to affect a personal interest, self-dealing is involved. This may involve taking "action in an official capacity which involves dealing with oneself in a private capacity and which confers a benefit on oneself" (Kernaghan and Langford 1990: 142). In policing, self-dealing may occur if a police officer seeks to acquire stolen property in the course of its otherwise legitimate disposal by the police. The attempt to gain such ownership may lead a police officer to dispose of goods other than within approved official procedures, thus constituting a conflict of interest breach. Self-dealing often involves a police officer performing his or her duty in such a way as to yield private or personal benefit rather than public benefit.

(b)   *Undue Influence, Preferential Treatment, and Influence Peddling*

Undue influence involves an associate of a police officer exercising influence over the performance of the official duties of the police officer (or seeking to do so). This can occur if an associate of a police officer seeks to use the association to gain preferential treatment in relation to a police matter. The discretionary elements within policing mean that there are potentially many instances where such influence could be applied. Undue influence could also potentially be exercised from inside the police force, if one officer seeks to influence a fellow officer in this manner.

Preferential treatment involves a police officer acting in a way that is partial to certain individuals (or appears to be so), especially those who have a familial or other personal relationship with the police officer. In contrast to undue influence, preferential treatment does not necessarily involve the associate of the police officer *soliciting* the advantage. Police officers are particularly vulnerable to this type of conflict if they are involved in, or can otherwise influence, investigations that involve friends, family, or other associates (Royal Canadian Mounted Police External Review Committee 1991: 66–69). A significant form of preferential treatment may arise from police discretion *not* to invoke the law (Goldstein 1960). This low-visibility act may have a significant impact at the point of entry into the criminal justice system and this remains one of the key areas of police activity that is inherently of low visibility (Lustgarten 1986).

Influence peddling involves the active solicitation of benefit in exchange for the exercise of influence. This takes preferential treatment a step further in so far as a police officer *actively seeks* a private benefit in return for an official favour.

In both undue influence and preferential treatment, the conflict of interest arises in relation to the general obligation of a police officer to be fair and unbiased in the performance of their duty. In relation to influence peddling, the problem is further compounded by the active solicitation of a private benefit. Undue influence, preferential treatment, and influence peddling almost always involve neglects of duty and are therefore conflict of interest breaches.

(c)   *Abuse of Office*

Abuse of office involves a police officer using his or her position to coerce others to provide private advantage for the police officer or his or her associates. Coercion may result from the capacity to affect (possibly negatively) the interests of the external party. This type of conflict of interest is like a negative form of influence peddling or preferential treatment. Consequently, a conflict of interest breach will often be involved in abuse of office.

(d)   *Private Payment for Public Acts*

This involves a police officer receiving private payment from an external party, and consequently becoming beholden to that party, even though the police officer may not be in a position to advance the specific interests of the external party. This latter element distinguishes private payment for public acts from straight-out bribery (Stark 2000: 68). The problematic nature of the beholdenness implicit in this category is not in the capacity of the police officer to directly affect the interests of the external party (in a *quid pro quo* arrangement that would be classified as bribery). The conflict of interest flows from the possibility that the external party may call on the police officer to advance the interests of some other *third* party (Stark 2000: 72).

In policing, the performance of a police officer's official duty may effectively confer private benefits on members of the public (such as lowered risk of becoming a victim of crime, or return of stolen property). If the private beneficiary seeks to privately reward the police officer in some way, this may have the effect of influencing the officer in the future performance of their duty, whether or not the reward was offered with such an intention. The anticipation of receiving such a benefit may also, *ex ante*, influence a police officer in the performance of their duty.

The receipt of private payment for public acts does not necessarily involve a conflict of interest breach, but does increase the likelihood of such a breach, providing a definite source of motivation for a neglect of duty in the future (through the possible creation of an obligation to the paying party).

(e)   *Acceptance of Benefits and Gratuities*

A police officer may be offered, and accept, any of a wide range of benefits of nominal or significant value from a private party, whether or not in 'return' for official acts. At the extreme, the acceptance of such benefits may constitute bribery; benefits obtained may be relatively minor but otherwise this type of conflict of interest is similar to private payment for public acts. Like private payment for public acts, the acceptance of benefits and gratuities does not of itself necessarily involve a conflict of interest breach, but does increase the likelihood of such a breach, providing a possible source of motivation for a neglect of duty coincident with the acceptance of the benefit, or in the future.

(f) *Use of Official Property*

The use of official property of any kind, varying from stationery through to office space, or computers, for activities not associated with the performance of official duties may give rise to a conflict of interest if it impacts on the performance of official duty. For example, if the use of such resources diverts them from official purposes and they are subsequently unavailable for official purposes, or if the desire to use official resources for private benefit influences the way official duties such as work allocation are performed. Problems may also flow from a desire to cover-up such unofficial use of police resources. Therefore, a breach of duty (conflict of interest breach) may or may not be involved with the private use of official (government) property.

(g) *Use of Confidential Information*

Use of confidential information may be construed as a subset of the use of official property, but its significance is such that it deserves separate attention in so far as it involves the use of a very particular, but intangible, form of government property (although it can, of course, be produced and used in a tangible form when printed out). Police have access to potentially large amounts of confidential information. The unauthorised access to such information, and particularly the disclosure of same, can have a negative impact on interactions between police and members of the public. If such information falls into the wrong hands (such as persons under police investigation or potential targets of police raids), directly or indirectly, it may compromise the integrity of police operations in the field (see Director—Police Integrity 2005c). The availability via computer of significant amounts of police information means that use (or disclosure) of confidential information is a particular problem for conflict of interest in policing. The problem of unauthorised access to and disclosure or other misuse of police information is regarded as dominating "corrupt activity" in British police forces (Miller 2003).

3 *Translating the Types of Conflict of Interest to the Domain of Policing*

Building from, and informed by, the types of conflict of interest outlined in the previous section, twenty-five separately identifiable types of conflict of interest behaviour were noted in the complaint case files examined for this study.

Table 2.2 summarises the areas that were derived from the complaint case file data in relation to the *private* realm. The table shows how each type of conflict of interest developed in this study is related to the types derived from the literature, discussed in the previous section. Three particular categories of conflict of interest problems were identified as emanating from the private realm: organisational involvements, family-based involvements, and problematic personal relationships. Each of these includes two or three different types of conflict of interest.

Table 2.2 shows the range of circumstances arising in a personal or private life that can interfere with a police officer's performance of public duty. In addition to the more general potential for personal advantage (financial or otherwise), familial and personal relationships, personal and private causes and interests, and problematic personal friendships and relationships have the particular potential to intervene and produce problems in judgment and poor policing outcomes. Many of these situations may be common traps for unwary or recalcitrant police officers where involvement in the private realm may provide particularly fertile ground for divided loyalties from officers.

Table 2.3 summarises the areas of conflict of interest that were derived from the complaint case file data in relation to the *public* realm. Three particular problem groups were identified, each consisting of two or three categories of conflict of interest: (1) the use and abuse of police powers and authority (consisting of three categories: intervention, action of involvement in police investigations and processes; use of police power to harass; and the exercise of improper influence in civil matters); (2) use and abuse of police resources (consisting of two categories: misuse of confidential police information; and misuse of other police resources); and (3) other aspects of police officers' actions and activities that may signify conflicts of interest (consisting of the categories of acceptance or procurement of goods and services; and breach of the law). Within each category are one or more identifiable types of conflict of interest.

Table 2.2: The Categories and Types of Conflict of Interest Used in This Study, Relating to the <u>Private</u> Realm

Literature types	Types of conflict of interest in this study	Category
Outside employment and post employment	Outside employment, or carrying on a business, without permission	*Organisational involvements*
Political involvement	Membership of an organisation involved in politics (for example, local council, political party)	
Other associational involvement	Engagement in civic, social, or other organised activities (for example, member of club, society)	
Personal conduct and personal relationships	Personal family law related problems	*Family-based involvements*
No equivalent category	Relatives and friends with family law and related problems	
Personal conduct and personal relationships	Facilitating intimate personal relationships, or (alleged) sexual misconduct/ impropriety	*Problematic personal relationships*
	Inappropriate relationship with a criminal, informer, or person/ business of ill repute	
	Other problematic personal relationships and friendships	
Private gain from public office	*Not used in this study*	

Table 2.3: The Categories and Types of Conflict of Interest Used in This Study, Relating to the <u>Public</u> Realm

Literature types	Types of conflict of interest in this study	Category
USE AND ABUSE OF POLICE POWERS AND AUTHORITY		
Undue influence, preferential treatment, influence peddling	Failure to act, due to a relationship with an involved party	*Intervention, action, or involvement in police investigations and processes*
Self-dealing	Delaying/discontinuing police processes, due to a relationship of an involved party	
No equivalent category	Taking police action against an opposing party	
No equivalent category	Involvement in an investigation or other processes in relation to an associated police officer	
No equivalent category	Other involvement, investigation, or intervention in a case with a personal interest	
Private payment for public acts	*Not used in this study*	
Personal conduct and personal relationships	Engagement in harassment	*Use of police power to harass*
	Harassment/discrimination	
Undue influence, preferential treatment, and influence peddling	Misuse of authority or position as a police officer in civil matters, with a personal interest	*Exercise of improper influence in civil matters*
	Other improper influence in a civil matter, with no personal interest	
Abuse of office	*Not used in this study*	

Table 2.3: The Categories and Types of Conflict of Interest Used in This Study, Relating to the <u>Public</u> Realm (cont.)

Literature types	Types of conflict of interest in this study	Category
USE AND ABUSE OF POLICE RESOURCES		
Use of confidential information	Access to, and personal use of, police information	*Misuse of confidential police information*
	Disclosure of police information to outside parties	
Use of government property	Misuse of police identity	*Misuse of other police resources*
	Other private use of police resources	
OTHER ASPECTS OF POLICE OFFICERS' ACTIONS AND ACTIVITIES THAT MAY SIGNIFY CONFLICTS OF INTEREST		
Accepting benefits and gratuities	Solicitation or acceptance of a gratuity, benefit, or advantage	*Acceptance or procurement of goods or services*
Self-dealing	Attempt to gain ownership of goods handled in an official capacity	
Personal conduct and personal relationships	Breach of the law whilst off duty	*Breach of the law*
	Breach of the law whilst on duty	
Public comment	*Considered as part of* disclosure of police information	

These categories of conflict of interest demonstrate the wide array of circumstances and range of scenarios that can lead a police officer into a conflict of interest situation, possibly resulting in various breaches of official duty. Drawing on the larger study of conflict of interest in policing in Davids (2005), this book provides analysis and discussion of conflicts of interest in relation to three aspects of conflict of interest[10] and related neglects or breaches of official police duty:

1.   those related to the private realm (Chapter Four);

2.   those related to the public realm that involve use and abuse of police powers and authority (Chapter Five); and

3.   those related to the public realm that involve use and abuse of police resources (Chapter Six).

The discussion in Chapter Four identifies and enunciates the identifiable relationships, involvements, and other circumstances in the private lives of police officers from which the conflict of interest complaint case files show that problematic conflicts of interest often arise. Conflicts are also shown to arise due to the nature of such relationships and involvements themselves, or the associations brought into being by them, and a range of associated conflict of interest breaches are examined.

The areas discussed in Chapters Five and Six involve actions or activities that are inherently at variance with duties that are fundamental to a police officer's position and role. Official involvement in relation to any of these matters usually represents conflict of interest breaches on some level. For example, at a general level, the mere fact of official involvement in a police

---

[10] The remaining areas that related to conflict of interest discussed in Davids (2005), namely acceptance or procurement of goods or services (including receipt of gratuities) and breach of the law are not included in this book because, on the basis of the cases examined it cannot be said that they always represent clear conflict of interest problems and likely breaches. In some instances, they may *produce* a conflict of interest, in others they may be a *manifestation* of a conflict of interest but they do not always represent obvious breaches of duty. Specific acts in these areas are often regarded as problematic because they breach specific regulations, not necessarily because they involve inherent conflicts of interest. As Davids (2005) shows, these areas may signify or give rise to conflicts of interest in any particular instance but conceptually, these areas are just as likely not to involve a conflict of interest as they *are* to involve such conflicts. Interested readers are directed to the broader study Davids (2005) for a discussion of issues such as gratuities and attempts to procure goods and services, along with the wider issue of police officers who breach the law (all in the context of conflicts of interest).

matter involving a friend or family member gives rise to a problem because the relationship may have an impact on the performance of duty. A more specific conflict of interest problem arises in relation to decisions or actions taken by a police officer (for example, a decision not to charge a friend or relative) because it may be difficult to judge the 'correctness' of the decision or action in so far as it cannot be regarded as having been taken without regard to personal interest (whether or not the decision or action may be regarded as 'objectively' appropriate in the circumstances). The particular on-the-job behaviours identified in Chapters Five and Six are associated with the private interests of the police officer or a friend, acquaintance or family, thus involving conflicts of interest and, as the discussion shows, often involving conflict of interest breaches.

CHAPTER THREE

Dealing with the Problem:
The System of Accountability

I Introduction

As argued in Chapter Two, conflicts of interest present a serious problem for public administration, in relation both to their potential to directly lead to breaches of duty on the part of public officials, and to the associated diminution in public trust in the integrity of public officials and institutions. Conflicts of interest may be manifested in many of the dimensions of day-to-day policing.

This chapter examines the day-to-day management of the problem within Victoria Police. The focus is on the regulatory environment faced by Victoria Police and the formal discipline system used within the organisation during the period under review to bring police officers to account for misconduct.

II Conflict of Interest and Police Misconduct

Whilst a range of causal factors can be identified as contributing to police misconduct, the evidence suggests that they are not always easily separable at an operational level. Conflicts of interest may interact with other recognised causal factors of corruption, but conflict of interest as a precursor to or cause of corruption is analytically distinct amongst both the work and non-work contexts that have been identified as providing the roots of corruption (see Miller 2003: 18–24, for example). Prima facie, a large proportion of unethical activity identified by Miller (2003: Ch. 2) could be seen to have its roots in conflict of interest, including: unauthorised disclosure of information, inappropriate associations, obtaining sexual favours, using position to obtain benefits, and inappropriate use of police information and databases. Together these categories constituted 62 per cent of all reports of unethical activity in

Miller's study, although the problem of conflict of interest was not explicitly recognised as a likely precursor to these activities.

A   Context: Empirical Evidence

Insight into the opportunities for conflict of interest can be gained by considering the context (relevant to the policing task) within which conflict of interest complaints arise. Familial and personal relationships, personal and private causes and interests, and the potential for financial or other advantage can lead an individual police officer into a conflict of interest situation involving the officer, his/her immediate family, or more distant family, friends, colleagues or acquaintances. Matters associated with family law, civil matters, criminal matters, or traffic related matters are prominent among the contextual setting in which conflicts of interest arise, accounting for 72 per cent of all complaints against police officers in this study. Figure 3.1 illustrates the context of conflict of interest complaints.

Figure 3.1: Context of Conflict of Interest Complaints

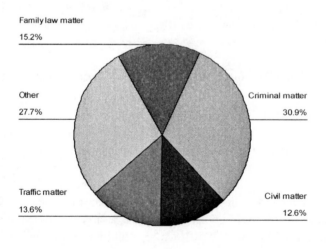

Table 3.1 provides greater detail for these categories, showing the extent of the involvement of the police officer, his/her immediate family, or more distant family, friends, colleagues or acquaintances.

Table 3.1: Context of Conflict of Interest Complaints
(by involvement of police officers)[1]

	Involves police officer or immediate family		Involves other family, friends, colleagues, acquaint-tances		No obvious direct connection to police officer		Total	
	N	%	N	%	N	%	N	%
Family law matter	27	5.0	29	5.4	26	4.8	82	15.2
Criminal matter	51	9.5	54	10.0	61	11.3	166	30.8
Civil matter	31	5.8	25	4.6	13	2.4	69	12.8
Traffic-related matter	31	5.8	23	4.3	19	3.5	73	13.6
Other							149	27.6
Total number of police officers							**539**	**100.0**

These results illustrate how daily police work puts police officers in conflict of interest situations such that *opportunities* and *motivations* for police misconduct in pursuit of a private interest come to the fore. Numerous opportunities in criminal, civil, family law, and traffic matters exist for a police officer to pursue a private interest at the expense of public duty. These contexts and activities are in many respects at the core of police work. The involvement and interests of self, family, friends or associates in the contexts within which a police officer works may also provide police officers with the motivation to pursue private interests.

---

[1] The table shows results in relation to *police officers*. Because some cases involved more than one police officer, the total is more than the number of cases in the study. (The breakdowns shown in Figure 3.1 are also relate to police officers rather than cases.)

B   *Regulatory and Enforcement Difficulties*

Law enforcement in particular areas, such as the regulation of illicit markets including drugs, prostitution and gambling, bring police to the "invitational edges" of corruption (Manning and Redlinger 1977), whereby they are exposed to the influence of 'sellers' who have little legitimate political influence. The prevalence of these criminal activities, and the possibility that some police may themselves have participated in them, make law enforcement in this area complex. The low managerial scrutiny to which many law enforcement activities are subjected means that individual police officers are often brought into an environment where conflicts of interest may be manifested through their contacts (legitimate or illegitimate) with ostensible criminal players.[2]

The specific types of conflict of interest outlined in Chapter Two and the distinction between the private and public involvements, activities, and relationships of a police officer, give rise to regulatory implications. In principle, regulation of the public involvements, activities, and relationships of a police officer presents a relatively straightforward structuring of the work environment, including the exercise of discretion. While opportunities for conflict of interest-related misconduct predominantly occur within the public realm, the motivations for that conduct emanate from the private realm and regulation of the private involvements, activities, and relationships of a police officer goes beyond the bounds of work and work duties. Regulation in this area thus presents a more controversial challenge (Davids 2006). Further, regulation and enforcement difficulties related to the low visibility of much police work are magnified in relation to attempts to regulate the private lives of police officers.

III   Accountability in Operation: The Victoria Police Discipline System

Three broad regulatory approaches are available for dealing with the problem of conflict of interest and associated disciplinary breaches:

---

[2] A stark example is provided by the case of the interaction of two detectives with major criminals through daily operations at the former Major Drug Investigation Division, as outlined in a report into the murder of police informants Christine and Terence Hodson in May 2004 (Director—Police Integrity 2005c).

1. Reducing the potential for conflict of interest, through policy and procedures regulating involvement in activities where conflicts may arise. For example, restriction and regulation of outside or secondary employment and various Victoria Police Manual (VPM) Instructions that relate to matters involving conflicts of interest. These include conflicts of interest in relation to assault investigations (VPM 108-7 (7.1.2)), reporting and investigating offences (VPM 108-2 and 108-3), and donations and sponsorships (VPM 205-5). These policies are enforceable and aimed at avoiding conflicts of interest that may arise during day-to-day policing.

2. Encouraging acceptable conduct and discouraging unethical conduct through the statements and guidelines in the Victoria Police Code of Conduct and organisational value statements, providing guidance to indicate expected standards when involved in areas or activities where there is potential for conflict of interest (such as policies relating to the acceptance of gifts and benefits); and

3. Legislative solutions, with provisions such as section 69(1)(g) of the *Police Regulation Act*, which prohibits police conducting businesses or engaging in outside employment without approval of the Chief Commissioner. The legislative option is largely the approach adopted for regulation of the financial interests of government officials in Canada and the United States of America—particular kinds of involvement are prohibited by law. Care needs to be taken because legislation may merely make potential wrongdoers more "crafty" and "careful" (McGuire 1983).

None of these approaches are without attendant problems and a combination of all three may be used. In Victoria, the provisions of the *Police Regulation Act* 1958 provide the overarching framework for disciplinary regulation, establishing a legislative and regulatory framework that governs both the expected standards of conduct of police officers and the processes and procedures for managing disciplinary breaches within the organisation. Although specific legislative solutions in relation to conflict of interest are not used, the general provisions of the Act, the associated Police Regulations, and the processes for managing disciplinary breaches within Victoria Police more broadly, all apply to conflict of interest situations.[3]

A   System Components

Formal systems of discipline combined with the practice of self-discipline on the part of individual police officers (that is, to fit the 'model officer' as presented to the new recruit), constitute the structures and environment through which police management seeks to effectively shape and define the conduct of police as employees. In its role as an employer, Victoria Police has rules and instructions that govern the workplace. Rules are found in several sources of authority:

♦   Sections 69–86 of the *Police Regulation Act* 1958 as amended, and associated *Police Regulations*;

♦   The *Public Sector Management Act* 1992 (applies to unsworn members of Victoria Police);[4]

♦   Parts V and VIA of the *Police Regulation Act* 1958 (in relation to Police Reservists and Protective Services Officers, respectively);

♦   The *Victoria Police Manual* instructions;

♦   The *Victoria Police Personnel Discipline Procedures Manual*;

♦   The *Victoria Police Hearing Officers Manual*;

♦   Police Academy Regulations;

♦   Training Department Guidelines;

♦   Victoria Police *Code of Conduct*;

♦   Victoria Police *Code of Ethics*; and

---

[3] I am grateful to Inspector Gary McColl and Sean Carroll, Discipline Advisory Unit, ESD, for providing information that was of assistance in preparing this section.

[4] The new *Public Administration Act* 2004 also applies to unsworn members, as did the *Public Sector Management and Employment Act* 1998 until its repeal in 2004. The *Public Sector Management and Employment Act* replaced the *Public Sector Management Act*.

◆   Victoria Police *Organisational Values* statement.[5]

The police discipline system is the core of the institutional process through which police management makes decisions regarding its employees (including police officers) who have allegedly breached their rules of employment. The discipline system itself underpins a formal organisational structure which is paramilitary in many of its characteristics.

There is often a tension between the prescriptive and structured organisational role for police officers and the actual experience of rank and file policing, and this is most telling when police are called to account through the discipline system. As Fielding (1991) has noted, sometimes police work can be a complicated and reflective activity that requires an officer to account unambiguously for ambiguous choices.

B   Disciplinary Procedures

In relation to conflict of interest breaches, the discipline system applies the disciplinary framework that applies to any type of police misconduct. That is, conflict of interest breaches (and conflicts of interest themselves) are judged according to the behaviour proscribed within police regulations enacted pursuant to a particular statute. Within Victoria Police, conflict of interest was not specifically defined as a form of misconduct within this regulatory framework until near the end of the period under examination here. In 1998 a new Code of Conduct was published, making specific mention of conflict of interest as a separate area of concern (Victoria Police 1998b). The earlier Code of Ethics did not make any specific mention of conflict of interest (Victoria Police, undated).

Consequently, conflicts of interest are dealt with under broader disciplinary rules. In Victoria, the principal regulatory form is section 69 of the

---

[5] Some of the relevant legislation underwent refinement and change during the period covered by this study, largely through changes introduced in 1988 and 1993, and then as a response to recommendations arising from Project Guardian in 1996 (Victoria Police 1996e, 1996d, 1996c, 1996b; The Ombudsman 2003). Subsequently, a complete overhaul of the oversight function of policing occurred through the establishment in November 2004 of the Office of Police Integrity (OPI) as a separate statutory body with a broad mandate to review police activity. Although many of these changes were important in their own right, as discussed later in this chapter, most had little substantive effect on the day-to-day processes and procedures within Victoria Police for dealing with conflict of interest within Victoria Police and for oversight of Victoria Police investigations.

Police Regulation Act,[6] which sets out the broad types of behaviour that may constitute the way in which misconduct can be framed. Both acts of malfeasance and genuine mistakes in judgment are handled through the discipline system:[7]

69. *Breaches of Discipline*

    (1)   A member of the force commits a breach of discipline if he or she—

        (a)   contravenes a provision of this Act or the regulations; or

        (b)   fails to comply with a standing order or instruction of the Chief Commissioner; or

        (c)   engages in conduct that is likely to bring the force into disrepute or diminish public confidence in it; or

        (d)   fails to comply with a lawful instruction given by the Chief Commissioner, a member of or above the rank of senior sergeant or a person having the authority to give the instruction; or

        (e)   is guilty of disgraceful or improper conduct (whether in his or her official capacity or otherwise); or

        (f)   is negligent or careless in the discharge of his or her duty; or

        (g)   without the approval of the Chief Commissioner—

            (i)   applies for or holds a licence or permit to conduct any trade, business or profession; or

---

[6] Prior to 1993 amendments to the *Police Regulation Act*, breaches of discipline were set down in section 81, with Part 4 of the Police Regulations providing various specific disciplinary regulations. Section 81 was replaced by section 69 in 1993, and Part 4 of the regulations was revoked. Therefore, from 1993, s 69 has been the key provision under which disciplinary matters are dealt with.

[7] The Victoria Police Management Intervention Model was introduced in 2006, providing a framework for managers to address lesser issues, such as minor mistakes in judgement and other areas where there is need for change, clarification, or update of policy.

(ii) conducts any trade, business or profession; or

(iii) accepts any other employment; or

(h) acts in a manner prejudicial to the good order or discipline of the force; or

(i) has been charged with an offence (whether under a Victorian law or under a law of another place) and the offence has been found proven.

(2) A member of the force who aids, abets, counsels or procures, or who, by any act or omission, is directly or indirectly knowingly concerned or is a party to the commission of a breach of discipline, also commits a breach of discipline.[8]

Section 71 of the *Police Regulation Act* provides that the Chief Commissioner of Police (or an authorised officer) may charge a member with a breach of discipline if, after a preliminary investigation, the Chief Commissioner (or authorised officer) "reasonably believes that a member of the force has committed a breach of discipline". Thus, whilst the existence of a conflict of interest may form the background to a charge or investigation, formally the basis of such a charge or investigation is that there is a reasonable belief that a police officer has breached a provision of section 69 of the *Act*.

Conflict of interest complaints are thus usually translated into identifiable neglects of duty and breaches of disciplinary provisions. These may be specific breaches under section 69 of the *Act*, such as failing to comply with a lawful instruction or engaging in unauthorised outside employment. Breaches of standing orders and instructions issued by the Chief Commissioner are dealt with under section 69(1)(b). In many conflict of interest cases the general provisions of section 69 of the *Act* are brought to bear, such as those dealing with disgraceful or improper conduct, bringing the Force into disrepute, or acting in a manner prejudicial to the good order of the Force. These general matters may be seen as very important in terms of conflict of interest, as they

---

[8] Subsequent amendments have not altered the effect of this section in relation to conflict of interest. A 2001 amendment inserted a new ss.69(1)(ab) in relation to compliance with directions under the *Whistleblowers Protection Act* 2001, and a 2004 amendment added a new section 69(3) relating to discipline breaches by police officers seconded to the OPI.

go to the heart of questions of impartiality, morale, and public trust, to which conflicts of interest can be so damaging.

Prior to 1993, the disciplinary provisions of Part 4 of the *Police Regulations* were significant, particularly Regulation 402 which listed a number of specific disciplinary breaches. Regulation 402 was brought to bear in many of the cases considered for this study. For example, if a police officer improperly disclosed information to an outside party, this may have represented a breach of Regulation 402(x), which stated in part that it is prohibited to "without proper authority show to any person outside the force any document or material under the control of the Chief Commissioner". The Part 4 Regulations were revoked in 1993 and effectively subsumed into the new section 69 of the *Police Regulation Act* as the provision under which action would be taken in relation to breaches of discipline.[9]

C   Complaints Against Police Officers

The system for dealing with conflict of interest matters within Victoria Police is complaints driven. This reflects a wider trend in which public complaints systems have become a crucial element of attempts in contemporary policing to validate notions of public accountability while dealing with internal management needs for mechanisms providing for discipline and organisational workplace consistency (Lewis 1997, 1999, 2000). In a complaints-driven system problematic situations come to attention principally as a result of complaints from a range of sources—usually members of the public.

1   Sources of Complaint

Anyone can complain about the conduct of police officers, including other police officers. There are two principal avenues through which complaints against the police may be lodged: directly with the police force itself, or to the office of the Victorian Ombudsman, which oversighted the police complaints process during the period of this study (this oversight function has been performed by the Office of Police Integrity since 2004). It should be noted that although the specific processes described in this section relate to the period

---

[9] In addition to the discipline action available in section 69, section 127A of the *Police Regulation Act* provides a specific criminal offence for police who without authority disclose information.

following the creation of the Ethical Standards Department (ESD) in 1996, similar processes previously existed under the former Internal Investigations Department and still exist internally within Victoria Police independent of the creation of the OPI.[10]

Complainants are required under section 86L(3) of the *Police Regulation Act* to be advised that they may also lodge a complaint with the Deputy Ombudsman (Police Complaints) (now the Director of Police Integrity). As a matter of practice and as required under Section 86N(2) of the *Act*, complaints made to the Deputy Ombudsman would routinely be referred to Victoria Police for resolution, with the Deputy Ombudsman following-up unresolved matters. The Deputy Ombudsman would closely oversee the investigation and review the resolution of complaints of serious misconduct.

Under section 86N(4) the Deputy Ombudsman was required to directly investigate complaints involving the Chief Commissioner or a Deputy of Assistant Commissioner, and empowered to investigate complaints made to his office where it was considered that such investigation was in the public interest or where the matter related to established practices or procedures of the Force that the Deputy Ombudsman considered should be reviewed. These provisions remain in place under the post-2004 OPI mandate. Explaining the rationale for this approach, the Director - Police Integrity has reported that matters involving service delivery or the performance of an individual officer are generally amenable to being handled by local police management and are therefore routinely referred back to Victoria Police for conciliation or informal resolution.[11] The OPI electronically tracks the progress of such complaints and may reassess unresolved matters and request Victoria Police to take further action (Director - Police Integrity 2006: 62). Broadly, under this approach the investigatory (as opposed to oversight) focus of the Deputy Ombudsman/OPI is on matters involving serious misconduct or systemic problems.

Where a public complaint is made to the police, the ESD must be immediately notified; the ESD in turn notifies the Deputy Ombudsman. A

---

[10] Discussion of the workings of the discipline and oversight system in the remainder of this chapter remains relevant under new investigation and oversight arrangements involving the OPI, with the OPI having taken on the functions of the former Deputy Ombudsman. In the succeeding discussion, any significant differences in the current arrangements from those that existed under the former Deputy Ombudsman mandate are noted.

[11] The Management Intervention Model introduced in 2006 provides the current practice for resolving such matters (see fn. 7).

complaint may be lodged in person, in writing (including by email), or by telephone. Where a complaint is lodged verbally, a member of staff takes a detailed statement which has the same status as received letters of complaint. There is an out-of-hours system for urgent complaints and a corresponding liaison out-of-hours system with the relevant section of the ESD.

Since the creation of the ESD in 1996, the Customer Assistance Unit is the filtering process for both telephone calls and written complaints that are made directly to the police. For complaints lodged by telephone, this unit considers the nature of the behaviour complained about and makes decisions about whether the complaint requires investigation or may be resolved and finalised over the telephone. During the time frame of this study approximately 90 per cent of all complaints received were resolved and finalised over the telephone in consultation with the complainant. Resolution could involve the Customer Assistance staff member explaining police policy or procedures to the satisfaction of the caller, and the complainant being satisfied that no further action is warranted or required. In the remaining 10 per cent of cases, the Customer Assistance staff member would pass the matter to an ESD investigator, who would contact the complainant, and the matter would proceed to investigation, with the creation of a formal complaint file. The creation of a formal complaint file merely indicates that an investigation into the complaint is underway and does not indicate that the police officer will become the subject of disciplinary charges.

Prior to 1997, internal complaints (that is, complaints about the conduct of one police officer by another member of the Force) could only be made through the internal processes of Victoria Police. Following the Operation Bart inquiry into the window-shutter kickbacks scam, which was brought to light when an internal whistleblower reported the matter to the Deputy Ombudsman, the *Police Regulation Act* was amended in 1997 at the suggestion of the Deputy Ombudsman, to permit internal complaints of serious misconduct to be reported directly to his office. These amendments also made it an offence not to report knowledge of serious misconduct on the part of fellow officers. Such reports are required to be made either to an officer of more senior rank than the member making the report, or to the Deputy Ombudsman (s 86L(2A)). For the purposes of this provision, serious misconduct is defined in section 86A as:

(a) conduct which constitutes an offence punishable by imprisonment; or

(b) conduct which is likely to bring the force into disrepute or diminish public confidence in it; or

(c)   disgraceful or improper conduct (whether in the member's official capacity or otherwise).

(a)   *Sources of Complaint: Evidence from this Study*

In this 10-year study, the majority of conflict of interest complaints (76 per cent) were lodged directly with Victoria Police. Table 3.2 breaks down these figures, showing both the source and destination of complaints.

Table 3.2: Breakdown of Source of Complaint (All Cases)

Source of complaint	N	%
Direct to police		
Internally-generated	59	15.7
Complaint by member of public	157	41.8
Complaint lodged through a solicitor	26	6.9
Complaint lodged through a legal aid organisation, etc	2	0.5
Complaint lodged from a public service organisation	8	2.1
Complaint lodged from another source	13	3.5
Unknown specific source	20	5.3
Total complaints direct to police	*285*	*75.8*
Direct to the office of the Ombudsman		
Complaint lodged by member of public	75	19.9
Complaint lodged through a solicitor	10	2.6
Complaint lodged from a public service organisation	4	1.1
Complaint lodged from another source	1	0.3
Unknown specific source	1	0.3
Total complaints direct to Ombudsman	**91**	**24.2**
Total number of cases *	**376**	**100.0**

* Source of lodgement was not able to be determined for one case.

The table demonstrates the significance of the office of the Ombudsman as a means for the lodgement of complaints. Almost 62 per cent of all conflict of interest complaints came direct from members of the public, and almost one-third of these (75 out of 232 complaints from members of the public) were lodged with the office of the Ombudsman. In eight of the ten years covered by this study, more than 20 per cent of all complaints were lodged directly with the Deputy Ombudsman, with the trend showing a generally increasing proportion of all complaints lodged in this manner. These findings reinforce the contemporary importance of the Deputy Ombudsman/OPI as an avenue for making complaints about police misconduct. The Deputy Ombudsman suggested that this trend reflects two key factors—"growing community awareness of the role of the Deputy Ombudsman, or a practical appreciation of the opportunity to lodge complaints with a specialist, independent, non-police authority" (The Ombudsman 1995: 21).

It is also of particular note that almost 16 per cent of complaints were internally generated—that is, they were made by a member of Victoria Police. This demonstrates a level of ethical awareness and concern in relation to conflict of interest on the part of at least some members of Victoria Police.

D   *Accounting to Complainants*

Feedback to complainants is an important aspect of public satisfaction with the accountability process. In many senses, the quality of reporting and feedback to complainants is as important as the quality of investigations themselves. Quality feedback is essential to securing and maintaining public confidence in the internal investigations and complaint handling processes (The Ombudsman 1995: 38).

The initial recipient of a complaint (that is, either the Deputy Ombudsman/OPI or Victoria Police) is responsible for writing to the complainant following the investigation to advise of the results of the investigation and of any action proposed to be taken (*Police Regulation Act*, s 86T).

E   *Investigation of Complaints*

Written complaints to the police usually result in a complaint case file. This file is allocated to an investigator who contacts the complainant and the matter proceeds from there. If a complainant wishes to withdraw a complaint this must be declared in writing, a process monitored by the Office of the Deputy Ombudsman, which will question the complainant as to whether coercion or pressure had been applied. If the complaint involves more than one officer, a single case file is created for all officers included in the complaint.

1   *Interviews*

Interviews with complainants are generally not taped. The final complaint statement includes a 'perjury acknowledgement', indicating that what is being alleged is true and acknowledging that the complainant may be liable to penalties for perjury if the statement is found to be untrue. There are no formal restrictions on who can be present during the interview of the complainant: this is a matter of discretion by the individual police officer taking the statement.

Police officers are not advised that a complaint has been made against them until they are about to be interviewed (due to the need for non-interference in the investigation). However, it is possible that, on occasion, some police officers do find out earlier about the existence of a complaint through informal communication channels within the organisation.

2   *Investigation*

Most investigations are carried out by ESD officers, however if a case file is sent out to the relevant Victoria Police Region for investigation, the investigation is allocated at the discretion of the divisional management. Also, a decision is made as to whether the complaint raises a management issue requiring a local management response (for example, time sheet breaches, misuse of a police vehicle, failure to wear appropriate uniform) or a more serious disciplinary issue requiring further investigation. If investigators within ESD are overloaded then a disciplinary investigation may be sent out to a local Police Region or District.

Police officers of the rank of senior sergeant or higher are able to conduct investigations in Regions; but must liaise with the Ethical and Professional Standards Officer (EPSO) and the Discipline Advisory Unit (DAU) within the ESD. Investigators cannot be from the same station as the officer complained about and in general they tend to be from a different Division in order to prevent or minimise collusion (and conflict of interest). Police officers under investigation can advise their Divisional Superintendent if they feel the person to whom the investigation has been allocated is biased against them and it can be allocated to another officer. Investigators tend to come from uniformed ranks, with detectives rarely involved in complaint investigations.

Within the ESD, management generally tries to allocate investigations to an officer of the rank of senior sergeant or above because only a senior sergeant or higher ranked officer can issue a demand under Section 86Q of the *Police Regulation Act*, which requires a police officer to answer questions or produce documents on demand. If a complaint is made against officers at the rank of Commissioner, Deputy Commissioner, or Assistant Commissioner, the Deputy Ombudsman must investigate the complaint (*Police Regulation Act*, s 86N(4)(a)). As noted above, the Deputy Ombudsman is also empowered to investigate complaints in matters where it is considered it to be in the public interest to do so, or where the subject matter of complaints relates to established police practices or procedures which he believes should be reviewed (s 86N(4)(b)).

3   Discipline Brief

Formal investigations on matters which are deemed to constitute a breach of discipline take the form of a preparation of a Brief. Guidelines mandate the information required:[12]

♦   A Discipline Inquiry Brief Head;

♦   Particulars of the breach, known as the Discipline Charge Notice (includes, for example, the acts, matters, things, or omissions said to constitute the breach);

♦   A list of witnesses, and a synopsis of their evidence;

♦   Witness statements, in chronological order;

♦   Documentary exhibits or photographs;

♦   Copies of tapes of interviews (transcripts are usually obtained only in relation to complex matters);

---

[12] The variation in circumstances of more complex cases may require more content in a discipline Brief. The DAU makes an assessment and recommends the requirements.

◆　A Human Resources Management report (in particular to outline past disciplinary breaches or similar matters);

◆　Legal opinions, if required; and

◆　A specification of Force Instructions or Directives that are alleged to have been breached.

4　*Investigation Timeframe*

The general guideline for finalisation of a complaint (investigation and making of a report by the investigating officer) is ninety days.[13] This research and the findings of a number of major Inquiries in Australia indicate that this outcome is often not achieved (Wood 1997b; Fitzgerald 1989). On occasion, there may be reasonable grounds for non-completion of an investigation within this time frame, and particular exceptions arise when criminal charges are pending against a police officer. In such circumstances, the matter proceeds to trial (or at least this option will be explored) and then the complaint will come back through the discipline process. Section 71(2) of the *Police Regulation Act* requires that if a serious charge (as listed in Schedule 1 of the Act) against a police officer is being contemplated the Director of Public Prosecutions must be consulted, leading to inevitable delays in finalising a matter.

After the investigation (or, where required, consultation with the Office of Public Prosecutions and the formal criminal process) a formal report from investigating officers proceeds to the DAU for oversight and comment on investigator recommendations regarding outcomes and discipline charges. The Deputy Ombudsman (Police Complaints) oversights the entire investigation and may pass matters back to Victoria Police for further consideration or investigation. Including these processes of oversight and review, most cases take at least up to six months to finalise.

5　*Role of the Discipline Advisory Unit (DAU)*

The DAU does not investigate every complaint, but it evaluates and assesses the quality of discipline investigations carried out by Regions and the ESD. In

---

[13] The OPI now advises complainants that on minor issues the matter should be finalised within 60 days.

addition, upon completion of an investigation file and, if relevant, a Discipline Brief, the file and Brief are forwarded to senior DAU staff, who assess whether formal disciplinary charges should be pursued through a Hearing. If so, the DAU prepares the necessary documents for a Discipline Hearing to be activated. The Unit also oversights management of these matters through to the hearing and documentation of the final result.

6   Discipline Hearings

The procedure to be followed at a Discipline Hearing is set down in section 75 of the *Police Regulation Act*. In general, the process is required to be as informal and untechnical as possible, and is designed to provide the person conducting the inquiry with a great degree of flexibility. If charges are laid the police officer must be given an opportunity to provide a written explanation of the matter (s 72).

(a)   Evidence on the Use of Disciplinary Hearings

Table 3.3 shows the breakdown of the use of Discipline Hearings in the cases examined for this research.

Table 3.3: Discipline Hearing Status (All Police Officers)

Discipline Hearing status	N	%
No hearing	466	86.9
Discipline Hearing held	36	6.7
Discipline Hearing scheduled but police officer resigned prior	20	3.7
Police officer used sick or other leave to stall process, then resigned prior to decision about Discipline Hearing	6	1.1
Discipline Hearing explored but insufficient evidence or grounds	8	1.5
Total number of police officers*	**536**	**100.0**

* Data not available for three police officers.

The table shows that in only 6.7 per cent of instances did matters proceed to a formal Discipline Hearing. In a small number of cases, a Discipline Hearing was explored, but failed to proceed because insufficient evidence against the police officer or insufficient grounds for such a Hearing. Discipline Hearings were scheduled, but not proceeded with, in a further 4.8 per cent of cases. The reasons for not proceeding to formal Hearings in these matters varied.

In the disciplinary cases of 20 officers, the police officers concerned chose to resign prior to the conclusion of formal discipline processes. For some of these officers, as the case discussion in following chapters will show, there seemed to be little doubt that resignation was a form of discipline avoidance. In practice this could be achieved by submitting a resignation notice with three months notice required under section 14 of the *Police Regulation Act* and following with a medical certificate for stress or related medical conditions until the expiration of the notice period.

In the disciplinary cases of a further six police officers, sick or other leave was used by the officer to stall processes, followed by resignation prior to a decision being taken about proceeding to a Discipline Hearing. The files suggested, however, that a Hearing would have been likely. For example, in two cases the police officers concerned resigned prior to completion of the investigation of the complaint against them, but they were nevertheless formally issued with an admonishment notice (in lieu of disciplinary charges), which stated that the police officer would have been dismissed if he had not resigned, and their personnel files were marked "never to be re-employed" (Cases 288 and 322). In matters such as these, the resignation of the officers concerned seems to be a clear tactic to stall or obviate the formal disciplinary process. However, the outcome (resignation) is generally regarded as representing a satisfactory resolution of the matter, and further action is not pursued. Nevertheless, this issue raises important questions regarding the public accountability of Victoria Police itself. A police officer who resigns whilst under investigation in order to avoid facing a disciplinary hearing also *ipso facto* effectively protects and maximises his or her employee retirements benefits. Under section 54 of the *Police Regulation Act* "[a] member of the force who for misconduct of any kind has been discharged or dismissed therefrom shall not be entitled to any pension or gratuity under this Division".

Thus, resignation in the face of possible dismissal effectively subverts some of the objectives of the complaints and discipline system, and this may be sending out the wrong message to other police officers. It is likely that public confidence in a system that allows recalcitrant police officers to resign and in so doing to protect their benefits may be diminished. From a management viewpoint, there are strong arguments for allowing such resignations as they result in the exclusion of undesirable employees from the workplace, they save resources, and they provide a definite outcome (whereas substantiation at the Discipline Hearing stage cannot be guaranteed). Balanced against this however is the point made by Commissioner Wood in the NSW Royal Commission into police misconduct, that resigning police are disinclined to assist investigators and they take with them key information regarding the behaviour and activities of other suspect police (Wood 1997a).

7 Outcomes: Determination

Charges that proceed to a Disciplinary Hearing will be found to be either proven or not proven. For investigations that are resolved without recourse to a formal hearing (the great majority), a range of possible determinations is available. Table 3.4 summarises the available determinations in these matters.

The various determinations shown in the table can be classified as to whether they are *in favour of the police officer*, *adverse to the police officer*, or *indeterminate* in nature. Findings that are clearly in favour of the police officer (withdrawn, no complaint, not substantiated, unfounded, or exonerated) or adverse to the police officer (substantiated) would generally be regarded as *definitive* findings. *Indeterminate* outcomes, are regarded here as findings neither for nor against the officer involved (lesser deficiency, conciliated, unable to determine, or not proceeded with due to resignation). *Lesser deficiency* is classified as indeterminate because it is a clear finding against a police officer, but not in relation to the substantive conflict of interest or conflict of interest breach which is the key focus of the complaint.

(a) Determinations: Evidence from this Study

Figure 3.2 shows the breakdown of determination of the investigation into all complaints against officers in this study.

Table 3.4: Possible Determinations

	Determination	Meaning *
1	Substantiated	Complaint found to be true
2	Lesser deficiency	A matter uncovered during an investigation not forming part of the complaint laid, requiring remedial action, such as a failure to complete an official document
3	Conciliated	A complaint involving either a misunderstanding or possible trivial breach of discipline has been discussed with the complainant who is satisfied with the explanation given or remedial action and requires no further investigation
4	Unable to determine	The available evidence does nor permit the Investigating Officer to establish whether the complaint is true or not
5	Not proceeded with (resigned prior)	The complaint is recorded as a file initially but is not proceeded with, due to the unwillingness of the complainant to supply information and is unwilling to withdraw the complaint or there is some other reason for being able to take the complaint further
6	Withdrawn	A complainant having made a formal complaint, of his or her own volition makes a written request that the complaint investigation cease
7	No complaint	A query or complaint by a person that is subsequently found to be an action sanctioned by law, or a complaint lodged by a third party which is denied by the alleged victim who has no complaint to make
8	Not substantiated	The weight of available evidence does not support the account of events as described by the complainant, but is weighted in favour of the account given by police members
9	Unfounded	The available evidence clearly establishes that there are no grounds for the complaint whatsoever
10	Exonerated	The evidence clearly establishes that a particular member is not involved in a complaint, or is completely free from blame

* Source: *Glossary of Terms Regarding Determination of Complaints*, Victoria Police.

Figure 3.2: Determination of Complaints (by police officer)[14]

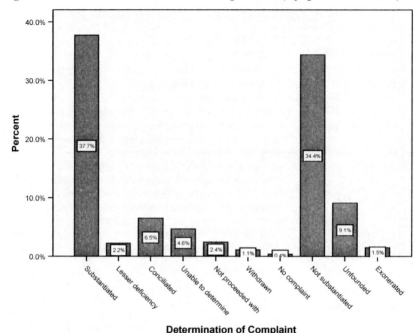

Determination of Complaint

Overall, most determinations (approximately 85 per cent) represented *definitive findings* for or against the police officer. The two that stand out in Figure 3.2 are 'substantiated' and 'not substantiated', each representing over 30 per cent of the total. Adverse findings were made against 37.7 per cent of officers. The high rate of substantiation found here must be contrasted with generally low rates of substantiation in other complaints against police— usually well under 10 per cent (see Goldsmith 1991b). Nevertheless, four important points need to be made in relation to this result.

First, this substantiation rate is not expressed as a proportion of all *allegations* but as a proportion of all officer cases. Where a single allegation

---

[14] The basis of this graph is matters against police officers, thus where more than one police officer was involved in a single complaint case file, for this research a separate determination was recorded for each police officer. The graph depicts the findings in matters against a total of 539 police officers. Determinations were not recorded for each allegation. Where a complaint contained several allegations against an officer, the most severe determination relevant to the issue of conflict of interest was recorded.

against a police officer was found to be substantiated, the matter was coded as 'substantiated', notwithstanding the findings in relation to all other allegations. This means that the figure of 38.5 per cent is not directly comparable with substantiation rates found in other research where the rate relates to allegations. The second point is that cases were coded as 'substantiated' whether the finding against a police officer was a formal or an informal one. Most complaint cases do not proceed to formal disciplinary hearings and formal findings are not made, however where a police officer was formally counselled, this was coded as a substantiated finding. Published statistics on findings in relation to formal Disciplinary Hearings are therefore not comparable.

Third, conflict of interest complaints studied for this research represent a relatively small percentage of all complaints against police. With approximately 1100 complaints against police (for all types of complaints) per year (The Ombudsman 1995), over the 10-year period of this study there would have been more than 10,000 complaints in total.[15] The 377 usable case files examined for this research therefore represent slightly less than 4 per cent of all complaints against police. This is a valuable sample, but it cannot be regarded as representative of all complaints against police.

Finally, certain conflict of interest complaints may be expected to have relatively higher substantiation rates than general complaints against police. For example, complaints relating to secondary or outside employment (unless vexatious or fictitious) would be expected to often result in a substantiated finding, due to the relatively easily provable nature of the complaint (through the use of tax returns or other third-party evidence, for example).[16]

Other analysis of definitive findings against police officers shows that there was no pattern of steadily increasing or decreasing substantiated findings over the period. Prima facie, this suggests that there has not been a differential application of the standards applied by the Internal Investigations Department or ESD over the period. Also, in four of the nine full calendar years (1989–1997) included in the analysis—1989, 1990, 1993, and 1995—the rate of substantiation versus non-substantiation was greater than 50 per cent, and in a

---

[15] The Ombudsman reported a total of 7962 complete complaint cases for the seven year period spanning 1988–9 to 1994–5 (The Ombudsman 1995: 18).

[16] As in any legal matter, the relationship between guilt or innocence, evidence, and ultimate findings is a complex one, and non-substantiation does not necessarily mean innocence. In relation to complaints against police, non-substantiation may be the result of an inability to corroborate a complainant's account of events.

fifth year—1991—an equal proportion of complaints were found to be substantiated and non-substantiated. This finding reinforces the concerns around the problem of conflict of interest during the period of analysis, as formally expressed by the Deputy Ombudsman and recognised by Victoria Police management.

8   Outcomes: Sanctions

Under the *Police Regulation Act* a range of penalties can be applied to police officers against whom formal disciplinary charges have been found proven. As at 1993, the available penalties were set out in subsections 1 and 2 of section 76 of the *Act*:

76. *Determination of the inquiry*

(1)   If, after considering all the submissions made at an inquiry the person conducting the inquiry finds that the charge has been proved, the person conducting the inquiry may make one or more of the following determinations—

(a)   to reprimand the member; or

(b)   to adjourn the hearing of the inquiry into the charge on the condition that the member be of good behaviour for a period not exceeding 12 months; or

(c)   to impose a fine not exceeding 40 penalty units; or

(d)   to reduce the rank or seniority of the member; or

(e)   to reduce the remuneration of the member; or

(f)   to transfer the member to other duties; or

(g)   to dismiss the member.

(2)   The person conducting the inquiry may also determine that the member make any restitution or pay any compensation or costs that are appropriate for that matter.[17]

---

[17] In 1999 amendments, the words "or on any other condition specified in the determination" were added to section 76(1)(b), and a new possible penalty was added as section 76(1)(ca): "to impose a period, not exceeding 2 years, during which the member will not be eligible for promotion or transfer to other duties".

The various sanctions are said to be not principally designed with a punitive intention, but with the intention of protecting Victoria Police and its reputation. Three further types of sanctions were available for cases that did not proceed to a formal Discipline Hearing: counselling (or Performance Improvement Notice), caution notice, and admonishment. These three sanctions are not available to Hearing Officers.[18]

(a) Development of the Sanctions Regime

Prior to 1993, counselling was the only formal administrative sanction available, although reprimands at District level could be issued by a high ranking officer (Regulation 402(2c)). In formal terms, counselling is not regarded as a sanction but as a remedial and developmental tool that is integral to staff management. Until the Project Guardian review in 1996, the details of a counselling were not required to be recorded at the police officer's station or on a member's personnel file. Station managers (or the superior officer who administered the counselling) were simply required to make a note on the member's personnel file that the counselling had occurred. Interviews conducted with first line managers from various districts as part of Project Guardian revealed that in relation to the use of counselling:

> Most [managers] utilise the informal counselling process that was generally described as a "quiet chat" that is not recorded. Formal counselling usually involved a private discussion in a supervisors' office and is recorded via a day book, diary, the stations [sic] personnel file or station discipline register (if kept). The transfer of information between supervisors is regarded as being ad hoc (Victoria Police 1996e: 26).

Even where counselling was conducted as a result of a complaint investigation the officer concerned was rarely provided any sort of written advice as to the nature and purpose of the counselling (Victoria Police 1996e: 26).

---

[18] The introduction of the Management Intervention Model in 2006 increased the range of outcomes/actions available in dealing with discipline issues. These now include counselling, education, and other preventative measures. Performance Improvement Notices have been replaced with structured accountable processes for both employer and employee, known as Performance Improvement Plans. Admonishment notices are still used and Caution Notices have been discontinued.

The Deputy Ombudsman (Police Complaints) expressed a number of concerns that counselling was an inappropriate level of administrative sanction, and he urged the introduction of administrative admonishments for cases where formal disciplinary charges were felt to be not warranted (for example, Case 24, 1989; Case 45, 1990). Partly as a response to these concerns, caution and admonishment notices were introduced in 1993, with the intended purpose being to "allow police supervisors and managers to take positive, direct and immediate disciplinary action in response to minor breaches of discipline or standards by subordinates" (Victoria Police 1996e: 21).

Caution and admonishment notices were used in situations when the circumstances of a case required more than counselling, but where a formal disciplinary charge was not appropriate. They were regarded as the first and second levels of the formal discipline process and were considered to be *administrative* levels of the formal discipline process to be used as a developmental tool, and not to be regarded as carrying a punitive sanction (this was emphasised in a number of cases that are discussed later in this book). They were, however, formally recorded and retained in a member's permanent personnel file.[19] A police officer could not be cautioned more than once for a similar breach within a twelve-month period. A second or successive similar offence would require a more serious outcome (Victoria Police 1996e: 28–29).

Admonishments were used for situations where the police officer had previously been cautioned over a similar situation, where the transgression fell short of warranting a disciplinary charge, or where the employee's prior work record was such that an admonishment notice would represent a satisfactory outcome in all the circumstances of the case (Victoria Police 1996e: 28–31; Victoria Police 1993b: 5.1–5.3). If a member had received two or more admonishments within a two-year period, a further admonishment could not be issued—formal disciplinary procedures would be required (Victoria Police 1996e: 29).

Caution notices could only be issued by Sergeants or superior ranks, and admonishments could only be issued by Inspectors or above (Victoria Police 1996e: 31). Prior to the issuing of either caution notice or an admonishment the

---

[19] Upon the handing down of a caution or admonishment the police officer could request a Review, however the grounds for review were limited and a review would not constitute a hearing *de novo*. The allowable grounds related to whether the issuing officer's decision was reasonable in all the circumstances.

police officer concerned was entitled to hear the allegations and provide a response to them. If the police officer failed to respond, the proposed notice could be issued without further reference to the police officer.

Although a caution notice was regarded by Victoria Police as of less gravity than an admonishment, the Project Guardian review found that in practice there was little distinction made and they were often issued for the same kinds of breaches. There was found to be little consistency in the issuing of caution notices, admonishments, or even counselling for similar disciplinary offences (Victoria Police 1996e: 30–31). Subsequently, the use of caution notices was discontinued in July 1997 and a recommendation from Project Guardian was that a formal counselling be recorded in the form of a Performance Improvement Notice (PIN) (Victoria Police 1996e: 25–28). The explicitly stated intended emphasis of a PIN was to be remedial action, not punishment. It was also recommended that admonishments be regarded as punitive (Victoria Police 1996e: 32, 34).

This discussion provides an insight into efforts made by Victoria Police to develop an appropriate sanctions regime for disciplinary matters that do not proceed to a formal hearing. A large majority of conflict of interest cases fall into this category.

(b) Sanctions: Evidence from this Study

Determinations—in terms of the most serious sanctions received by each police officer—are shown in Table 3.5. Counselling, caution notices, admonishments, and resignation during investigation are all regarded as sanctions for the purposes of the table. The range of determinations and sanctions outlined above were used to code outcomes for police officers subject to adverse findings in the conflict of interest complaint cases examined in this study. In addition, if a police officer resigned during an investigation or prior to a formal investigation commencing (but after the receipt of a complaint), thus effectively avoiding any ultimate (perhaps likely) sanction outcome, this was also coded as an outcome analogous to a sanction.

Table 3.5: Sanctions in all Cases with Adverse Outcomes

Sanction	N	%
Counselling (or Performance Improvement Notice)	66	33.2
Caution notice	12	6.0
Admonishment	38	19.1
Reprimand	4	2.0
Transfer	1	0.5
Demotion	1	0.5
Fine	20	10.1
Dismissal	5	2.5
Resigned during investigation	25	12.6
Good Behaviour Bond	1	0.5
No sanction	21	10.6
Other[20]	5	2.5
Total*	**199**	**100.0**

* of the 207 officers subject to an adverse determination (substantiation), sanction data was unavailable in eight instances.

Table 3.5 clearly shows that where a sanction was applied, counselling was the most common outcome—applied in more than one-third of all matters in which an adverse finding was made against a police officer. Given that counselling is regarded as developmental rather than a disciplinary measure, the

---

[20] "Other" includes sanctions that are not part of the formal disciplinary structure, such as the withdrawal of a police officer's approved driving certificate for a police officer who was convicted on a careless driving charge. This meant that the police officer could no longer drive police vehicles.

extensive use of this sanction may be regarded as a 'soft' option. However, the Project Guardian review found that most police officers do in fact regard counselling as punitive rather than developmental (Victoria Police 1996e: 30). It was reported that officers regard counselling as "disheartening" and that it "decreased their morale". Paradoxically, this suggests that the formal intent that counselling be used for developmental and training purposes is not fulfilled in practice and it may be concluded that developmental and training needs are not being met. This is particularly unfortunate in the case of conflict of interest, as the development of an understanding of the significance of conflict of interest, its potential to impact on a police officer's performance of duty, and the deleterious effect it may have on public perceptions of policing, are all central to effectively dealing with the problem. If these understandings are unable to be achieved through formal or informal counselling processes that result from the disciplinary system, it may be concluded that the problem of conflict of interest is not being effectively dealt with at the level of police culture. The development and introduction in 2006 of a Best Practice Training package dealing with conflict of interest (Victoria Police 2006) represents a welcome development that may go some way towards meeting training and developmental needs in this area.

After counselling, the next most common *sanctions* were cautions and admonishments, but it is perhaps most surprising to find that in almost 15 per cent of cases with outcomes adverse to the police officer, the officer concerned either resigned or was dismissed. As discussed earlier, resignation and dismissal may be linked to the extent that it is likely a number of officers who have engaged in serious misconduct resigned prior to a hearing rather than face dismissal. In relation to cases that proceeded to a formal Hearing which resulted in an adverse finding, the lesser sanctions of fines (which were mostly under $1000), reprimands, and good behaviour bonds were the most common outcomes.

Overall, apart from the resignations and dismissals, the picture presented here is one that suggests sanctions are not generally applied at a high level. It may be suggested that the limited use of formal Discipline Hearings, given that a higher standard of evidence is required for such a hearing to result in a substantiated outcome, may in fact make little overall difference to the sorts of sanctions that are imposed in conflict of interest cases.

F   *Review and Oversight*

A significant aspect of the police disciplinary system is the capacity for findings and determinations to be challenged both by the member concerned (or the Police Association), and by superior oversighting officers. The role of the Deputy Ombudsman (Police Complaints) in oversighting internal investigations, or conducting his own investigations into alleged police misconduct is also a central part of the accountability process. Although the Deputy Ombudsman played an important function during the timeframe of this study and, as case studies in later chapters of this book will show, had an influence in the final disposition of many cases, this role was one that was constrained by legislation and limited resources. To a large extent, these limitations have been recognised in recent years, both as a result of political pressures and representations from the Office of the Ombudsman. The formation of the OPI as a separate statutory authority with greatly enhanced independence, powers and resources is clearly an attempt to address this situation and overcome these deficiencies.

1   *Internal review*

Complaints procedures adopted by Victoria Police include considerable internal processes of oversight prior to final determinations. Investigations, proposed determinations, and sanctions are reviewed by senior ESD staff (Internal Investigations Department staff prior to 1996) and in many cases there is considerable interaction between original investigators and reviewing officers. Where initial investigations have been conducted within a Police District rather than by an ESD member, the internal oversight is particularly vigorous. ESD members are in a position to take account of policy considerations of which individual members in Districts may be unaware, and to apply consistent expectations and standards across a large number of cases.

(a)   *Internal review: Evidence from this Study*

Table 3.6 shows evidence from this study where, in the course of internal processes of review, superior or reviewing officers challenged preliminary determinations and/or sanctions proposed for at least one police officer involved in the matter.

Table 3.6: Internal Review of Preliminary Determinations

Status	N	%
Internal review		
Determination and sanction changed	29	7.7
Determination only changed	2	0.5
Sanction only changed	19	5.1
No change to determination or sanction	46	12.3
No challenge	**279**	**74.4**
Total*	**375**	**100.0**

* Not known for two cases

In almost three-quarters of cases, there was no internal challenge, and in just over half of the cases where there was an internal challenge the internal review process resulted in a changed determination and/or sanction. These findings are significant because the effective operation of internal review processes is an important consideration in debates about whether the police can be trusted to police themselves. This study found that in just over one-quarter of cases the internal review process resulted in some level of criticism of initial investigations or recommended outcomes. The language of such criticisms was not tempered in such a manner as to diminish its effect, and reports of reviewing officers suggested a genuine critical gaze over the evidence and reasoning in these cases.

Whilst critical literature on policing suggests that police cannot be trusted to police themselves, this research provides evidence of vigorous disagreement and questioning of both investigations and outcomes from within Victoria Police itself. These processes are independent of the external oversight of the Deputy Ombudsman. Without dismissing the possibility that this external oversight could have a 'backwards' effect on the rigour of internal oversight mechanisms, it may be concluded that claims that police cannot be trusted to police themselves are too simplistic because the evidence presented here indicates that there is much less cohesion and 'rubber-stamping' within the organisation than might be thought. The analysis in Chapters Four to Six provide detail of how these internal processes of criticism and review play out in individual cases.

2 Grievances

Following an adverse determination, the police officer concerned may object to an aspect of an investigation or outcome by lodging a grievance. In this study, grievances were lodged in respect of only 5.6 per cent of all police officers' cases and in more than half of these (3.4 per cent), there was no change to either the determination or sanction. This suggests that the grievance procedure, while an important element of procedural fairness, has little influence on the overall outcomes in conflict of interest disciplinary cases.

3 Police Association Involvement

The Police Association has a potential role in supporting member officers who are the subject of conflict of interest complaints. Although this involvement represents an intervention in support of the individual interests of the officer rather than being necessarily focused on the public interest, it is an important part of the natural justice accorded to the officer.

The evidence in this study showed that the Association became involved in less than 10 per cent of conflict of interest cases (involving 49 out of 519 police officers where this information was available in the files). Little of a definitive nature can be said about the Police Association involvement on the basis of the data in the case files, but it was notable that in almost 86 per cent of the matters where the Police Association became involved (involving 42 police officers), there was a determination that was adverse to the police officer, and Police Association involvement was higher in matters where more serious sanctions resulted. The Police Association became involved in only 4.5 per cent of all cases which resulted in a counselling, but was involved in 27.5 per cent of cases that resulted in dismissal or resignation. Prima facie, this suggests that the Police Association tends to become involved in more serious cases.

4 External Oversight

For most of the timeframe of this study, the Deputy Ombudsman (Police Complaints) had a statutory responsibility under the *Police Regulation Act* to oversee the investigation of all public complaints against police. The Deputy Ombudsman was a separate statutory person with distinct statutory responsibilities from those of the Ombudsman, whose wider role is to inquire and investigate matters relating to government administration. The statutory responsibilities of the Deputy Ombudsman related specifically to investigating complaints of police conduct and reviewing police internal investigations. In 1995, the then Deputy Ombudsman, Barry Perry, was appointed as Ombudsman, and the government decided to effectively merge the two roles from July 1996. The new Ombudsman simultaneously served in the statutory office of Deputy Ombudsman (Police Complaints) and restructured the Ombudsman's Office into two discrete jurisdictions (General and Police) each with a Senior Assistant Ombudsman (The Ombudsman 1997a: 5). Although important from an organisational perspective, these changes had no substantive effect on the nature of the oversight functions performed by the Office or investigatory powers.

Amendments to the *Police Regulation Act* in 1997 required that Victoria Police notify the Ombudsman of the commencement of internally generated investigations of serious misconduct by police, providing for the subsequent review and monitoring of such investigations by the Ombudsman. These amendments gave statutory authority to a previous informal arrangement (see also The Ombudsman 1998b: 19), meaning that the Office of the Ombudsman had the *potential*, at least, to oversight all complaints against police, although a number of constraints on the performance of this function remained (discussed below).

The Deputy Ombudsman's role was to monitor the progress of an investigation as it was being conducted and to comment on the adequacy of the investigation, findings, and proposed sanctions. If a case was not resolved within three months, progress reports were required to be sent to the Deputy Ombudsman after a further three months and thereafter at regular intervals (Internal Investigations Department 1996). During the latter period of this study it became the practice of the then Deputy Ombudsman to regularly visit the ESD to discuss investigations in progress (The Ombudsman 1995: 25–26). Notwithstanding potential arguments around the notion of 'agency capture', supporters of this practice argued that it generated a greater insight into the processes of investigation undertaken, and allowed the Deputy Ombudsman, on occasion, to be proactive in commenting on investigations as they proceeded, rather than reacting after a matter was finalised.

(a)   *Changes to Oversight Arrangements Post-1998*

As indicated earlier in this chapter, the creation in late 2004 of the Office of Police Integrity (OPI) meant that the external oversight function was established within an independent statutory office with significant financial resources and investigatory powers. The former statutory role of Deputy Ombudsman (Police Complaints) was subsumed by the new statutory role of Director of OPI. As reported in the first OPI Annual Report, this development was:

> … in response to widespread concern within the Victorian community about the integrity of its police and the effectiveness of arrangements for oversight and review of police conduct. There was a succession of revelations about the activities of the criminal world, its alleged links with certain police members and its impact on policing practice. This justifiably magnified community concern about police integrity (Director—Police Integrity 2005b: 6).

An interim step was the establishment in mid-2004 of the position of Police Ombudsman as a separate statutory officer (replacing the Deputy Ombudsman (Police Complaints)), with increased resources and investigatory powers. Although a separate office, the Ombudsman, George Brouwer, occupied the roles of both Ombudsman and Police Ombudsman.[21] Increased investigatory powers not previously held by the Deputy Ombudsman (Police Complaints) included the power to conduct hearings, seek and execute search warrants, and to obtain evidence in the manner of a Royal Commission.

The Police Ombudsman was empowered under section 86NA of the *Police Regulation Act* to conduct certain "own motion" investigations independent of the making of a complaint:[22]

> … in respect of any matter that is relevant to the achievement of his or her objects, including but not limited to—
>
> (a)   an investigation into the conduct of a member of the force; or
>
> (b)   an investigation into police corruption or serious misconduct generally; or

---

[21] A new section 6A(2) of the *Ombudsman Act* provided that "The office of Police Ombudsman is to be held by the person who holds office as Ombudsman".

[22] This effectively mirrored a power held by the Ombudsman in relation to his general jurisdiction.

(c)   an investigation into any of the policies, practices or procedures of the force or of a member of the force, or the failure of those policies, practices or procedures.

Therefore, the Police Ombudsman (now the Director of Police Integrity) was accorded wide and independent investigatory powers including the power to initiate investigations and to re-investigate complaints already dealt with by Victoria Police. This development provided for a "more energetic, proactive oversight and review of policing" (Director - Police Integrity 2005b: 6). Although these powers were significant, the Police Ombudsman was still required to inform the Minister for Police and Emergency Services and the Chief Commissioner of Police before conducting an own motion investigation, and it was required that the Chief Commissioner be provided the opportunity to comment before a report adverse to Victoria Police was made. A further constraint was that police members seconded to the office of the Police Ombudsman to assist with investigations remained under the direction of the Chief Commissioner and could not be directed by the Police Ombudsman.

In late 2004, the Victorian government responded to concerns expressed by the Police Ombudsman and formed the OPI, with further increased powers, resources and independence. The Police Ombudsman became the Director of Police Integrity.[23] The Director is now not required to inform the Minister and the Chief Commissioner before conducting own motion investigations, and seconded police members are subject to the sole direction of the Director. As noted in the first Annual Report of the OPI:

> In the interests of securing public confidence in policing and in the oversight arrangements, a credible review body must not only be independent of police and government. It must also have a substantial

---

[23] The legislation provides that the Director, Police Integrity must be the Ombudsman (*Police Regulation Act* section 102A(2)), whose status as an independent officer of the Parliament is assured by section 94E of the *Constitution Act* 1975 (see Director—Police Integrity 2005b: 7). Although the same person continued to fill both statutory roles, by 2006 the offices of the OPI and the Ombudsman were organisationally separated (Director—Police Integrity 2006). In the initial phases of the establishment of the OPI, administrative and organisational support was provided by the Office of the Ombudsman, allowing the OPI to become fully operational at an early stage of its life (Director—Police Integrity 2005b: 18). By mid-2006, the two organisations had completely separate administrative arrangements, and the Ombudsman's office subsequently moved to separate premises (Director—Police Integrity 2006: 29). In late 2007, the Victorian government announced its intention to formally and fully separate the roles of the Ombudsman and the Director – Police Integrity, including the occupancy of these positions.

investigative capability. Its powers, processes and staff must be robust (Director—Police Integrity 2005b: 7).

In addition to the oversight of police internal investigations and the conduct of its own investigations, the objects of the OPI are "to assess policies, practices and procedures which guide police to see that they promote the highest professional, as well as ethical, conduct" on an ongoing basis (Director—Police Integrity 2005b: 9). The powers of the OPI include independent search and seizure and a capacity to use surveillance devices (Director—Police Integrity 2005b: 10). The OPI undertakes follow-up assessment of the implementation of its recommendations and may take further action (investigation or recommendations) if deemed necessary.[24] The Director, Police Integrity describes these arrangements as a "permanent anti-corruption body" for policing, with standing powers that are in most respects equivalent to those of a Royal Commission (Director—Police Integrity 2006: 9). These powers are ongoing and do not end with the tabling of a Commission Report.

As noted earlier in this chapter, the oversight function of the Office allows the Director to investigate a complaint against police if to do so is deemed to be in the "public interest". The OPI has noted that factors considered relevant in determining whether it is in the public interest for a matter to be investigated are:

–   whether the alleged conduct has attracted public interest, apprehension or concern;

–   whether the matter concerns conduct affecting a large number of people or a large number of particular groups of people;

–   whether the substance of the alleged misconduct relates to OPI's investigative priorities;

–   whether the matter involves Force policies, procedures and practices;

–   the complaints history of the officer or officers involved; and

–   issues involving public confidence in the public complaint investigation process.

(Director - Police Integrity 2006: 62)

---

[24] By 2005–06 almost 3000 complaints against police had been received and the Office of Police Integrity had heard evidence from 75 witnesses (Director—Police Integrity 2006: 9).

In summary, the post-1994 arrangements for external oversight and independent investigation of complaints against police have been considerably strengthened in terms of power and resources. Since its formation, the OPI has been active in a number of major investigations into police practice (Director - Police Integrity 2005b, 2006). In many senses, this marks a turning point in oversight of the police disciplinary system. Transcending its former heavy reliance on police investigations of complaints, the OPI has its own proactive intelligence and assessments, and it aims to utilise these in 70 per cent of OPI's investigations into corruption and serious misconduct cases (Director - Police Integrity 2005b: 9). Since its inception the OPI has conducted a number of high profile investigations, enquiries, and reviews. These have been conducted independently, as one would expect of a permanent anti-corruption body, and in some cases in conjunction with the Ethical Standards Department (ESD) of Victoria Police.

(b)   *External Oversight: Evidence from this Study*

Tables 3.7 and 3.8 show the impact of the oversight of the Deputy Ombudsman in the period under review. The Deputy Ombudsman had the option to comment on the investigation and outcomes in individual cases and to argue for changes in findings or determination/sanctions. There was also the option to comment on the overall policies and procedures followed by Victoria Police, as evidenced by processes followed in investigating particular complaints, and to argue for changes in these policies and procedures. In all cases the recommendations of the Deputy Ombudsman were not binding on Victoria Police, but, as illustrated in the analysis in Chapters Four to Six, the interactions between the Deputy Ombudsman and Victoria Police were often vigorous and productive.

Table 3.7 provides detail of the extent of the Deputy Ombudsman's comments on the adequacy of the outcome in relation to investigation of conflict of interest cases in this study.

Table 3.7: Comments by the Deputy Ombudsman

Deputy Ombudsman Comments	N	%
No adverse comment on investigation and outcome	317	84.8
Unhappy with initial investigation/outcome; requests revision	23	6.1
Argued for different determination/sanction; Victoria Police agree	14	3.7
Argued for different determination/sanction; Victoria Police disagree	12	3.2
Adverse comment on outcome, but concedes evidentiary problem	8	2.1
Total *	**374**	**100.0**

* Data not available for three cases

Overwhelmingly (in almost 85 per cent of cases), the Deputy Ombudsman found no reason to make any formal comment on the Victoria Police processing of complaints. This signified—sometimes explicitly—that he was satisfied with the processes and outcomes in these cases. In the remaining 15 per cent of cases, the Deputy Ombudsman's comments can be characterised as falling into one of four groups. First, they could be an expression of dissatisfaction with some aspect of the investigation or outcome in a case and a request for revision and did not necessarily involve an argument for a change in the determination of the matter. In all cases, Victoria Police revisited the matter and provided further advice to the Deputy Ombudsman. Secondly, the Deputy Ombudsman could specifically argue for a change in the determination. Thirdly, he could argue for a change in the proposed sanction (usually this involved an argument that the proposed sanction was inadequate). Arguments for increases in sanctions were made in 6.9 per cent of all cases. Victoria Police considered the Deputy Ombudsman's suggestions in all instances, and in just over half of these cases agreed to increase the sanction. Finally, in a small number of cases (2.1 per cent) the Deputy Ombudsman expressed dissatisfaction with the outcome in a case, but nevertheless conceded that the outcome was acceptable in the circumstances. This was as much an expression of frustration that the state of the evidence or legal advice in a case meant that it seemed that an officer would be inadequately dealt with.

The results of the Deputy Ombudsman's oversight are significant both in that they portray a general satisfaction with internal Victoria Police processes and outcomes, and that where this was not the case Victoria Police were generally responsive to the comments of the Deputy Ombudsman. This evidence therefore suggests that the oversight of the Deputy Ombudsman, at least in relation to complaints of conflict of interest, makes an important contribution to the rigour and integrity of internal investigations processes.

However, as noted earlier, there remained a number of constraints on the powers and capacities of the office of the Deputy Ombudsman. Although the value of the Deputy Ombudsman's oversight is clearly evident both in the results presented here and in case analyses in Chapters Four to Six, this is not to conclude that it was *sufficient*. Clearly, the rigour of an investigation can be as much a question of resource allocation and budget as it is a matter of the intent and skills of the investigator. All other things being equal, the increase in funding and attendant increase in powers granted to the OPI since 2004 provide for further enhancement of an important monitoring and oversight role while adding an independent investigatory function.

(c) *Issues of Policy and Procedure: Evidence from this Study*

The Deputy Ombudsman also had the capacity to comment on wider matters of policy and procedure within Victoria Police which, while arising in the context of a particular complaint, were not necessarily related to the specific circumstances of a particular case.

Table 3.8 shows the extent of the Ombudsman's comments on the overall policies and procedures adopted by Victoria Police in the conflict of interest cases examined for this research.

Table 3.8: Recommendations from Ombudsman

Recommendations	N	%
No policy implications mentioned	327	87.4
Recommended procedures, etc. be changed: Police agree	40	10.7
Recommended procedures, etc. be changed: Police disagree	7	1.9
Total *	374	100.0

* Data not available for three cases

As was the case with the Deputy Ombudsman's comments on specific investigations, overwhelmingly (87.4 per cent of cases), there were no formal recommendations for changes in Victoria Police policy and procedures. Where such recommendations were made, Victoria Police agreed in almost all instances and made adjustments to policy or process accordingly.

Again, these results exhibit the value of the oversight function carried out by the Deputy Ombudsman and indicate a preparedness on the part of Victoria Police management to respond productively to such comments. With the recent strengthening of the powers of the OPI, clusters of complaint, such as particular types of conflict of interest as outlined in the following chapters, may be able to be acted upon as systemic issues warranting attention.

(d) *External Oversight: Concluding Note*

The findings presented in Tables 3.7 and 3.8 show that the Deputy Ombudsman (Police Complaints) performed an important function in the system of accountability for individual police officers as well as an effective element in attending to the wider accountability of Victoria Police as an organisation. Combined with processes of internal review, the model of external oversight should mean that complaint cases are investigated and assessed in a thoroughgoing and independent manner (resource allocation and managerial will permitting). The increased independence, investigatory powers, and financial resources accorded to the OPI since 2004 have undoubtedly enhanced this function.

However, overall these processes, whilst of value and effective, remain centred on a reactive model of *ex-post* passive accountability. This is also true of the police discipline system as a whole—problems are generally dealt with reactively, after they arise rather than through processes of developing *ex-ante* responsibility and accountability. In dealing with the specific problem of conflict of interest (and police accountability more generally), the development of active responsibility is vital. The remainder of this chapter addresses these issues.

IV   Building Accountability

A   *The Importance of Culture*

The hierarchical nature of the police discipline system typifies classical, traditional forms of bureaucratic accountability. Reliance on a notion of hierarchical responsibility encourages passive or reactive responsibility and is unlikely to be successful in developing forms of active responsibility that may prevent problems from arising in the first place. These questions are particularly important, given the power and authority vested in the police, and their need to retain legitimacy in the eyes of the public and the government.

While the central problem in conflict of interest seems to emerge at an individual level (for example, as an individual police officer pursues private interests), effectively dealing with the problem requires action at the collective and cultural level within policing. Police organisations can be seen as micro-communities, characterised by particular and distinct cultures and rules of action and interaction. Accountability forms a basic constituent of relationships inside and outside police organisations, making them intelligible, meaningful, and, to some degree, controllable. The way police officers are rendered accountable to themselves and to others will provide an important input into the production and reproduction of police culture.

Whilst a particular incident or act of misconduct may be attributed to a single police officer or identifiable group of officers, it is much less certain that the causal factors for such misconduct can be so attributed. It has been established that police culture, organisational factors, and the socio-political context also play significant roles. An excessive focus on individual misconduct can direct attention away from key structural and organisational sources of problems (Crank 1998: Ch. 18). Ultimately, change in policing, and in police culture, requires a change in the way police and policing are conceived both within police organisations themselves and within the general population (Dixon 1999c; Reiner 2000).

B   *Evidence on the Culture of Conflict of Interest*

If conflict of interest is to be addressed at the level of police culture, the attitudes and activities of senior members of the organisation may need to come under scrutiny. This is because processes of enculturation within a police organisation mean that senior officers have a significant influence on new constables once they are on the job.

Illustrating the significance of this issue, this section presents evidence of the rank and seniority of officers involved in conflict of interest complaints.

1   Rank and Position of Police Officers

It is noteworthy, and perhaps surprising, that many of those complained against had considerable levels of experience and, at the rank of sergeant and above, were likely to have had management and supervision responsibilities. Table 3.9 compares the rank composition for Victoria Police as a whole (based on an average for the years 1988–1998) with the conflict of interest complaint cases. This shows that the senior ranks of Sergeant and above were over-represented in complaints, compared with the ranks of Constable and Senior Constable.[25]

Table 3.9: Rank Structure of Victoria Police compared with Conflict of Interest Complaints

Rank		Victoria Police officers *		Conflict of Interest Complaints	
	1988–1998	N	%	N	%
Constable [#]		2718	28.5	118	22.2
Senior Constable [#]		4528	43.6	220	41.4
Sergeant		1675	17.9	111	20.9
Senior Sergeant		520	5.6	47	8.9
Inspector or above		420	4.5	35	6.6
Total†		9860	100	531	100

* Based on figures obtained from: Victoria Police (1988; Victoria Police 1989, 1990, 1991, 1992, 1993a, 1994, 1995, 1996a, 1997, 1998a). [#] Excluding the years 1988 and 1989—in these years published figures combine the ranks of Constable and Senior Constable.
† Total excludes 3 unsworn members and 5 police officers for whom rank data was not available.

---

[25] An examination of the rank structure proportions for each of the 10 years reiterates this conclusion, indicating that the 10-year averages are not distorted by fluctuations from year to year. In addition, this conclusion is not affected by the higher number of complaint cases in the years 1994–1996, because in these three years the ranks of Sergeant and above represented lower proportions of the total Force than the 10-year average.

Table 3.10 adds a further dimension to this analysis by showing the outcome of complaint cases in terms of final determinations for all police officers, by rank.

Table 3.10: Determination by Rank

Rank	Determination of complaint						Total	
	Adverse to police officer		Indeterminate		In favour of police officer			
	N	%	N	%	N	%	N	%
Constable	50	42.4	20	16.9	48	40.7	118	100.0
Senior Constable	85	38.6	35	15.9	100	45.5	220	100.0
Sergeant	43	38.7	11	9.9	57	51.4	111	100.0
Senior Sergeant	14	29.8	7	14.9	26	55.3	47	100.0
Inspector or above	11	31.4	5	14.3	19	54.3	35	100.0
Total*	203	38.2	78	14.7	250	47.1	531	100.0

* Total excludes 3 unsworn members and 5 police officers for whom rank data was not available.

Whilst the senior ranks had lower substantiation rates, the rates are nevertheless of considerable concern, and the over-representation of senior ranks in conflict of interest complaints is problematic. The Ombudsman, in his final report on the window-shutter kickback scam (The Ombudsman 1998b) singled out the ranks of Sergeant and Senior Sergeant for particular criticism. He noted that it was Sergeants and Senior Sergeants who control the day-to-day operations of the police force and it is they who are largely responsible for making or breaking the standards of acceptable conduct and ethical behaviour established by Police Command. The Ombudsman noted that the effective working environment and ethical behaviour of members below this rank is set by these middle-level managers. In spite of this level of seniority and responsibility within the police force, the Ombudsman expressed regret that:

> ... a large number of sergeants and senior sergeants, in particular, have actively obstructed the investigation and actively encouraged subordinates to do the same. Furthermore, there is evidence that some

supervisors have colluded with or pressured subordinates to make statements which minimise the supervisor's involvement. A number of such supervisors I believe have escaped disciplinary action. (The Ombudsman 1998b: 55–56)

If conflict of interest is to be dealt with effectively at the organisational level, the leadership shown by the senior ranks in these matters clearly needs to be addressed.

2   Level of Experience

Further exacerbating the problem of leadership, most officers complained against were experienced officers. Where years of service data was available in the case files (474 police officers – approximately 88 per cent of the total), only 15 per cent of officers complained against had less than five years of service. The breakdown of officers' experience in terms of years of service is shown in Figure 3.3.

Figure 3.3: Years of Service of Officers Complained Against

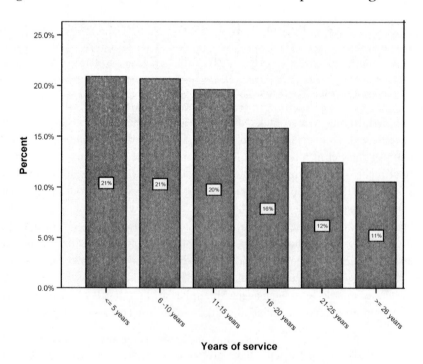

Years of service

This figure depicts a situation that is of considerable concern in relation to the building of accountability within policing because it suggests that police officers with significant levels of experience become involved in claims of conflict of interest. Working from the right side of the graph, looking at the last two bars, it can be seen that some 23 per cent of all conflict of interest claims are made against officers with more than 21 years of police experience. Combining the last three bars shows that 39 per cent of all claims are made against officers with more than 16 years of service.

It is evident that overwhelmingly it was *experienced* police officers who were the subject of conflict of interest complaints—79 per cent of officers complained against had at least five years of service to the Police Force. Table 3.11 illustrates a further aspect of this problem, showing the determinations for these 474 police officers, by years of service.

Table 3.11: Determination by Years of Service

Length of service (years)	Determination of complaint						Total	
	Adverse to police officer (substantiated)		Indeterminate		In favour of police officer			
	N	%	N	%	N	%	N	%
<= 5	38	38.4	21	21.2	40	40.4	99	100.0
6–10	29	29.6	15	15.3	54	55.1	98	100.0
11–15	38	40.9	11	11.8	44	47.3	93	100.0
16–20	24	32.0	12	16.0	39	52.0	75	100.0
21–25	25	42.4	6	10.2	28	47.5	59	100.0
>= 26	13	26.0	7	14.0	30	60.0	50	100.0
Total	167	35.2	72	15.2	235	49.6	474	100.0

Again, this reiterates the problem by showing that relatively high substantiation rates are evident across the board. These results are in contrast with a generally held view that it is younger, less experienced constables who are likely to attract the bulk of complaints (and adverse findings).

3   Gender

Given the prominence of rank and years of experience in conflict of interest complaints statistics, it is interesting to note that an examination of gender yields a different result. Of all complaints lodged against police officers during the period, 93.1 per cent were against male officers and 6.9 per cent female officers (data unknown in two instances out of 539). For the period of the study, this percentage may be contrasted with the overall makeup of the Force as a whole. For the 11 years covered by Victoria Police Annual Reports in the period 1987/88–1997/98, the average percentage of female members (excluding reservists and public servants) was 14.1 per cent (Victoria Police 1988, 1989, 1990, 1991, 1992, 1993a, 1994, 1995, 1996a, 1997, 1998a).[26]

An Australian National Police Research Unit study of perception of ethical dilemmas among police officers, offers some assistance in interpreting this result. The study involved asking police officers to rank a set of scenarios in terms of how they and other officers might react to the circumstances and events portrayed in the scenarios. The research found that female police officers (recruits and constables) held themselves to higher standards than did 'typical' officers (see Huon et al. 1995). Other research has indicated that female police recruits belong to an 'outgroup' and may not be part of the police 'brotherhood', thus giving rise to independent perceptions on ethical issues, or, at least, to exclusion from 'the take'. It may be that differential socialisation of men and women police officers in a strong male police culture may account for a lower complaint rate against women police officers (Huon et al. 1995; Wood 1997a).

In a Queensland Criminal Justice Commission report analysing assault complaints against Queensland police officers, 95 per cent of the officers involved in the alleged conflictual events were male. This indicated "a significant overrepresentation of males". At the time of the study, women police officers constituted 9 to 12 per cent of the make up of the state's police

---

[26] It is not possible to compare the proportion conflict of interest complaints against female police officers with the proportion of all complaints against female officers (that is, involving allegations relating to matters other than conflict of interest), as published complaint statistics are not broken down by gender.

force, and most of those female police officers were employed in the 'front line' ranks of constable and senior constable where the likelihood of being the subject of an assault complaint is present (Criminal Justice Commission 1997). Other internal studies conducted by the Queensland Police Service (cited in the Criminal Justice Commission report) confirmed that "males were more likely than females to attract more serious misconduct complaints". In a separate Criminal Justice Commission publication specifically addressing gender and ethics in policing (Criminal Justice Commission 1996), the Commission examined complaints against Queensland police for the years 1992–1995. This study found that female officers of the rank of constable or senior constable were less likely to attract misconduct complaints, in general, than their male counterparts.

Lersch and Mieczkowski (1996) cited a range of United States research that indicates that women police officers are perceived more favourably by members of the public as more competent, more respectful, and having greater listening ability than their male counterparts. Other research cited by Lersch and Mieczkowski indicates that female police officers are less likely to be involved in violent confrontation, have a general calming effect, are less likely to be involved in deadly force incidents, and attract far fewer complaints from the public than their male counterparts.

Patterns of complaint and discipline investigations against women police officers may also be affected by micro decisions within the organisation. Research in the United States of America on gender disparity in supervisory decisions about whether to proceed with a complaint investigation against female officers suggests that the decisions of middle management supervisors may also go some way to explaining the apparent lower incidence of female police misconduct (Hickman et al. 2000). The authors of the Queensland Criminal Justice Commission report on gender and ethics in policing (Criminal Justice Commission 1996) suggested that their research supported the view that female police officers are generally less confrontational in their manner and more adept at handling conflict.

In summary, the under-representation of female officers in conflict of interest allegations, relative to their total proportion of police numbers, is reflective of other research showing that female police officers may exhibit different ethical standards to their male counterparts, and are less likely to be involved in, or attract, complaints of misconduct.

C   *Conflict of Interest and Police Accountability*

In order to develop a detailed understanding of the nature of the problem of conflict of interest and how it is dealt with, the next three chapters examine and analyse the conflict of interest complaint cases included in this study. Chapter Four focuses on the private realm—sources of conflict of interest originating in the private relationships and involvements of police officers—and how this may play out in terms of breaches of duty. Chapters Five and Six focus on the public realm—how conflicts of interest play out in terms of their effect on the performance of official police duties. Chapter Five examines the use and abuse of police powers and authority, such as inappropriate involvement in police investigations and processes. The focus of Chapter Six is on how conflicts of interest may be manifested in the use and abuse of police resources such as police information and police identity.

The final chapter of the book considers issues relating to how conflict of interest might be better dealt with, focusing on questions of police accountability and its relationship with public trust in the integrity of police officers and police organisations as a whole.

CHAPTER FOUR

The Private Realm:
Relationships and Involvements

I   Introduction

The realm of police discretion and authority combined with the low visibility of much day-to-day police work provides numerous opportunities for the advancement of private interests (including those of family, friends, and acquaintances). This chapter seeks to identify the circumstances in the private lives of police officers from which problematic conflicts of interest often arise. Specific conflicts of interest related to (or sourced in) private relationships and involvements were able to be identified in approximately one-third of all the conflict of interest complaint case files examined (132 occurrences). In examining these private relationships and involvements, the chapter moves beyond a general notion of 'private interests' to articulate specific forms of private interest that give rise to conflicts of interest. In other cases, the alleged conflicts are more general, such as the pursuit of a private financial advantage for the police officer or seeking to advance the interests of a friend.

Eight broad areas of private relationships and involvements are discussed in this chapter. As shown in Table 4.1, these are organised into three analytical groups: organisational involvements; family-based involvements; and problematic personal relationships (and associated personal conduct). The area of problematic personal relationships represents just over 40 per cent of the total identifiable conflicts of interest in this area. The other two areas—organisational involvements and family-based involvements—each involve close to 30 per cent of the total identifiable conflicts.

Although there may be some intersections with a police officer's public (official) involvements (for example, in relationships with informers) the problematic aspects of these relationships and involvements relate principally to personal conduct within the private domain of a police officer's life.

Table 4.1: Cases of Conflict of Interest—Private Relationships and Involvements

Category of conflict of interest	Total Occurrences	
	N	% (n=132)
Organisational involvements		
Outside employment, or carrying on a business, without permission	27	20.4
Membership of an organisation involved in politics (for example, local council, political party)	5	3.8
Engagement in civic, social, or other organised activities (for example, member of club, society)	6	4.5
CATEGORY TOTAL	**38**	**28.8**
Family-based involvements		
Personal family law related problems	9	6.8
Relatives with family law and related problems	31	23.5
CATEGORY TOTAL	**40**	**30.3**
Problematic personal relationships		
Facilitating intimate personal relationships, or (alleged) sexual misconduct/impropriety	30	22.7
Inappropriate relationship with a criminal, informer, or person/business of ill repute	9	6.8
Other problematic personal relationships and friendships	15	11.4
CATEGORY TOTAL	**54**	**40.9**
OVERALL TOTAL	**132**	**100.0**

The conflicts of interest discussed in this chapter do not inherently or necessarily result in conflict of interest breaches (neglects of duty), but they do elevate the chances of such breaches occurring. As the analysis shows, when such matters come to attention (often when a complaint is made against police) they do often involve breaches of duty. It is often the case, therefore, that breaches of duty are involved in the use of police position to engage or attempt to engage in intimate personal relationships, or in illicit or improper sexual conduct. Inappropriate relationships with criminals, informers, and persons or businesses of ill repute will also usually involve a breach of duty. In regard to sexual impropriety, in so far as such activity will almost always breach disciplinary regulations, it would probably involve a conflict of interest breach, although the pursuit of personal relationships is itself not necessarily problematic.

The distinction between conflicts of interest and conflict of interest breaches is generally not drawn in the conflict of interest literature but it is important for clearly understanding the nature of the problem. This distinction separates the sources of problems (conflicts of interest) from the manifestations or results of those problems (breaches of duty).

A *Note on method and terminology*

Many of the cases examined were characterised by more than one type of conflict of interest, therefore each case was coded with up to two conflict of interest category types. Across the entire study of 377 cases, 523 separate instances of conflict of interest allegations were coded in this way. Of these, 132 related to the private realm, and are included in the analysis in this chapter. The remaining 391 instances related to aspects of the public realm, and are discussed in Chapters 5 and 6.

In Chapters 4 to 6, where the discussion refers to "cases" or "complaints, unless otherwise specifically stated, this relates to one of the total 523 instances of conflict of interest allegations contained within the 377 cases.

II   Organisational Involvements

Outside organisational involvements of a police officer have the potential to impact on the performance of official duties. A range of issues relating to outside organisational involvements have been canvassed by a number of authors (e.g. Independent Commission on Policing for Northern Ireland 1999; Kleinig 1996; Davis 1982; Elliston and Feldberg 1985; Kingsley 1996; Macintyre and Prenzler 1999; Miller *et al.* 1997; Neyroud and Beckley 2001) but for the present analysis the key conflict is between those duties and obligations and the personal interests of the police officer or those of an employer or other organisation with which the police officer is involved.

Table 4.2 summarises the findings in complaints relating to organisational involvements. Secondary employment and private business involvements represented the most significant problem in this area (27 out of 38 complaints). Two other groups of problems also emerged from the complaint case files: membership of organisations involved in politics, such as local/municipal councils; and involvement in civic, social, or other organised activities. For the secondary employment and private business cases, 19 resulted in substantiated findings. Although the total number of cases is relatively low, the high substantiation rate (70.4 per cent) demonstrates that where allegations do arise in this area, it is generally indicative of a definite conflict of interest, and often a conflict of interest breach. This may partially reflect the fact that secondary employment may be easier to substantiate because there is often a documentary trail (with the secondary employer and taxation authorities, for example) which provides evidence to support claims made. Other types of conflict of interest allegations often rest on verbal evidence that cannot necessarily be corroborated.

The small number of complaints in relation to membership of organisations involved in politics and involvement in civic, social or other organised activities means that generalisation is difficult, although it is possible to say that the problems are not significant in the overall picture of conflict of interest. Nevertheless, awareness of the possible conflicts of interest in these areas is necessary, especially in light of the public prominence of cases related to political involvement.

Table 4.2: Findings in Complaints Relating to Organisational Involvements

Category of conflict of interest	Determination						Total Occurrences	
	Finding against police officer (sub-stantiated)		In-determinate finding[1]		Finding in favour of police officer[2]			
	N	%	N	%	N	%	N	%
Outside employment, or carrying on a business, without permission	19	70.4	4	14.8	4	14.8	27	100
Membership of an organisation involved in politics (for example, local council, political party)	1	20.0	0	0.0	4	80.0	5	100
Engagement in civic, social, or other organised activities (for example, member of club, society)	3	50.0	2	33.3	1	16.7	6	100
TOTAL	23	60.5	6	15.8	9	23.7	38	100

(1) *Indeterminate finding* = Lesser deficiency, Unable to determine, Conciliated, Not proceeded with (resigned prior).

(2) *Finding in favour of police officer* = Withdrawn, No complaint, Not substantiated, Unfounded, Exonerated

A   *Outside Employment and Business Arrangements*

There are two key aspects of the conflict of interest problems related to the outside employment and private business arrangements of police officers: the potential for outside employment duties, allegiances, and commitments to interfere with the actual performance of public duties; and potentially negative impacts on public perceptions of police integrity. The public perception problem essentially relates to the belief of members of the public as to whether police officers perform their duty in an unbiased manner. Where a police officer is seen to 'serve two masters'—the police force and his or her secondary employer—members of the public may understandably question which set of interests are prioritised by the police officer.

These problems have led Victoria Police, in common with many other police forces around the world, to put in place strict rules regarding the circumstances in which police officers may undertake such activity. Approval from the Chief Commissioner[1] must be sought in order to participate in outside or secondary employment, including private business activities. Section 69(1) of the *Police Regulation Act* provides that a breach of discipline is committed when a police officer, without approval:

(i)   applies for or holds a license or permit to conduct any trade, business or profession; or

(ii)   conducts any trade, business or profession; or

(iii)   accepts any other employment ...

The Victoria Police Code of Conduct provides police officers with some detail of the rationale behind this provision, arguing that police officers must be 'fit to perform' police work, and that:

Approval to engage in outside employment will not be granted if it is likely to:

- interfere with the effective performance of your official duties

- create or appear to create a conflict of interest

- reflect adversely on the Force.

Approval to engage in outside employment is suspended during any period of absence from the Force on paid sick leave.

(Victoria Police 1998b: 26)

This remains a contentious area of police regulation because police officers often wish to engage in outside employment to supplement their family incomes, arguing that their inability to do so would effectively penalise them financially. In addition to the provision of supplementary income, involvement in outside employment may facilitate the development of new skills and may

---

[1] Prior to amendments in the early 1990s, the approval had to be sought from the relevant State Government Minister. In practice, the Minister's authority was delegated to the Chief Commissioner.

assist the building of community relations (Royal Canadian Mounted Police External Review Committee 1991: 44). It is also accepted that police officers may wish to engage in outside employment and related activities (including voluntary activity) to relieve stress and provide relaxation. However, even though it may be accepted on the one hand that police, like anyone else, should have the right to earn extra income, on the other hand "there are few areas where a police officer can work without the potential for conflict of interest" (Moss 1997b: 10).

1   *Importance of Perceptions*

At all times police management and individual police officers must attempt to ensure that police officers do not become engaged in activities that may give rise to a perception of conflict of interest, or where they may actually experience such a conflict. For police management, the key concern with outside employment is not the employment *per se*, but the underlying nature of the employment and the fact that the *particular* activities engaged in may conflict with the individual's duties as a police officer.

A further key concern is the potential for police officers engaging in outside employment to bring discredit upon the Force. Some employment areas have the potential, by their very nature, to negatively impact on the Force. For example, for police officers stationed as Traffic Operations Group members, private involvements in areas that have direct association with their police duties, such as operating as a licensed motor car trader, operating as a driving instructor, or involvement with a vehicle towing firm, may conflict with duties as a police officer. As explained in Chapter 2, conflict exists whether or not there is any actual impact on the performance of police duties.

In rural locations or small communities, such concerns might be exacerbated. For example, one case examined for this book involved a police officer who had obtained permission to conduct outside employment in the form of running a used car dealership (licensed motor car trader). When the matter came up for review as a result of a conflict of interest complaint, the officer's senior sought to have approval withdrawn, stating that such activity "in a small community adversely reflects upon the Victoria Police Force and his ability to successfully carry out his duties" (Case 122). The police officer claimed that as a police officer he was well known in his local community, and that it was consequently impossible for customers dealing with his car dealership not to know that he was also a police officer. He also stated that "several" of the people he had spoken to thought it was "terrific" that he had permission to operate as a licensed motor car trader in addition to his work as a police officer. In resolving this case, the police officer was given new approval to conduct business as a licensed motor car trader, however new restrictions were added to the approval, including that he was required to operate outside his Police District area. In addition, he was instructed that the employment must not impinge upon his police work in terms of hours worked, that he must not expect any preference in terms of rostering, that he must not work while on leave, and that he must never wear his uniform during his outside employment (Case 122).

In such cases, the core concern relates to situations where a police officer has both official (police) and non-official dealings with a person. The potential exists for direct or indirect pressure to be exerted in relation to non-official (non-police) dealings. The problem exists in terms of the perception of the public as well as in relation to specific actions undertaken by the individual officer. Public perceptions of an individual's activity are possibly as important as the actual facts in a given case. In a case involving a police officer working as a driving school instructor, the officer argued that his actions in conducting his private business were *in fact* impartial and not affected by any conflict of interest. Whilst accepting that there could be conflicts if he was called upon to deal with an offending current or former student, he argued in effect that he had not actually been shown to have acted in a way that conflicted with his police duties. In support, the police officer cited the fact that he had issued a traffic infringement notice to an ex-student, and that most of his students did not know he was a police officer. The investigating officer agreed, concluding that the police officer had not compromised his position as a member of the Force and had not used his position as a police member to gain advantage in his outside employment or to disadvantage his opposition. The Deputy Ombudsman also concurred with these views. Nevertheless, the officer was reprimanded for operating outside employment without permission and he agreed to cease operating as a driving instructor, handing the business over to his wife (Case 23). This resolution was perhaps understandable in terms of seeking to minimise the impact on the police officer, who had not been shown to have abused his position or breached his duties, but the conflict of interest problem was not thereby eliminated. The source of the conflict of interest was merely shifted from the police officer's private interests to those of his wife. It was not recognised that new conflicts could flow from the potential for the police officer, in his official capacity, to take action with the intention and/or effect of benefiting his wife's business activity.

A more obvious conflict of interest problem arises if a police officer conducts off-duty business interests whilst in police uniform. A complaint against an officer who conducted business as an unlicensed motor car trader (selling cars for a friend) was found to have been substantiated following evidence that he conducted business whilst in police uniform. The concern was that this had the effect of giving an official imprimatur to his private activity, thus creating an advantage in a commercial transaction. The police officer also signed a statutory declaration, in his capacity as a police officer, for a party to a disputed commercial transaction with which he was involved (Case 79).

2   *Impact on Police Duties*

In some areas of activity the problem lies in the way the police officer's outside employment may impact on the conduct of police duties. For example, an officer who had a commercial arrangement with a heavy vehicle towing firm had a complaint against him substantiated on the basis of the fact that he not only received free benefits from the firms (including a mobile telephone, phone calls, and diesel fuel), but that he specifically breached police regulations by carrying a mobile phone whilst on duty, in order to inform his (outside) employer of heavy vehicle accidents. A police management concern was that particular police officers might be targeted in such cases, as heavy vehicle towing was not part of the Victorian legislated tow-truck allocation system, meaning that the first truck to attend the scene of an accident would have the best chance of securing the business (Case 262).

Associations of an informal nature with tow-truck operators are also particularly sensitive. A police officer who had previously been admonished for unprofessional behaviour in relation to a close, although informal, association with a towing company where his best friend worked (Case 126) was the subject of a complaint that included involvement in similar circumstances with the same towing company. In this second complaint it was alleged that the police officer had a formal arrangement with the towing company that involved the provision of information that assisted them to obtain towing contracts prior to other towing companies being informed (the metropolitan tow-truck allocation system did not apply in the provincial location involved in this case). The complaint involved evidence that the police officer had made a telephone call to the towing company to provide information that was of assistance to the company in its business dealings. It was also found that in his general association with the company and its employees the police officer engaged in conduct likely to bring the Force into disrepute, for which he was admonished (Case 251).

Private business interests can also have an impact on the way officers interact with members of the public in the course of their duties. A case illustrating this problem related to the interests of two police officers engaged in a business partnership (a farm). One of the officers had permission to engage in outside employment while the other did not. The allegations included claims that the police officers had tried to recruit labour for their private business from private citizens who attended the police station and had used various police resources to assist in the running of the business (Case 370). The investigating officer felt that the private business concerns of the two police officers had had a deleterious impact on their general performance of police duties, and that they may have used police resources (motor vehicles) in their private business. The outcome of the case was that the police officer who did not have permission to engage in outside employment was admonished, but the other officer resigned prior to the disciplinary charge proceeding, ostensibly due to ill health.

3   Surveillance and Security Work

Private surveillance and security work is an area of ongoing concern as it may give rise to an increased risk both of conflict of interest breaches and negative public perceptions of the police force. Given the nature of the work, this is an attractive area of outside employment for police due to the somewhat similar skills required and their attractiveness to an employer. Key problems for police management are, on the one hand, the potential for the misuse of police information and other resources in the furtherance of private surveillance and security work and, on the other hand, the potential for such employment to deleteriously impact on the performance of police duties. There were seven cases in this area in the complaint case files; two are discussed here to illustrate the sorts of problems that may arise.

The first case involved a police officer who served in a senior capacity on the local municipal council. He used his position to organise police officers to undertake after hours security work in guarding a council building site (Case 95). The work was paid for by the council via cash cheques, and the police officers involved were not identified and the police officer who was the subject of this complaint would not disclose the names of the other officers involved. He refused to disclose the names even when directed to do so by a superior officer and was consequently charged with a discipline breach of failing to comply with a lawful instruction given by a member above the rank of senior sergeant, under s 69(1)(d) of the *Police Regulation Act*. He was also charged under s 69(2) with aiding, abetting, and procuring unnamed members of the Force to breach discipline regulations (to accept outside employment without permission). The police officer attempted to justify his actions by stating that he had seen a pressing need for security at the council building and the interests of the ratepayers were served by the outcome he had procured. He did not regard the good order and discipline of the force as coming into question as a result of these actions. This case generated considerable controversy and was written up in the local press. The police officer who had organised the security work was admonished.

The second case embroiled a number of police officers who were members of a state-wide police unit (Case 345). It was alleged that they had a formal arrangement to conduct regular (off duty) surveillance work for a Private Agent. No permission had been sought to undertake the outside employment. A large number of police officers were suspected as being involved in the formal arrangement and disciplinary charges were brought against five officers, including the Officer in Charge of the unit. Not only were they engaged in unauthorised outside employment, but it was alleged that they utilised police information (motor vehicle checks), vehicles, radios, and mobile phones in the furtherance of their outside employment. The employment was organised by liaison between a Detective Sergeant and the Private Agent with whom he had a longstanding professional and social relationship. The liaison involved the distribution of jobs to the various police officers, collection of handwritten surveillance reports from them and delivery to the Private Agent, and payment of cash monies to the officers for work performed. It was also apparent that other members of the unit had unwittingly become involved, by conducting motor vehicle checks for their colleagues, of whose unauthorised surveillance activities they were unaware.

It was argued by the five police officers that prior to the matter coming under investigation they had met to discuss coming forward to the ESD to admit their involvement in these matters, as they were aware that their behaviour was a breach of discipline. In response to the investigation, the police officers offered the following: they had performed the unauthorised surveillance for the money, and they had only conducted the surveillance activities on rostered days off or after duty. Each member agreed that in the surveillance work they had used police vehicles, radios and, where present, mobile telephones. One of the police officers explained her conduct by suggesting that she only undertook the work if it did not interfere with her police work, did not involve any criminal activity, and did not involve any other officer. She said she was "worried about setting a bad example". At the time of examining this case file, it was not possible to determine what sanctions were applied against four of the police officers involved as these matters had not progressed to finalisation of sanctions, but in the remaining case the police officer was initially to be fined $2500, but the matter was adjourned on condition that she be of good behaviour (effectively, a good behaviour bond), and the charge was later dismissed upon the expiration of the good behaviour period without further incident.

Summarising the conflict of interest that often arises in this area is the general inability of police officers engaged in outside surveillance and security work to clearly separate it from police work—a feature of all of these cases. The appropriation of police resources for private benefit, the misleading of colleagues, and a general lack of cooperation with investigators, are all indicative of the problems that may flow from this form of engagement.

4   Outside Employment While On Leave

Outside employment for police officers whilst on long service leave or recreation leave is specifically prohibited under the *Employee Relations Act*, even where it is argued that the work conducted has no direct bearing on the police officer's duties as a member of the Force, there is no contact with the public, limited contact with other staff of the outside employer, and no use of investigative skills. Employment with the Army Reserve may present particular problems for police management, although there is a tendency to support such employment. This is the case even when it is undertaken on a full-time basis whilst the police officer is on leave from the Force—such full-time employment would seem to be prohibited under the *Employee Relations Act*.

The support for full-time employment with the Army Reserve whilst on leave does not go unquestioned or uncontested, however, as illustrated by a case involving a police officer who worked full-time in the Army Reserve whilst on long service leave. Although there was ultimately found to be no conflict of interest or breach of discipline, the senior police officer who had lodged the initial complaint expressed disappointment with this outcome. His objections were multiple: that a member could be allowed to work full-time for the entire recreation leave period; that his employment had been considered under the same category as Training Camps and Courses for no economic benefit whereas he had clearly been receiving pay; and that emotional pleas from the member to not be punished for 'serving his country' had been taken into account. Part of the argument made was related to the need for a police officer to have genuine rest and recreation from their police work (Case 291).

The workforce procedures relevant during the time frame of this study included a declaratory statement that "there must be no conflict of interest between the functions and responsibilities of a member, reservist or protective services officer and any private pursuits" (10.2.1). Further in relation specifically to membership of outside voluntary organisations, in particular fire services or other emergency services, they stated that police duty must come first and the officer may be recalled in emergencies, disasters or other unusual events (10.3).

5   Private Business Activity

A major concern with involvements in private business, including family businesses, is that police officers may intervene or otherwise become involved in civil disputes in relation to the business. These involvements may be, or may be perceived to be, inappropriate. Sometimes only seemingly minor misdemeanours are involved, such as using a police station as the registered address of a private business, but other cases involve much more fundamental conflicts of interest, often involving the disputes of a civil nature that arise from time to time in private business activity. The most overt problems relate to circumstances where police officers use their police position and authority or police resources to further their private business interests in such disputes.

Illustrating the problems was a case involving a police officer who was a director of three family companies run by his mother. These interests had been declared in a letter to the Victoria Police personnel department but they had not been officially approved in accordance with usual procedures. A complaint arose after one of the family companies dismissed a director, leading to a dispute between the police officer's mother and the dismissed director, including an allegation of assault. Although this specific allegation was not substantiated, it was found that the police officer had inappropriately used his authority in a civil dispute. He was counselled for carrying on a business without the Chief Commissioner's approval—a finding based on the fact that declaration of interests in a letter to personnel did not constitute obtaining permission from the Chief Commissioner (Case 49).

Most complaints in relation to private or family business involvements involve individual police officers, but the problems may be magnified if officers involve other officers in their personal business affairs. In a complicated case in this category, one police officer involved another senior officer who travelled in a police vehicle to a neighbouring district, where they also recruited a further two members from another police station to assist in the forcible eviction of a person from family business premises. The police officer had inherited a controlling share in the business from her deceased estranged husband and this action was part of an attempt to take physical control of the business from another family member. The police officer had not sought approval to be involved in the private business and she was initially admonished but following the lodgement of a grievance the penalty was reduced to a counselling, due to the fact that it was her husband's business and that he had died only a short time before (Case 12).

The senior officer who had assisted the police officer with the eviction was also counselled for entering into a civil dispute involving a fellow police officer and for leaving his district without permission. Nevertheless in objecting to his counselling, he refused to see it from the public perspective and would not concede that he had not displayed fairness and impartiality. Notwithstanding this objection, the counselling was deemed to have been justified in the circumstances. Indeed, in an Internal Investigations Department interview with the female police officer who actually achieved the business victory, it emerged that the attendance and forcible eviction at the business had been instigated by the senior officer when she had telephoned him for advice. It was his decision to travel with three other experienced officers to the neighbouring district, and to enlist the assistance of two more officers from that district.

6   Post Employment

None of the cases examined for this research involved post-employment conflicts of interest, where the potential for future employment with an outside organisation has an influence on the manner in which a police officer interacts and deals with that organisation. However, Ayling and Grabosky (2006: 675) discuss divided loyalties that arise in the context of potential 'poaching' of police employees by private contractors. Given the increasing private use of policing (Davids and Hancock 1998; Ayling and Grabosky 2006) the possibility for post employment relationships to influence the performance of police duties—including administrative duties—is something police management must be aware of.

B   *Political Interests*

Many police services attempt to exercise a degree of control over members in relation to political expression and engagement in political activity. For example, in England and Wales, under Police Regulations of 1995 (Regs 9-11& Sch 2, para 1) it is stated that "in particular a member of a police force shall not take any active part in politics". In Canada, the *Charter of Rights and Freedoms* means that only "reasonable limits" on political participation are permitted. Such limits and restrictions are sought because personal opinions expressed publicly (even when the member is off duty) might convey an impression of official sanction. Further, the behaviour of individual police officers may colour attitudes to the Force as a whole.

Two competing principles are often at work in this domain: first, the impartiality of police officers (in perception and fact); secondly, the rights of police officers, as citizens, to freedom of expression, assembly, and association. In Victoria, the type of specific prohibition or limitation on participation in politics referred to above is not in place,[2] and there is a recognition that a balance must be struck between the need to maintain both the actuality and appearance of impartiality in the police force, and the democratic rights of individual police officers to engage in political activity.

The potential for *any* elected member of a local government body to be involved in conflicts of interest is widely recognised (see Independent Commission Against Corruption 1997), and the danger is no less present for police officers who occupy local elected office. Indeed, for police officers who serve as members of local government authorities, it may be said that they are subject to conflict of interest problems both in their roles as police officers *and* as elected officials.

Several cases in this study demonstrate the sorts of conflicts that active involvement in local political activity can give rise to, even where the evidence does not necessarily suggest that a police officer has actually misused an official position to gain an advantage in relation to political activity. In the first

---

[2] In the past, involvement in politics, including membership of political or industrial organisations (including trade unions) was prohibited, as, indeed, was the right to vote. Enhancements of industrial and political rights for police officers, both individual and collective rights, were made gradually, to the point where it is now accepted that individual police officers may stand for parliamentary and local government election (Finnane 1994: Ch 2).

case, a complainant alleged several minor matters against a police officer who had recently defeated the complainant in municipal elections. Although all matters were found to be unfounded, the case demonstrated how the mere act of a police officer becoming actively involved in the political arena can draw criticism (Case 94).

More specific allegations of action against competing candidates in relation to local electoral processes may also arise. In such a case, a local councillor alleged that a police officer had effectively teamed up with a local council opponent of the complainant councillor. The substance of the allegation was that the council opponent and the police officer harassed and intimidated him (the councillor) during an election campaign. This case received widespread media attention and resulted in a major police investigation involving a large amount of time and resources and resulting in an extensive complaint case file (over 400 pages). However, the investigation was unable to produce independent evidence in support of the complainant's allegations and was found to be unsubstantiated (Case 108).

The general concerns with involvement in local government have led the Deputy Ombudsman to suggest that the interests of neither the Police Force nor the public are well served when police officers serve as municipal councillors (Deputy Ombudsman comments in relation to Case 95),[3] however evidence from this study suggests that police management have taken the view that, although there is always a potential for conflicts of interest to arise, police officers should be permitted to serve as municipal councillors (comments from Chief Superintendent Internal Affairs Department, Case 95).

C   Civic, Social, or Other Organised Activities

A range of civic, social, and other community-based associations that a police officer may have can potentially give rise to conflicts of interest but regulation of particular associational involvements is difficult because in their private lives police officers will invariably be members of sporting, social, professional, or community groups. Proscription of membership of particular

---

[3] Case 95 was the matter discussed earlier in this chapter, involving a police officer who served in a senior capacity on a local municipal council and who had used his position to organise police officers to undertake after hours security work for the council.

organisations is of limited utility from a regulatory point of view because such prohibitions are limited to the particular *organisations* whereas conflicts of interest are more likely to relate to particular *activities* which may or may not necessarily be exclusively associated with the organisations in which membership is proscribed.

Membership of some organisations may be felt to be clearly at odds with police membership. For example, membership by British police officers in the National Front, despite the organisation being legal, is likely to cause an affront to many as it raises an array of racially sensitive issues that relate to the daily activities of policing. For other organisations which are less overtly damaging, while they are not as obvious there may still be problems. For example, freemasonry in Britain has been regarded as an arena of particular and ongoing concern because the Articles of the organisation demand a bond of loyalty from their members and this may place them in a possible conflict of interest with their police force (Topping 1997). In addition, issues of the secrecy associated with the organisation have also been raised (Neyroud and Beckley 2001).

The issues involved in private engagement in civic, social and other organised activities by police officers are always sensitive because although it may be felt that it is asking too much of police officers to forfeit their rights to freely associate in legal organisations, it must be recognised that conflicts of interest may arise. In the Victoria Police complaint files examined for this book, three key areas of concern emerged: active involvement in sporting and social clubs, involvement in sporting teams, and membership of school councils (see Davids 2006, for more discussion of this area).

1 Sporting and Social Clubs

Sporting and social clubs are an area of active involvement for many people, so involvement of police officers in such organisations is to be expected. However, this involvement may give rise to particular situations where complaints of conflict of interest are likely to arise.

In one case, problems arose because a police officer held a position of authority (club captain) in a cricket club that served alcohol, and which was frequented by patrons aged below the legal drinking age. Following a social event where a liquor licence was required to serve alcohol, a member of the club lodged a complaint including allegations relating to the police officer's involvement with the liquor licence, under-age drinking and various other alleged breaches of licensing requirements which it was claimed the police officer had knowledge of. It was also alleged that the police officer had failed to assist in an assault/damage incident in the club car park. Although the indeterminate nature of the evidence in this case resulted in an "unable to determine" finding, the case illustrates how private involvement in sporting clubs can give rise to problems in relation to the police officer's official role and duties as a police officer (Case 252).

At other times involvement in sporting clubs may give rise to vexatious or vindictive complaints against police officers by disgruntled parties. For example, in one case the complainant had an ongoing dispute with the club committee of which the police officer happened to be a member. The complainant had failed in an effort to be elected to the club committee and, in an apparent effort to place blame with others, tried to cast a wide net. The allegation against the police officer was found to be not substantiated and it was commented that the police officer had been unfairly caught up in a wider dispute (Case 136).

These cases indicate some of the problems that may arise in the context of private involvements in sporting and social clubs. The difficulties in effectively regulating involvement in this area without putting in place a blanket prohibition means that there is a clear need for broader awareness of the problem of conflict of interest and the circumstances in which such conflicts can arise.

2 Sporting Teams

Whilst membership of sporting teams does not seem problematic in itself and is clearly desirable for the health and recreation of police officers, whether as spectators, players, or officials, police officers need to be careful not to get so involved in these private activities that they misuse their status as police members. A case that was ultimately conciliated under the Victoria Police Public Incident Resolution procedures illustrates how this may happen.

In this case, a police officer who served as a local football club official exerted police authority following a match which he viewed as a spectator. He observed an on-field behind-play incident and after the game attended the umpire's room whereupon he produced his police badge and started questioning the umpires about whether any of them had witnessed the event (as he had) and what action was to be taken regarding the incident. None of the field umpires proposed to take the matter further based on the police officer's report as they had not seen the incident in question, but the police officer himself compiled an official crime report in relation to the on-field matter. The head umpire subsequently expressed concern in relation to the powers of off-duty police in such circumstances and the apparent conflict between the police officer's personal interest in the club and his role as a member of the police force in relation to the matter (Case 371).

In what may be regarded as an ironic twist to the story, one of the umpires officiating in the match was also a serving police officer who stated to the investigating officer that he was "most surprised" to be interviewed by the police officer. This police officer had not disclosed or attempted to utilise his status as a police officer during the discussions in the umpire's room, illustrating how he, at least, had been able to keep his police position separate from his sporting engagement.

3   School Councils

Like sporting and recreational pursuits, involvement in school councils and other civic interests is *prima facie* desirable in terms of a police officer's family and community responsibilities, but conflict of interest problems can still arise when an individual police officer behaves inappropriately in relation to such civic duties.

An exemplar case involved a police officer who, in a private capacity attended a meeting of the school council of which he was an office bearer. The particular problem in this case arose because he was on duty and in full police uniform, including revolver and baton, and had left his station for two hours. The complainant raised issues of misuse of police time and resources (a police vehicle). The key issues did not relate to his membership of the school council *per se*, but concerns over the police officer's performance of official duties, including neglect of supervisory duties when away from the station, and use of police position and resources to further a private activity. The complaint was substantiated and the police officer was admonished (Case 228).

III   Family-based Involvements

Sometimes private family and personal involvements become problematic in such a way as to impact on the performance of a police officer's duties. A police officer's involvement in personal family law and other relationship problems, or such problems encountered by the officer's close family, has the potential to put the police officer in situations where conflict of interests may arise. In the research for this book, 40 complaint case files involved such circumstances.

Table 4.3 summarises the findings in these 40 cases. Nine cases involved allegations that a police officer had breached his or her duty in the context of personal difficulties relating to a family law context. There was an even spread of determinations in this category, with one-third of cases resulting in findings against the police officer, one-third of cases resulting in findings in favour of the police officer, and one-third of cases with an indeterminate outcome. The largest number of complaints (31 cases) alleged that a police officer had in some way become implicated in family law related problems of relatives. In more than half of these cases, there was a finding in favour of the police officer. Overall, one-quarter of the 40 cases in this category as a whole resulted in substantiated complaints, indicating that most allegations were *not* supported by the evidence. Despite the low substantiation rates relative to other areas under examination in this book, as with all areas of conflict of interest an awareness of the possible conflicts that may arise in the context of family-based involvements is important.

The complaint case files demonstrate that many of the problematic elements of these cases are not immediately apparent in the relationship, but are only manifested when a police officer does certain things in respect of that relationship (such as accessing police information about an estranged partner or disclosing information to a relative with family law difficulties). Therefore, whilst having a family law or related problem (or having family or friends with such problems) gives rise to a *latent* conflict of interest, the conflict may be actualised if the police officer is in a position (as a police officer) to further his or her own interests in respect of that relationship. Such problems are a common thread in many conflict of interest cases.

The complaint case files also show that problematic relationships expose police officers to a range of allegations of conflict of interest that might be based on misperceptions that an aggrieved party attributes to otherwise perfectly legitimate police behaviour (on- or off-duty). They are also vulnerable to unfounded or vexatious allegations.

Table 4.3: Findings in Complaints Relating to Family-based Involvements

Category of conflict of interest	Determination						Total Occurrences	
	Finding against police officer (substantiated)		In-determinate finding[1]		Finding in favour of police officer[2]			
	N	%	N	%	N	%	N	%
Personal family law related problems	3	33.3	3	33.3	3	33.3	9	100
Relatives with family law related problems	7	22.6	7	22.6	17	54.8	31	100
TOTAL	10	25.0	10	25.0	20	50.0	40	100

(1) *Indeterminate finding* = Lesser deficiency, Unable to determine, Conciliated, Not proceeded with (resigned prior)

(2) *Finding in favour of police officer* = Withdrawn, No complaint, Not substantiated, Unfounded, Exonerated

A   *Personal Family Law and Related Problems*

Family law and related problems present difficulties for any person. For a police officer, the stresses and strains of such problems, combined with the power and position of individual officers, leaves them vulnerable to poor judgment, inappropriate action, and unacceptable behaviour in situations where they are unable to separate their police duty from their private pressures, relationships, or difficulties. The complaint case files reveal a range of alleged conflict of interest breaches relating to use of police information, harassment, and abuse of position.

1   *Use of Police Information*

In the course of official duties police officers have access to a range of personal and sensitive information about individuals, thus it is logistically a relatively easy matter to access information desired for personal reasons in the context of family law or related difficulties. Conflict of interest problems relating to misuse of police information are analysed in detail in Chapter Six, but at present it is sufficient to note that allegations of inappropriate access to police information in relation to personal problems may be difficult to prove, given: (1) the range of circumstances in which individual officers may legitimately access records; (2) the range of sources of information that police may have, and (3) the possibilities that colleagues may access data on behalf of another police officer, whether surreptitiously or not.

Despite the above comments, some matters are more clear-cut. In a case involving two police officers who had formerly been involved in a personal relationship, the complainant said she had been continually harassed by the other police officer after the breakdown of the relationship. She also alleged that he had misused the police database to obtain her current address and vehicle details. The male police officer made cross allegations that she had also misused police records and abused her position in relation to interactions with him. The allegations were substantiated for both officers, and they were both admonished (Case 152).

It may also be the case that a complainant *assumes* a police officer has obtained information using illegitimate means even where this is not the case. For example, when an allegation was made that a female police officer had used police information systems to track her ex-husband (in relation to problems with maintenance payments), an investigation found that she had not actually used the police data system. The woman had obtained information about her ex-husband from some source, but she refused to name the source, and no evidence could be found that she had obtained the information from police sources (Case 120).

2   Harassment

In more serious cases, police officers may engage in harassment of ex-partners. Where it was found that a police officer had breached an intervention order taken out against him by his ex-*de facto* partner, by harassing and stalking her, the police officer in question was transferred from a country location to the city (Case 200). In another case, the allegation (although unable to be determined) was that the police officer was harassing a man who was going out with the police officer's estranged spouse. The complainant alleged that he had been pulled over in his motor vehicle three times in 10 days, almost immediately after commencing the relationship with the woman (Case 220).

3   *Abuse of Position*

Personal family law problems may provide the *context* in which a police officer exercises improper influence in a manner inconsistent with his or her official duties. In one case, an off-duty police officer was involved in a road rage incident with another driver. During the subsequent altercation the police officer produced his police identification. In interview, he stated that he had been in the midst of a particularly difficult and acrimonious separation from his wife of 20 years and that he had been receiving counselling. The case was resolved amicably when a conciliation meeting was convened. At this meeting, the police officer unreservedly apologised for his actions. The complainant also accepted a degree of responsibility for the confrontation, and stated that she was fully satisfied with the conciliated resolution of the matter (Case 90).

Police officers are also vulnerable to allegations of abuse of position in relation to family law related matters. One complaint involved an allegation that a senior police officer had abused his position in having police attend during the handover of his children for a custody visit on the ostensible basis that a breach of the peace might arise. This case was conciliated (Case 340).

B   *Relatives and Friends with Family Law and Related Problems*

Family relationships and disputes may give rise to a similar array of behaviours and similar allegations to those discussed above, although the cases examined for this book reveal a greater range of problem areas here. The cases show how police officers may be accused of inappropriately intervening in private disputes; using police information inappropriately; carrying out police duties with a lack of impartiality; misusing their police position; or involving themselves in or pursuing personal relationships with people involved in family law disputes and with whom they have come into contact in the course of their police duties.

1   *Involvement or Intervention in Family Law Matters*

If a police officer intervenes in a private dispute, this may involve actions taken outside the area of responsibility or duty of the individual officer, or may involve inappropriate application of normal duties. Any time that police officers get involved in private disputes where emotion and friendship are involved, complaints are possible.

A complaint case involved a police officer who became involved in a friend's domestic dispute in that the police officer went to the former marital home of his friend (who was subject to an intervention order) in order to retrieve property for his friend. The complainant (the friend's ex-spouse) claimed that the police officer tried to gain entry by using his authority as an officer but the complainant refused. In an ensuing altercation, the police officer's foot was said to have been caught in the front door and the door was damaged. The police officer in this case was counselled about his lack of partiality in involving himself (and invoking police authority) in a matter that did not relate to his duty (Case 147).

Police activity outside the district where a police officer is stationed is clearly outside the realm of normal duty, and is often a manifestation of a conflict of interest. A police officer in one case involved himself in a third-party private matter by attending the home of one of his relations to intervene in a custody dispute. He travelled out of his district to do so and ignored the fact that local police had attended the matter that same day. It was recommended by the original investigating officer that the police officer be counselled, but on internal review the sanction was increased to a reprimand— an outcome with which the Deputy Ombudsman concurred (Case 43).

2   Use of Police Information

In a case involving the disclosure of information in a family custodial dispute, a female police officer made inquiries to obtain information about sexual abuse allegations against the man who was the father in the family that had custody of a young child who was a member of her (the police officer's) extended family. She disclosed this information to some of her extended family members. The allegation against this police officer was initially found to be *not* substantiated, because she had her senior officer's go-ahead to retrieve and use the information, but following intervention from the Deputy Ombudsman, the police officer was counselled about the matter (Case 255).

In another case involving a complaint of inappropriate access to the police database, a male police officer alleged that a fellow female police officer who was a friend of his ex-wife had undertaken an unofficial database check on his new partner's vehicle. The finding in this case was that it was not substantiated (Case 375).

3   *Complaints and Allegations*

If there is any possible *perception* of conflict of interest in a matter, entirely legitimate police officer involvement in family disputes may give rise to complaints, especially where there is a conflictual family law context. Where matters do not proceed well for one party to a dispute, other causes to which problems can be attributed may be sought. In such a case, a police officer was a co-parishioner of the complainant's ex-wife. The complainant (ex-husband) had been granted only restricted access to their child and assumed, because things had not gone well, that the police officer had somehow interfered in the case. There was no evidence to support the complaint however it was conciliated (Case 206).

The mere presence of a police officer in domestic disputes where the officer has a connection to one of the parties may give rise to problems. A police officer complained against was located at the station where the complainant went, by arrangement, to pick up his son for access visits. The complainant alleged that the police officer was now seeing his estranged wife, and behaved in an intimidating fashion when the complainant picked up his son at the police station. The police officer had also accompanied the complainant's estranged wife to the former joint property to assist her collect her personal belongings. The matter was conciliated, but the police officer was required to stay away from the station at the times the complainant was to pick up his son, and not have any contact with the complainant (Case 93).

Complainants may seek to cast a relatively wide net in finding a source of their problems. For example, a female complainant (along with her father) alleged that six police officers were biased against her in favour of her ex-*de facto* partner in several police matters. On investigation, it seemed that five of the police officers had been caught up in an allegation that really related only to one of the officers. This police officer, in the course of his duties, had been an informant to an intervention order taken out by the former *de facto* spouse of the complainant, and she alleged that the police officer was assisting her ex-*de facto* spouse on an ongoing basis. The other police officers had at various times attended domestic disputes at the complainant's residence, but no personal connections were evident. None of the allegations made by the complainant were substantiated (Case 222).

4   Domestic Disputes of Friends

Involvement of police officers in the domestic disputes of friends often presents a situation where complaints of conflict of interest will arise, particularly if the evidence suggests that a police officer has acted outside the course of normal duty.

One such complaint involved an allegation of involvement as a third-party to a personal dispute outside police responsibilities. In this case the police officer's station was not even in the area in which the complainant lived, and the police officer's involvement outside his locality was specifically mentioned in the complaint. A friend of the police officer's brother was the former boyfriend of the complainant's new girlfriend, and the allegation related to a telephone call between the police officer and the complainant. The police officer explained his actions by saying that he was merely trying to resolve a problematic "love triangle" situation prior to it deteriorating to a situation of domestic violence, but that he realised he should not have intervened in this way without an official police report being made to him for investigation. Given the facts of the case, the police officer's admissions and his expressions of regret, the matter was conciliated and the police officer was informally counselled (Case 273).

5   Overstepping Duty

Involvement or intervention in disputes, such as those detailed above, may be passive and/or well-intentioned but at other times involvement or intervention may be more active and punitive. For example, a senior police officer in one case directed reluctant subordinates to go outside their patrol area to target a person (the complainant) who was subsequently booked for a traffic matter. On investigation there was found to be an acrimonious relationship between the police officer's daughter and the complainant, who was the ex-son-in-law of the police officer who had issued the direction to the other officers. The senior officer received a caution, but no action was taken against his subordinates (Case 137).

In another example illustrating the extremes to which individuals may go, two police officers (senior detectives) travelled interstate, used police computers, and conducted ostensibly official inquiries—all the while purporting to be on official duty—as part of a private (paid) arrangement with a friend to locate his estranged wife and children. Penalties imposed on these officers included a fine and transfer, and one subsequently resigned (Case 300).

6   *Harassment*

Police officers who attempt to use their police position of authority to intimidate or harass civilians are clearly liable to complaint in any circumstances; this is especially the case where one person in the matter is in a problematic relationship. In one such situation, two police officers were alleged to have harassed and victimised a motorist, the sister of whose ex-*de facto* spouse was now living with one of the police officers, in a house formerly owned by the complainant. The complainant alleged that the police officers had pulled him over several times over a period of a few months; when they pulled him over again and asked him for his identification, the complainant uttered an obscenity saying they knew who he was. He was subsequently charged with failing to produce his name and address when requested (a charge that was later withdrawn). One of the police officers in this case resigned prior to any adverse finding against him; the other (who lived with the complainant's ex-*de facto* spouse) was counselled regarding his failure to avoid a conflict of interest (Case 159).

Another complaint revolved around a domestic dispute between a police officer's parents-in-law and the police officer's wife. She had taken out an intervention order against her father (the police officer's father-in-law), who subsequently claimed the police officer (son-in-law) had telephoned him and threatened his life. Although the finding in this particular matter was "unable to determine", the case helps to illustrate the problems in this area (Case 235).

7   *Lack of Impartiality*

If a police officer has relatives or friends with family law problems, or when an aggrieved party believes that a police officer has a connection with a party to a family law dispute, a complainant may allege that the police officer has used his or her position to favour one party over another when attending to police duties.

One case centring on an allegation of failure to carry out duties impartially involved a claim from a member of the public who reported an allegation of harassment to police. The police officer involved had personally known the man complained against for 20 years and the complainant believed that the officer would not investigate the harassment allegation impartially. This matter was ultimately conciliated (Case 171).

IV Problematic Personal Relationships

Beyond problems that arise from family-based involvements, other personal relationships of a police officer may become problematic if they have an impact on the performance of the official duties. In the complaint files examined, two particular groups of problematic personal relationships stood out.

The first group involved situations where a police officer sought to facilitate intimate personal relationships (sometimes explicitly unwanted on the part of the other party), or engaged in (alleged) sexual misconduct or impropriety. In this context, a range of conflicts may arise between the personal desires of the police officer and police duty. These areas are particularly problematic if a police officer tries to use his position to further these relationships, and may include attempts to facilitate or further relationships with persons encountered in the course of police duties.

The second group of problems arose in relation to allegedly inappropriate relationships with criminals, informers, or persons/businesses of ill repute. Officially sanctioned relationships with such persons or organisations may be problematic in relation to the questionable ethics of covert policing and the use (or misuse) of informants (Fitzgerald 1989; Wood 1997a; Independent Commission Against Corruption 1994a; Brodeur 1995; Feldberg 1985; Kleinig 1996). Police officers inevitably come into contact with criminals, informers, and participants in regulated industries such as gaming and prostitution in the ordinary course of police duty but where the association extends beyond the confines of the job into the private realm, a range of problems may emerge.

In addition to these two groups, some other problematic personal relationships and friendships were identified. These included associations with tow-truck operators, *indirect* associations with suspected criminals, and problems with neighbours. A total of 54 cases involved allegations relating to problematic personal friendships. The outcomes in these cases are summarised in Table 4.4.

130

Table 4.4: Findings in Complaints Relating to Problematic Personal Relationships

Category of conflict of interest	Determination						Total Occurrences	
	Finding against police officer (substantiated)		In-determinate finding[1]		Finding in favour of police officer[2]			
	N	%	N	%	N	%	N	%
Facilitation of personal relationships, or (alleged) sexual impropriety	22	73.3	1	3.3	7	23.3	30	100
Inappropriate relationship with a criminal, informer, or person/business of ill repute	2	22.2	2	22.2	5	55.6	9	100
Other problematic personal relationships and friendships	5	33.3	2	13.3	8	53.3	15	100
TOTAL	**29**	**53.7**	**5**	**9.3**	**20**	**37.0**	**54**	**100**

(1) *Indeterminate finding* = Lesser deficiency, Unable to determine, Conciliated, Not proceeded with (resigned prior)

(2) *Finding in favour of police officer* = Withdrawn, No complaint, Not substantiated, Unfounded, Exonerated

The overall substantiation rate in this group was 53.7 per cent (29 cases). This is the largest number of substantiated complaints arising from the types of private relationships and involvements identified in the case files, indicating that problematic personal friendships are a significant problem in relation to conflict of interest. Amongst these cases, the facilitation of personal relationships and conduct involving sexual impropriety stands out, with a very high substantiation rate of over 73 per cent of the 30 cases involved in this category. This overall outcome is heavily influenced by the one-third of these complaints (10 out of 30) that were related to a particular problem that arose in one particular location (the Maryborough complaints, discussed below)—nine of these 10 cases resulted in the substantiation of at least one allegation. Despite the significance of this particular sub-group of cases, the cases considered will show that the problem is more widespread. Both the total number of complaints and the high overall substantiation rate in this area presents clear cause for concern, given the sensitivity of this area and the often-serious nature of allegations.

Nine cases involved allegations that a police officer maintained an inappropriate relationship with criminal, informer, or person/business of ill repute. Despite the relatively small number of cases, the outcomes in these cases, with substantiated outcomes in two cases, and findings in favour of the police officer in five cases indicates that such allegations of conflict of interest are difficult to substantiate. Where such relationships are maintained beyond the confines of the job, problems in relation to the public perceptions of policing are likely to arise. Both police officers and police management must take care to separate work and non-work relationships and activities. Where the complainant in such cases is a criminal, informer, or person/business of ill repute, the credibility of the complainant may become an issue in two ways: allegations from such complainants may be lacking in substance; or a police officer may use the likely lack of credibility with which complaints would be regarded as a form of exploitative lever in such a relationship.

Other problematic personal relationships, including personal friendships and neighbourhood relationships, were involved in 15 cases, five of which resulted in findings that the allegation was substantiated.

A   Personal Relationships, or (Alleged) Sexual Misconduct/Impropriety

The general principle that police officers should be permitted to engage in private relationships, and private life more generally, unhindered by regulation from their employer—a freedom available to ordinary citizens—is quite reasonably qualified in so far as a police officer may use his or her position to prey on the vulnerable. In relation to the area of sexual misconduct or impropriety, police management can take action against individual police officers under the provisions of s 69 of the *Police Regulation Act* which prohibits any conduct that "is likely to bring the Force into disrepute or diminish public confidence in it" (s 69(1)(c)) or is judged as "disgraceful or improper conduct (whether in his or her official capacity or otherwise)" (s 69(1)(e)).

1   *Relationships in the Course of Police Work*

In instances where a police officer becomes involved in a close personal relationship with a person with whom he first came into contact during the course of his police duties, the police officer may be subject to various allegations.[4] If a police officer uses his official position to facilitate personal relationships or to engage in sexual misconduct or impropriety, there is always a conflict of interest involved. The conflict is between the police officer's private interests in pursuing or engaging in this particular relationship, on the one hand, and good order and discipline within the Force and the reputation and public perception of the Force (and a police officer's duty to maintain these), on the other. In circumstances where the police officer has (or has had) official police dealings with the other party to the relationship or activity, the conflict of interest is even clearer. Whether such matters also involve conflict of interest breaches (neglects of duty) will depend on the circumstances of the particular case.

Where the other party is (or was) involved in a pre-existing relationship, an obvious source of complaint is the aggrieved third party. In such a case from the complaint case files, a police officer was engaged in an extra-marital affair with a woman who had previously sought police assistance in taking out and enforcing an intervention order against her husband. The aggrieved husband complained that the police officer had engaged in improper conduct. The complaint was substantiated and the police officer admonished partly on the basis of an argument that the small country town location exacerbated the potential damage to the reputation of the Police Force. It was acknowledged that the officer did have a sexual relationship with the complainant's wife and that this was 'improper conduct' which would be subject to disciplinary action. Nevertheless it was acknowledged by police management that there was no evidence that the relationship had contributed to the breakdown of the marriage, nor that this breakdown was a result of collusion between police and his wife or that the police action in relation to the intervention order was improper (Case 173).

---

[4] All of the conflict of interest cases in relation to alleged facilitation of personal relationships, or (alleged) sexual misconduct/impropriety involved male police officers. Consequently, unless otherwise specifically required, the male third person pronoun ("he" or "his") will be used in the remainder of this section.

Despite this eventual outcome, there was a significant degree of debate and disagreement within Victoria Police in relation to whether the issue was essentially a moral matter in which police management had no right to interfere in a police officer's personal life. After some investigation and comparison to an earlier case, the Assistant Commissioner decided that an admonishment was still appropriate in the present case, mainly due to effect on policing effectiveness and public confidence and the attraction of critical media publicity caused by such cases.

The case is an important one in illustrating a central element of many conflict of interest cases: the need to maintain public confidence in policing and the importance of appearances of integrity. This may stand in contrast to the intrusion in the private life of police officers that may be implicit in attempts to maintain that public confidence.

In cases where relationships turn sour, the other party may herself become a complainant. Such was the situation for a police officer who became involved in a consensual relationship with a woman who had sought police assistance during a difficult separation from her husband. When she subsequently discovered that the police officer was also involved in a relationship with another woman, she lodged a complaint, including allegations of sexual assault. The police officer admitted sexual foreplay had occurred, but denied intercourse had taken place. He claimed the activity was consensual and denied that there had been any use of force. The assault allegations were found to be unproven, but the allegation of conduct likely to bring the Force into disrepute was substantiated and the police officer was counselled. The Deputy Ombudsman felt that a reprimand may have been more appropriate, although he conceded he did not have sufficient information about the background of the police officer, and deferred to Victoria Police to make the final judgment (Case 41).

Complaints of inappropriate use of police position may also arise following the cessation of a relationship. In a case where a police officer had instigated the break-up of a longstanding relationship with a woman who had been the ex-*de facto* of a criminal against whom she became an informer, the woman subsequently complained that he had exploited her vulnerability in order to commence and continue the relationship (Case 351). In an internal review of this complaint, a general concern was noted in relation to police officers becoming involved with vulnerable or susceptible women met in the course of police duties. It was further noted that Victoria Police concerns arose because a number of women had made complaints about the conduct or relationships of police officers in such situations.

Despite the problems evident in the cases cited above, not all complaints against police officers in this area are found to be problematic for the Police Force. It is recognised that extra-marital relationships do happen and that they are not *per se* "disgraceful or improper" or "likely to bring the force into disrepute". A case that illustrates this involved a police officer who slept with a married woman (who had pre-existing marriage problems) whom he had initially met in the course of his duties. Following the Internal Investigations Department investigation, it was concluded that the relationship between the police officer and the woman was not the cause of the problems between the woman and her husband (the complainant). The police officer did not carry on the relationship whilst on duty and there was no evidence that he had used his position as a police officer in any way (Case 2).

Engagement in sexual misconduct or impropriety represents a clear conflict of interest breach in terms of a police officer's duty not to bring discredit to the Force, and not to engage in "disgraceful or improper conduct". The facilitation of personal relationships, even if such relationships would otherwise be regarded as legitimate, may similarly represent a conflict of interest breach if the police officer uses his official position in order to further his interests in the relationship.

2   *Use of Police Information in the Context of a Relationship*

Whilst sexual relationships with other parties may or may not be regarded as problematic *per se*, the misuse of police information in the context of a personal relationship is always regarded as a serious disciplinary matter. Illustrating the problems, in one case, three separate complainants all alleged that a police officer had made inappropriate approaches to their wives, had used his position and police resources to access their phone numbers and addresses, and had pursued them whilst on duty. In this case, it was felt that the police officer was a 'womaniser' and that, in the small town setting, he had behaved inappropriately. He was counselled about the need to maintain prudence in relation to private relationships. Following this disciplinary outcome, the police officer objected to the counselling and resigned. When he subsequently tried to withdraw his resignation, the Chief Commissioner refused to allow him to do so (Case 19).

In another case, a police officer used the police database to obtain personal information on a woman whom he then contacted with a view to commencing a relationship. The woman complained that the police officer telephoned her and visited her many times and that she felt "spooked" by his interest in her. At the time this police officer had two separate pending allegations of sexual harassment by female police officers, both of which were also found to be substantiated. The police officer resigned on short notice during the investigation. This occurred prior to the formulation of disciplinary charges against the police officer, and the effective date of his resignation would have precluded the completion of the necessary formalities. The Assistant Commissioner (Internal Affairs Department) therefore directed that the police officer be formally admonished in relation to each of the matters alleged against him, and it was requested that letters detailing the scope and outcome of the investigation be attached to his personnel file (Case 113).

3   Inappropriate Relationships and Behaviour

Some private relationships an individual police officer may wish to pursue are regarded as problematic by their very nature. In cases where there is a sexual element to the relationship, a distinct possibility exists that the police officer has abused his position in establishing or continuing such a relationship.

In a complaint against a police officer who allegedly pursued two underage girls for sexual favours, it was alleged that the police officer gave the girls gifts, wrote personal letters and offered lifts in his vehicle. During the investigation, the police officer was interviewed by a senior officer within the Internal Affairs Department, but he refused to answer questions due to his concerns about his evidence being used "in relation to possible criminal matters". Despite his non-cooperation the complaint against the police officer was substantiated, and a Discipline Board hearing was scheduled, but he resigned prior to the hearing (Case 35).

4   The Maryborough Complaints

During the period of research, a series of allegations involving sexual misconduct on the part of a number of police officers at a Victorian country police station received wide media attention. The Maryborough complaints later erupted into a major scandal revolving around a series of allegations involving sexual misconduct between 1988 and 1997. The matter involved 12 police officers stationed at the Maryborough police station. The Deputy

Ombudsman (Police Complaints) made an official report on the matter to the State Parliament (The Ombudsman 1997b).

All of these cases involved allegations of sexual misconduct on the part of a large number of police officers, including inappropriate intimate relationships with women (Case 326), sexual (or otherwise 'disgraceful') misconduct whilst on duty (Cases 288, 322, 328, 330, 334), and sexual (or otherwise 'disgraceful') misconduct with children (minors) (Cases 325, 327). In several cases, the complaints alleged misconduct on the part of one or two police officers, although many of the cases involved numerous allegations (Cases 323, 330, 334). Complaints in one case came from multiple complainants (Cases 325, 330, 334). In all, 10 of the complaint files examined for this book involved the Maryborough investigations (although one was separate to the main investigation—Case 322). As noted, the complaints involved various details of sexual misconduct on- and off-duty. Allegations were found to have been substantiated in nine of the 10 cases (the tenth complaint, which had come from the ex-spouse of the police officer involved, was found to be vexatious—Case 263). In the nine substantiated complaints, sanctions applied were as follows:

♦ Fines, transfers, demotion (Cases 323, 325);

♦ Admonishment (Case 326);

♦ Dismissal from the Police Force (Cases 327, 330, 334);

♦ Police officer resigned prior to completion of investigation (Cases 328, 288).

The misconduct on the part of the Maryborough police officers was viewed with such seriousness that in one case where the police officer resigned prior to completion of investigation, he was nevertheless formally issued with an admonishment notice (in lieu of disciplinary charges). The notice stated that the police officer would have been dismissed if he had not resigned, and his personnel file was marked "never to be re-employed" (Case 288).[5] This case involved a married police officer who was involved in a longstanding consensual extra-marital sexual relationship, with a range of activity whilst the police officer was on-duty.

---

[5] The file of the police officer in Case 322 was similarly endorsed.

B   Relationships with Criminals, Informers, or Persons/Businesses of Ill Repute

Relationships with convicted criminals or informers can give rise to problems, as can associations with persons of ill-repute or those engaged in the conduct of certain regulated business sectors such as the sex or gaming industries. These relationships may expose a police officer to situations where specific conflicts of interest (and, indeed, corrupt behaviours) may emerge. In addition, the effect on public perceptions and the image of the police force may be particularly problematic if police officer associations with such persons are publicly known.

Some private relationships of police officers may involve an extension of relationships that are conducted partly in the course of their on-duty interactions, including relationships with informers and convicted criminals (important sources of information that assist in the conduct of police work), and people suspected of having committed or being engaged in the conduct of criminal activity (whether or not this suspicion is held by or known to the individual police officer). The latter category includes known, alleged, or suspected drug dealers. In addition, the status of prostitution as an industry that is regulated by police means that the on- or off-duty attendance of police officers at licensed or unlicensed brothels can present particular problems in terms of conflict of interest.

In general, some of the conflicts in regard to personal (and/or professional) associations in this category relate to a police officer's choice of friends and acquaintances, where a police officer's connections present an inherent conflict of interest due to security concerns and risks (see Davids 2006 for further discussion).

1   Informants and Convicted Criminals

Policing is clearly subject to process corruption in relation to the use of informants. Individual police officers may think that the granting of undue favours to informants is acceptable if they are perceived to be consistent with the overall ends of policing. If informant/police officer relationships are established at or develop to a personal level, which may or may not include intimate interpersonal relations, conflicts of interest will be involved. Where problems arise in a police–informer relationship or police officer misconduct occurs in the context of the relationship, the informant may *inform on* the police officer by lodging a formal complaint (Billingsley *et al.* 2001).

Any kind of non-official relationship with a criminal or suspected criminal may be an indication of a wider problematic relationship, but some cases involve direct evidence of the police officer acting at variance with police duties in favour of such a person. For example, a police officer was found to have an inappropriate relationship with a suspected drug offender who was under telephone surveillance, and the relationship was discovered as the result of a taped conversation between the two wherein the suspected offender asked the police officer to supply information from the police database. The police officer complied with the request, and he was found to have failed to comply with an instruction from the Chief Commissioner (database access protocols) and to have engaged in conduct likely to bring the Force into disrepute. Formal discipline charges against the officer did not proceed because he took extended sick, recreation, then long service leave, then resigned (Case 289).

Even where police take a complaint very seriously, if there is insufficient corroborating evidence, allegations made by a convicted criminal will likely prove to be an unsatisfactory basis for a finding against a police officer. When a complaint from a prisoner alleged numerous instances of misconduct on the part of a particular police officer, including that the police officer had undertaken security work for him (the prisoner), the police officer concerned claimed that the relationship between he and the prisoner had been simply a police/informer relationship (the criminal was an informer). Although the police officer formally (through his solicitors) advised the Internal Affairs Department that he did not wish to be interviewed in relation to any criminal or disciplinary allegations arising from the alleged association with the complainant, he was interviewed by the Internal Affairs Department, following instructions from an Acting Chief Superintendent. However, acting on legal advice, the police officer refused to answer any questions (in relation to this and other allegations against him). When he was instructed to answer questions under (then) s 86Q (2) of the *Police Regulation Act*, he continued to refuse to do so. During his interview, the police officer sought an assurance from the Department that any answers he would give to questions would not be used against him (Case 91).

On each occasion where the police officer asked for this assurance, the interrogating police officer responded in the negative and it was noted that this left him with a "common law right defence" to a charge under s 86Q(2), against self-incrimination. Despite the police officer's refusal to assist the investigation, the initial recommendation within the Internal Affairs Department was that the complaint be regarded as substantiated, but the normal review of the investigators' recommendations overturned this, citing the concern that, since the police officer would not answer questions, the only evidence available was from the complainant, who was regarded as an extremely unreliable witness (in previous court cases, he had proved his unreliability and had even been previously convicted on a perjury charge). Therefore it was recommended that the officer not be charged.

The reviewing senior officer called for legal advice regarding the police officer's refusal to answer questions, as required under s 86Q(2) of the *Police Regulation Act*. That advice agreed with his legal analysis of the issues and the police officer's privilege against self-incrimination was regarded as entitling him to refuse to answer questions. Ultimately, because of evidentiary problems, the final determination in this case was "unable to determine".

These cases demonstrate that complaints made against police are often difficult to substantiate. The nature of both allegations made and the background of the complainant means that they must be treated with concern, but care. Recent outcomes from Commissions of Inquiry, Royal Commissions, and other special-purpose inquiries in other jurisdictions reveals that such claims can, on occasion, be the tip of the corruption iceberg (Fitzgerald 1989; Finnane 1994; Wood 1997a; Kennedy 2004a). The management of relationships with informants thus needs to be dealt with on a systematic basis through the use of organisational controls of informant handling (Billingsley *et al.* 2001).

2   Suspects in Criminal Investigations

In addition to care in relationships with convicted criminals and informers, police officers must also ensure that their relationships with people who may be suspects in criminal investigations are beyond reproach or suspicion. Complaints in this area may express allegations at a very general level or may be quite specific. For example, a complaint was received from a government agency involved in industry regulation that a police officer may have an improper relationship with a suspected criminal (Case 128).

The police officer, who had some knowledge of cars, had an association with a mechanic who was under investigation for suspected criminal activity, and the complainant felt that the police officer may have had knowledge of such activity and/or been complicit in it. The police officer had assisted the mechanic compile an official report in relation to the roadworthiness of a vehicle. The Internal Affairs Department investigation found that a "quasi-business relationship" existed because of the suspect's mechanical ability and knowledge but there was no evidence of a social affiliation and therefore the alleged improper relationship was not substantiated. However, it was concluded that a conflict of interest could have been construed in his relationship with the mechanic and that his actions in assisting the mechanic had been inappropriate. The investigation concluded that the police officer had shown poor judgment in his association and that his level of experience suggested that he should have known better.

3 Persons Associated with Regulated Industries

Various allegations of conflict of interest may arise where ex-police officers conduct business in certain industries and serving police officers maintain relationships with these ex-police officers. Close relationships with proprietors of regulated industries and their business establishments, such as hotels and brothels, may magnify a police officer's motivation to neglect duty in the furtherance of private interests. In addition, the potential for damage to public perceptions of policing is high because such relationships are often conducted in public places.

The problem that such relationships may give rise to is illustrated by a complaint that alleged that an assault at a hotel whose owners were ex-police officers was not investigated because of the relationship between the owners and serving police officers (Case 338). Even though this complaint was found to be not substantiated, the problem of perceptions is clearly illustrated.

Relationships with owners of hotel venues, whether they are ex-police officers or not, may give rise to perceptions of conflict of interest, but relationships with the owners of brothels are likely to be even more problematic. A complaint that raised particular interest within Victoria Police alleged that on-duty police officers regularly frequented a particular brothel (said to be owned by a major underworld figure), engaged in sexual activity, and received a range of discounts at the brothel. The brothel in question was operated by former Victoria Police officers. The complaint of improper conduct in this instance was found to be not substantiated, but it was found that attendance at the brothels was more frequent than officially notified to police, as required under established procedures (Case 339).

The case attracted media attention, including a television investigative feature. Police management recognised that police attendance at, and use of the services of, brothels could become a problem, and that a proactive response would be desirable. Consequently, the Victoria Police Risk Assessment Unit reviewed the file in this case, and the wider issues involved in police attendance and use of services at brothels.

The Risk Assessment Unit identified three key areas involved with police officers attending brothels. These were on duty attendance at licensed/unlicensed brothels, off duty attendance at licensed/unlicensed brothels, and potential compromise. In regard to the first, the report recommended that police officers be reminded of their duty to report visits; in regard to the second, the report advised that although there is no legal obstruction to police officers visiting brothels, they must be aware of the issue of potential compromise. Particular concerns in relation to potential compromise included attempts by criminal elements associated with prostitution to exert influence over members, leverage that may be obtained over a member who did not wish off-duty attendance at a licensed brothel to become known to others, and attempts to negotiate discounted prices for brothel services.

C   Other Problematic Personal Relationships and Friendships

A small number of additional cases involve other problematic personal relationships or friendships. These include close friendships with tow-truck operators, *indirect* associations with suspected criminals (not related to police work), and problems with neighbours.

1   Personal Friends and Acquaintances

Police management does recognise that most private relationships cannot be proscribed, but individual police officers are required to recognise the potential for problems of conflicts of interest in terms of the performance of official duties and in relation to public perceptions. One case illustrates the problems clearly, showing that even if a police officer may not have acted at variance with his or her duty, some close personal associations can give rise to particular problems.

The police officer concerned in this matter had a close personal family friendship with the operators of a towing and panel beating company and was frequently seen as a passenger in a marked company vehicle driven by his best friend, who was employed by the company. The situation was exacerbated by the provincial city location of the police officer and the tow-truck company.

The police officer was advised that members of the public and other tow-truck operators would be likely to perceive a conflict of interest in such circumstances and this could tarnish the professional image of police in general, even if his intentions were honourable. He was admonished for his unprofessional conduct in relation to a specific complaint that he spoke inappropriately to a driver to whom he issued a Traffic Infringement Notice following a collision. Although he agreed that the language he had used towards the complainant was inappropriate, the police officer asked for a review of the sanction, arguing that his driving around with his friend was a purely social matter and that the use of the business vehicle (including the police officer's presence in it) had the approval of the manager of the company. The vehicle in question was a business sedan driven by his friend for work and recreational purposes; it was the only vehicle his friend had access to. The police officer denied he ever rode in a tow-truck and he strongly denied any improper behaviour or actions whilst a passenger in the tow-truck vehicle, or any other vehicle (Case 126).

A senior officer reviewed the matter, including a lengthy interview with the police officer to clarify some of the issues. The outcome was that the admonishment was felt to be appropriate. The reviewing officer's comments acknowledged the friendship and the difficulty of the situation, but nevertheless noted that, as the location was a country town, it could damage the professional image of police in general.

The matter did not end there, however, because the police officer was the subject of three separate subsequent complaints, lodged independently, that included allegations of closer involvement with the same towing company. These complaints alleged that the police officer had an arrangement with the towing company that involved the provision of information that assisted them to obtain towing contracts prior to other towing companies being informed. The investigation found that the police officer had made a telephone call to the towing company to provide information that was of assistance to the company in its business dealings. It was concluded that in his general association with the company and its employees he engaged in conduct likely to bring the Force into disrepute. As a result, it was proposed to admonish the police officer (Case 251).

However, in reviewing the file, the Deputy Ombudsman argued that, following this second matter (Case 251), a further admonishment would be insufficient:

In relation to the previous case [Case 126] I referred to the loss of credibility of [the police officer] and pointed to his continuation as a member of [the Victoria Police unit in that locality] as being a considerable challenge to his superiors. It seems to me that [the police officer] is continuing his inappropriate relationship and if he persists in this way I believe that his position at [the Victoria Police unit in that locality] would be untenable and an embarrassment to the Force.

If the incidents referred to in this file had occurred after [the police officer] had been admonished for the previous matter, I would be suggesting that a further admonishment was inadequate. In any event, I believe that consideration should be given to whether admonishments are adequate ...

(Comments from the Deputy Ombudsman, Case 251)

The comments of the Deputy Ombudsman were taken on board, and the police officer was issued with a preliminary Discipline Procedure Notice. He was charged with three offences: engaging in conduct likely to bring the Force into disrepute, improper conduct, and engaging in conduct likely to diminish public confidence in the Force. He pleaded not guilty, but the first two charges were found to have been proven. The police officer was fined and transferred to another location.

This case demonstrates how difficult it can be to regulate the private lives of police officers. The case represents an important example of the limited capacity of regulation to deal with the specific problem of conflict of interest It may be argued that self-regulation is what is most needed in the context of day-to-day policing. In this case, the police officer had difficulty separating his personal and professional lives and he did not understand the nature of the conflict of interest involved. The problem could ultimately only be effectively dealt with by physically removing the police officer from the location in which the problems were arising. Thus, the principal aim of the disciplinary outcome was to eliminate any similar conflicts of interest in relation to future matters.

2   *Problem Neighbours*

Several cases involved problematic relationships between a police officer and his or her neighbours. Problematic officer–neighbour relationships involved a range of complaints alleging inappropriate involvement in civil matters, failure to act against other neighbours, inappropriate involvement in a case, and misuse of police resources.

Two of these matters involved allegations that the police officer had become involved in attempting to facilitate civil settlement of disputes, based around a problem dog, between other neighbours. In one case, the matter was found to be unfounded (Case 4), but in the other (Case 28), the police officer was counselled in relation to a procedural matter, and the neighbour who had prompted the complaint (the party in opposition to the complainant) was charged with criminal damage (in relation to the incident the police officer had attempted to have settled civilly).

Some cases involved neighbourhood disputes over noise. One case involved an ongoing dispute over neighbourhood noise. The complainant alleged that her husband had been threatened by the police officer during a dispute about noise from the stereo of the daughter of the couple. In this particular dispute, the police officer had not actively participated in a deputation from various neighbours to the complainant, but perhaps his position as a police officer had provided the complainant with a convenient target for complaint. There was no evidence that the police officer had in any way used his police position to advance his private position in the neighbourhood dispute, and the complaint was unfounded. Indeed, the investigators found that the police officer himself had become a 'victim' in the matter, because he was a police officer, and that the officer had become frustrated in attempting to deal with this situation in a way that reconciled his position as a police officer and a member of the community (Case 245).

In another neighbourhood dispute over noise, two police officers who shared a unit were involved in an ongoing dispute with neighbours in an adjacent block of units, about noise, parking, and associated issues. The complainant alleged that the police officers attempted to use their authority in their own favour in relation to these disputes, but the Internal Investigations Department investigation showed that the police officers had not done anything wrong in relation to the matter. Indeed, it was felt that the complainant may have been trying to use the police complaints system to 'get at' the police officers in relation to their ongoing dispute, when if there was any substance to the complaints, civil action would be more appropriate (Case 182).

Despite this finding, another investigating officer, accompanied by another police officer, visited the complainant and attempted to settle the matter, suggesting a number of possible solutions to the parking aspects of the complaint. They also suggested that there should be no ongoing communication between the police officers and the complainant (since such communication seemed destined to end in argument). The investigating officer later spoke to the two police officers complained against and they agreed with the suggested points of conciliation. However, a further complaint was made by the complainant to the Deputy Ombudsman (Case 307). Ultimately, the police officers decided to settle the matter by moving residence.

These cases, in particular those involving neighbourhood disputes, illustrate some of the difficulties faced by police officers in normal life. Neighbourhood disputes are not uncommon in the wider community, so it is to be expected that police officers will, from time to time, become involved in such matters. Even though police officers may personally attempt to ensure that they do not use their police position to further their own interests in such contexts, other people who know their occupation may read events differently. Such interpretation may be genuine, but it can also be malicious or vexatious. If a police officer takes any action that can be misinterpreted, he or she may contribute to a complaint. The possibility that a police officer has attempted to exercise improper influence, or otherwise acted inappropriately, cannot be ignored.

Yet a police officer who is aware of these difficulties may become frustrated with an apparent inability to act freely as a normal citizen in relation to neighbourhood disputes. A prerequisite to effectively dealing with these issues is that police officers understand the problem of conflict of interest in terms of a need to separate personal interests and professional position, even though this may be difficult to achieve at all times. Public understanding in such situations may be more difficult to achieve, especially if particular members of the public feel aggrieved and seek a party to 'blame'.

V   Discussion

Whilst a general principle that police officers should be permitted to freely engage in personal associations and relationships seems *prima facie* reasonable, on the grounds that intrusion into anyone's private life should be minimal, the cases discussed in this chapter demonstrate how this principle must be qualified in certain circumstances. Not all interests that give rise to conflicts have been specifically identified and analysed in the chapter, because many conflicts arise from what may be described as the 'general' private interests of a police officer, or the family, friends, or associates of a police officer (such as general financial interests).[6] The chapter has analysed a range of identifiable circumstances arising in the private realm where police officers are often found to be in situations of conflict of interest. This discussion section comments on the types of measures that may reduce such incidences.

A   Organisational Involvements

Three areas of organisational involvements within the realm of the private life of police officers have been identified as giving rise to particular conflict of interest problems. These are: outside employment or carrying on a business without permission; membership of an organisation involved in politics; and engagement in civic, social, or other organised activities.

1   Outside Employment or Business Venture Without Permission

Most of the problems that arise in this area stem from situations where police officers have *not* sought appropriate permission, suggesting not only that they have not complied with the relevant police rules, but that they neither have an adequate appreciation of the reason for the rules nor of the conflicts of interest that may flow from outside employment or private business arrangements. Thus the approval process for outside employment may be seen as an *ex ante* attempt to deal with the problem of conflict of interest in this particular domain. The absence of more conflict of interest cases in relation to *approved* outside employment suggests that the approval process is substantially successful in this regard.

Nevertheless, the high substantiation rate in cases involving allegations involving outside employment (70.4 per cent—19 of 27 cases) means that this area remains a cause for concern in relation to conflict of interest. As the case files show, not all problems are able to be anticipated, and three sets of particular difficulties may arise. The first relates to private business interests with which close members of a police officer's family (for example, the police

---

[6] In addition, in the contemporary environment where significant use is made of private provision of various aspects of the policing function, including procurement from private providers, police management also needs to be aware of the potential for conflicts of interest in contract and tender assessment and awarding processes (see Ayling and Grabosky 2006: 674–675).

officer's spouse) are involved. The second set of difficulties relates to the definition of 'employment', which apparently does not include voluntary work, work performed without remuneration, or work with the Army Reserve or emergency services. The third area of difficulty relates to unanticipated problems in approved employment or business arrangements. These sorts of problems are perhaps unavoidable; however, it may be argued that a clearer appreciation and understanding by police officers both of the reason for the rules, and of the conflicts of interest that may be involved in outside employment or private business arrangements, could make the rules themselves more meaningful and boost compliance both with the letter and the spirit of the rules.

2   Political Interests

Involvement in political activity is a part of social participation, and this ought not be arbitrarily denied to citizens who 'happen to be' police officers. However, there is a need to clearly delineate between political activity conducted as a private citizen, and the authority and prestige of the official position of a police officer. Whilst *particular* areas of outside employment can be *ex ante* recognised as more likely to give rise to conflict of interest problems, and thus not authorised, a similar situation does not seem to apply to political involvement.

Consequently, prohibitive rules do not seem to present a likely solution to the conflict of interest problems that may arise when a police officer is privately involved in the political arena. Once again, a heightened appreciation and understanding of the problem of conflict of interest, and its potential relation to breaches of official duty, seems apposite.

3   Engagement in Civic, Social, or Sporting Activities

Involvement in sporting and social clubs, sporting teams, school councils, and other organised civic and social activities, takes the issue of conflict of interest a further step away from what might be regarded as 'reasonable' regulation of the private lives of police officers. The identification of such involvements as part of the normal realm of private, family, and community engagements and the variability of possible activities with which one may be involved mean that police forces are reluctant to even attempt to regulate such involvements.

Although only a small number of complaints involved this category of conflict of interest, it can be said that a heightened appreciation and understanding of the problem of conflict of interest is warranted. This particularly relates to the potential link between such conflicts of interest and breaches of official duty. Regulation that limits types of civic, social, or other organised activities in which police officers may participate, will alone be likely to be insufficient to deal with the problem. Thus an enhanced understanding of the issue, and of the *personal* responsibility involved in sometimes complex ethical situations, would seem to be a necessary precondition to effectively dealing with this problem.

B   *Family-based Involvements*

The difficulty with regulating a range of organisational involvements, even where they are able to be associated with conflict of interest in a general sense, is magnified in relation to personal involvements. Whilst it is at least theoretically feasible to regulate private *organisational* involvements, it is near impossible to prescribe the sorts of *people* a police officer may associate with, or not, in his or her personal life.

The substance of the complaints discussed in this area was of varying quality, and some were largely the result of assumptions made by complainants on the simple basis of perceived associations. It should be noted also that the tensions and emotions involved in family law and other problems arising from people's personal friendships and relationships mean that complainants may interpret *legitimate* police involvement in matters as being wrong, inappropriate, or impartial.

Whilst these problems of perception and interpretation are themselves very difficult to regulate, a clear understanding on the part of police officers as to when it may be more appropriate to actively *not* involve themselves in particular matters, must be an important aspect of dealing with this problem area. This understanding needs to be cognisant both of the problem of conflict of interest itself and the likelihood that even legitimate or impartial involvement may give rise to perceptions of conflict of interest.

The area of 'domestic disharmony' may assume greater significance in the profile of conflicts of interest as police are increasingly involved in disturbances that arise around family law problems. This is a contemporary area of conflict of interest that police officers need to be aware of when they are called upon to deal with such issues, or find themselves in a personal situation that involves domestic disharmony.

C *Problematic Personal Relationships*

The cases in this area demonstrated a range of problems that can flow from situations where a police officer seeks to facilitate intimate personal relationships or engages in (alleged) sexual misconduct or impropriety, or engagement in private relationships with criminals, informers, or persons/businesses of ill repute. Both the number of cases and the high overall substantiation rate in this group (53.7 per cent—29 of 54 cases), and particularly in relation to close and intimate relationships (consensual or not) indicates that conflicts of interest in relation to problematic personal relationships present a definite problem for policing.

It is possible to regulate on-duty activity, such as attendance at brothels, but it is very difficult to otherwise regulate who police officers may associate with in their private time. Victoria Police management have recognised these difficulties, and, as has been indicated through discussion of the files, demonstrated awareness that greater consideration of and reflection on the issues is required amongst police officers of the potential compromise that may flow from their private associations in particular areas.

An enhanced understanding of various forms of problematic personal relationships on the part of police officers, and the conflicts of interest that may arise in such relationships is a necessary precursor to dealing with such problems. These areas constitute 'shades of grey' in professional integrity, but recognition of them as key variables in operational decision-making is a step in the direction of active accountability.

CHAPTER FIVE

The Public Realm:
Use and Abuse of Police Powers and Authority

I   Introduction

Chapters Five and Six focus on aspects of the public life, or official duty of police officers. These two chapters analyse situations in which a police officer is either *brought into a position* of conflict of interest or *acts on* a conflict of interest in various ways that involve the pursuit of private interests. The problem of conflict of interest is significant in the public realm because, despite normative statements proscribing a range of behaviours which would fall under the rubric of conflict of interest, studies of police ethics reveal a propensity by officers, at least in some jurisdictions, to tolerate a range of conduct that is unethical and/or prohibited. Previous research has shown how such conduct may include misrepresentation in an accident report; avoidance of a random breath test; running a check on an attractive woman; striking a detainee who assaulted a police officer; and making a personal pick up outside a patrol area (see, for example Criminal Justice Commission 1995; Macintyre and Prenzler 1999).

A   *Conflict of Interest Groups*

Seventeen broad areas of police officer actions and activities emerged from the complaint case files. These are organised into three groups for the purpose of the analysis. The relative distribution amongst the three groups is shown in Figure 5.1.

Figure 5.1: Conflict of Interest in the Public Realm

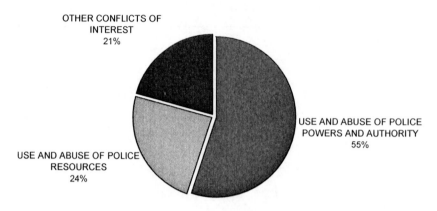

OTHER CONFLICTS OF
INTEREST
21%

USE AND ABUSE OF POLICE
POWERS AND AUTHORITY
55%

USE AND ABUSE OF POLICE
RESOURCES
24%

It is clear from Figure 5.1 that the most significant area of conflict of interest in the public realm is the *use and abuse of police powers and authority*, comprising over half of all alleged conflicts of interest in the public realm. These cases are discussed in this chapter while Chapter Six discusses the other key area of *use and abuse of police resources*. Table 5.1 summarises the three groups, and the various categories and types of conflict of interest within each group.

As explained at the end of Chapter 2, the *other areas* of conflict of interest included in the wider study on which this book draws (Davids 2005), namely acceptance or procurement of goods or services (acceptance of gratuities being a part of this problem) and breach of the law, are not included in this book because, on the basis of the cases examined, it cannot be said that they represent clear conflicts of interest in and of themselves in all cases. These areas may signify or give rise to conflicts of interest in particular instances, but they do not always represent obvious breaches of duty (and thus *conflict of interest* breaches), except where the act is regarded as problematic because in itself it represents a breach of regulations and not because it involves a conflict of interest. Davids (2005) shows that these areas may signify or give rise to conflicts of interest in any particular instance but conceptually, these areas are just as likely *not* to involve a conflict of interest as they *are* to involve such conflicts. Nevertheless, cases in this area were included in the wider pool of conflict of interest complaint cases examined and they are included in Figure 5.1 and Table 5.1 to clearly show the relative scale of the problem represented by the conflicts of interest discussed in Chapters Five and Six.

Table 5.1: Cases of Conflict of Interest—Public Actions and Activities

Category of Conflict of Interest	Total Occurrences	
	N	%
USE AND ABUSE OF POLICE POWERS AND AUTHORITY (discussed in Chapter Five)		
Intervention, action, or involvement in police investigations and processes		
Failure to Act, Due to a Relationship with an Involved Party	45	11.5
Delaying/Discontinuing Police Processes, Due to Relationship with an Involved Party	11	2.8
Taking Police Action against an Opposing Party	44	11.3
Involvement in an Investigation or Other Processes in Relation to an Associated Police Officer	7	1.8
Other Involvement, Investigation, or Intervention in a Case with a Personal Interest	11	2.8
CATEGORY TOTAL	118	30.3
Use of police power to harass		
Engagement in Harassment	26	6.7
Harassment/Discrimination	3	0.8
CATEGORY TOTAL	29	7.4
Exercise of improper influence in civil matters		
Misuse of Authority or Position as a Police Officer in a Civil Matter, with a Personal Interest	42	10.7
Other Improper Influence in a Civil Matter, No Personal Interest	26	6.7
CATEGORY TOTAL	68	17.4
USE AND ABUSE OF POLICE RESOURCES (discussed in Chapter Six)		
Misuse of confidential police information		
Access to, and Personal Use of, Police Information	19	4.9
Disclosure of Police Information to Outside Parties	39	10.0
CATEGORY TOTAL	58	14.9

Misuse of other police resources		
Misuse of Police Identity	15	3.8
Other Private Use of Police Resources	22	5.6
CATEGORY TOTAL	37	9.5
OTHER ASPECTS OF POLICE OFFICERS' ACTIONS AND ACTIVITIES THAT MAY SIGNIFY CONFLICTS OF INTEREST (not discussed in this book: see Davids 2005)		
Acceptance or procurement of goods or services		
Solicitation or Acceptance of a Gratuity, Benefit, or Advantage	29	7.4
Attempt to Gain Ownership of Goods Handled in an Official Capacity	7	1.8
CATEGORY TOTAL	36	9.2
Breach of the law		
Breach of the Law Whilst Off Duty	15	3.8
Breach of the Law Whilst On Duty	30	7.7
CATEGORY TOTAL	45	11.5
OVERALL TOTAL	391	100.0

B   Use and Abuse of Powers and Authority

The remainder of this chapter discusses the three categories of problems in relation to the use and abuse of police powers and authority. The three categories include nine different specific types of conflict of interest. Figure 5.2 shows that *intervention, action, or involvement in police investigations and processes* is the largest category, with 55 per cent of the total conflicts of interest in the area of use and abuse of powers and authority. The second largest category is the *exercise of improper influence in civil matters*, which involved 32 per cent of the total conflicts of interest in this area. The third category is the *use of police power to harass*, which involved 13 per cent of the total conflicts of interest in this area.

Figure 5.2: Use and Abuse of Police Powers and Authority

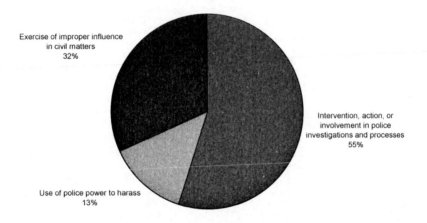

Exercise of improper influence
in civil matters
32%

Intervention, action, or
involvement in police
investigations and processes
55%

Use of police power to harass
13%

II   Intervention, Action, or Involvement in Police Investigations and Processes

The disinterested independence, both in fact and appearance, of police processes is central to their integrity. A threat to this independence is presented by the intervention, involvement, or other action in relation to police procedures in which a police officer has a personal interest, or which involves a family member, friend, or associate.

The outcomes of the complaint cases in five key areas of involvement in official police processes are summarised in Table 5.2. Of the five areas, the most significant in terms of number of cases involved allegations that police officers had either failed to act against a party with whom the police officer/s concerned had some connection, or had taken police action against a party to whom the police officer/s concerned was opposed in some context. A total of 89 occurences involved allegations in these two areas. The substantiation rates in these two groups, at 17.8 per cent and 34.1 per cent respectively, were relatively low when compared to the other groups, but nevertheless were not insignificant. The overall substantiation rate of 33 per cent for all cases involving alleged inappropriate intervention, involvement, or action in police investigations and processes indicates that this area presents a significant problem for police management, going to the heart of impartial performance of fundamental police duties.

Table 5.2: Findings in Complaints Relating to Intervention, Action, or Involvement in Police Investigations and Activities Processes

Category of conflict of interest	Determination						Total Occurrences	
	Finding against police officer (substantiated)		In-determinate finding[1]		Finding in favour of police officer[2]			
	N	%	N	%	N	%	N	%
Failure to act, due to a relationship with an involved party	8	17.8	10	22.2	27	60.0	45	100
Delaying/discontinuing police processes, due to relationship with one of the parties	5	45.5	0	0.0	6	54.5	11	100
Taking police action against an opposing party	15	34.1	4	9.1	25	56.8	44	100
Investigating associated police officer	4	57.1	2	28.6	1	14.3	7	100
Other involvement, investigation, or intervention in a case with a personal interest	7	63.6	1	9.1	3	27.3	11	100
TOTAL	39	33.0	17	14.4	62	52.6	118	100

(1) *Indeterminate finding* = Lesser deficiency, Unable to determine, Conciliated, Not proceeded with (resigned prior)

(2) *Finding in favour of police officer* = Withdrawn, No complaint, Not substantiated, Unfounded, Exonerated

Many of the issues at stake when police officers become involved in official police processes in relation to matters in which they have a direct or indirect personal interest came to attention in a prominent case in 1994 that resulted in a Deputy Ombudsman's report tabled in the Victorian Parliament (The Deputy Ombudsman (Police Complaints) 1995). The key focus of this report reflected continuing concern with issues of conflict of interest in such matters. It was noted that whilst conflicts of interest often could not be avoided altogether, a police officer could avoid continuing involvement in subsequent action and thereby avoid breaching the duty of disinterestedness, a

> ... problem continually confronted by police members both senior and junior. Being approached by a friend or acquaintance of any degree is not a matter which in reality can be avoided. However, what can be avoided ... is the involvement of the member approached in the issues which are of concern or the subject of the approach. That involvement is easily avoided by the member who is approached by directing the enquirer to a more appropriate member to deal with the matter. In such circumstances in my view the object of the police member approached should be to avoid performing any duties or undertaking any work in relation to the matter raised with him by the friend or acquaintance. Doing so denies the opportunity for any conflict to arise between the member's professional duties and obligations, on the one hand, and on the other hand his personal connections with the friend or acquaintance ... (The Deputy Ombudsman (Police Complaints) 1995: 27).

The Deputy Ombudsman recommended that the Force review its training, operational procedures, and professional ethics and standards to ensure that there were clear and comprehensive instructions in place regarding conflicts of interest (The Deputy Ombudsman (Police Complaints) 1995: 28). The Chief Commissioner of Police responded by stating that training, operating procedures, and professional ethics and standards would be reviewed in the manner suggested by the Deputy Ombudsman.

A   Failure to Act Due to a Relationship with an Involved Party

The first group of cases involved claims that a police officer failed to act, or to act with sufficient severity, in relation to matters in which it was claimed that the police officer had a relationship (or similar association) with the party against whom allegedly insufficient action was taken. Five distinct circumstances in this group have been identified from the case files:

♦   failure to act against family, friends or colleagues;

♦   failure to act in which a complainant *assumed* a conflict of interest although none was found;

♦ failure to act in which the complainant seemed to have vexatious motives in alleging a conflict of interest;

♦ civil resolution of a matter sought, giving rise to a complaint of conflict of interest for not taking police action; and

♦ a direct conflict of interest between the police officer's official duties and private business interests.

1   *Family, Friends or Colleagues*

In the course of ordinary duties a police officer may be called upon to undertake policing tasks in contexts where friends or acquaintances of the police officer are involved. If an aggrieved party or a member of the public perceives that the officer has failed to take appropriate police action against a particular party in such circumstances, complaints of conflict of interest are likely to ensue.

Some complaint cases relevant to this area involved traffic-related matters. In one serious case it was alleged that a police officer had falsified an accident collision statement in order to protect one of the vehicle occupants, who was a brother-in-law of a police officer at the same station. The vehicle occupant was a passenger of the vehicle, but the complainant alleged he was in fact the driver, and that the falsification was to protect him from the possibility of losing his licence. The complaint was made anonymously, and was found to be unfounded on the evidence (Case 373).

Other cases related to policing activity, or perceived lack thereof, in relation to hotels/nightclubs and a restaurant. For example, in one case, it was alleged by a group of local residents that police were not appropriately policing a nightclub because the police were regular patrons at the venue, and that some police members worked there (secondary employment). The complaint alleged that police had not acted on evidence that the nightclub was in breach of the Liquor Control Act, particularly in regard to alleged underage consumption of alcohol. It was also alleged that Private Inquiry Agents had observed on-duty police visiting the premises but ignoring breaches of the Act whilst they were on the premises (Case 52).

In response to the complaint, police inquiries showed that many arrests had been made at the nightclub and reports relating to the running of the nightclub and recommending a review of the venue's licence had been sent to the Liquor Licensing Commission. It was acknowledged that the complainant's comments relating to the perceived non-enforcement of breaches of the Act were a matter for genuine concern. However, the claim that police effectively 'turned a blind eye' to such breaches was deemed to be unfounded; there was no evidence to suggest that police members did work at the premises; and the claim that police members had close connections with the management of the venue was found not to be supported. This case demonstrates the problems that can arise where members of the public perceive a conflict of interest, even where there is insufficient evidence to demonstrate such conflicts.

The cases discussed above involved relatively minor incidents. More serious are criminal matters where there is an alleged failure to act due to a claimed relationship with an involved party. Two cases illustrate the problems.

The first case involved a serious traffic matter, where a driver caused significant damage and a large fire when he crashed into two shops. The driver allegedly decamped from the scene. A complaint, in the form of a series of accusatory questions including a suggestion that the driver was over the legal blood alcohol limit and had been drinking with police officer friends prior to the incident, was lodged by the man's insurer which was liable for third-party property damage caused. The complaint insinuated that a named detective, alleged to be a personal friend of the driver, attended the accident scene before the Traffic Operations Group and had assisted the driver in various ways, and that one result was that charges were not laid against him (Case 261).

The evaluation resulting from the Internal Investigations Department investigation rebutted all the allegations implied in the complainant's questions, and the allegations were therefore found to be unsubstantiated. It was found that the named police officer was not known to the driver and he did not attend the scene of the accident. Prosecution of the driver was correctly not approved as there was no evidence of his blood alcohol level at the time of the accident (his blood alcohol level was only tested some time later). There was no evidence that the driver had been drinking with any Victoria Police members prior to the collision.

In the second case, a person was alleged to have molested a male youth and to have said to the youth that if he (the youth) complained it would do him no good because he (the offender) had friends who were police officers. Upon investigation, the alleged offender denied all aspects of the allegation. In relation to the claim that he had police officer friends who would fail to take police action against him, this was found to be unsubstantiated. It was found that, while a number of police officers had visited the offender over a number of years in his professional capacity as a chiropractor/masseur, there was no evidence "whatsoever" that any member had tried to interfere with or influence the investigative outcome as alleged by the complainant. The police brief against the alleged offender was marked "not authorised" but this was because it was felt to have little hope of succeeding due to the passage of time from the alleged offences, evidentiary problems in relation to consent, and associated matters (Case 141).

These cases again illustrate the vulnerability of police officers to assumptions made by complainants on the simple basis of perceived or manufactured associations (or alleged friendships), whether valid or not.

2   Relationship Assumed by Complainant

Sometimes there is no *evidence* of any relationship between the police officer and the party allegedly benefiting from a failure to take police action, yet a complainant *assumes* that such a relationship exists and that the failure to take action is linked to the assumed/alleged conflict of interest.

One such case involved a woman in the midst of a bitter divorce and custody battle. She had alleged sexual abuse by her estranged husband—an ex-police officer—on their daughter. When no action was taken against the man, the woman believed that it must have been because he exerted influence over the police officers investigating the matter. However, the Internal Investigations Department investigation found that there was no evidence to support this allegation and it was concluded that charges had not been laid against him due to conflicting evidence in relation to the allegation (Case 166).

Several other cases involved complainants making similar assumptions of an association between police and alleged offenders. In one of these cases, a youth used open hands to punch an intoxicated man on the chest. The man fell and suffered a fractured skull and brain haemorrhage as a result of hitting his head on the pavement. He subsequently died from these injuries. The youth was charged with recklessly causing serious injury, but the deceased man's son wanted him charged with manslaughter. When the desired charges were not laid, the complainant assumed there *must* be a connection between the police officers involved and the offending youth. A companion of the youth (who was with him at the time of the accident, and did not assist the injured/deceased man) was a retired police officer's son, but there was no evidence of any connection between that man and the police officers involved in this case. The complaint was found to be unsubstantiated (Case 217).

Another case involving an alleged failure to lay appropriate criminal charges involved allegations of conspiracy between police, the courts, and other parties in failing to prosecute a woman for allegedly menacing the complainant with an imitation firearm. Amongst other allegations, the complainant had alleged that he had been threatened in this manner by the mother of his girlfriend. He alleged that a police officer involved was associated with the other party. The complainant had written to the Deputy Ombudsman, a local magistrate, his local Member of Parliament, and the Victoria Police ESD. In addition, he erected signs near the police station, and picketed the police station. There was no evidence to support his assertions of an association between the other party he was in dispute with and any police officer at the station (Case 271). The original complaint was lodged in 1996, and in early 1998 the ESD received a further letter from the complainant stating that no charges had been laid after he was threatened by a gun. However, no new information to justify reopening the case was received.

Here, despite there being no evidence of any association between an alleged offender and a police officer, the complainant could not let go of his perception, demonstrating the potential vulnerability of police officers to unsubstantiated claims of conflict of interest.

3 Relationship Claimed by an Apparently Vexatious Complainant

In this group of cases, a police officer's failure to act in relation to a particular matter gave rise to a complaint, but the complainant seemed to have vexatious motives in alleging a conflict of interest. In all these cases, the finding was that the allegation was unsubstantiated or unfounded. Two cases serve to illustrate the types of situation that may arise.

In one case it was anonymously alleged that a person who was a drug dealer was being protected because of a relationship with a police officer. Investigations revealed that the alleged drug dealer was in the midst of a bitter custody battle, and the evidence suggested that the complaint may have been fabricated (Case 132).

Other cases involved failure to take action in relation to allegations of criminal conduct. One case involved members and ex-members of a motorcycle gang and the death of one member who was believed by one group of people to have been killed by members of the other group. It was alleged that the police officer involved did not appropriately investigate their allegations of murder, but there was no evidence to support either the original allegation or the allegation of conflict of interest. It seemed apparent that the complainants were vexatiously using the police complaints system (Case 178).

Like other cases in which a complainant may have nefarious motives, these cases illustrate the vulnerability of police officers to vexatious (and mistaken) complaints. This vulnerability flows from three factors that are difficult to avoid: the visibility of police as they go about their duties, the discretion inherent in many aspects of policing work, and the authority police carry as part of their role.

4   Civil Resolution Attempt Sparks Complaint

Some cases involved allegations claiming that a police officer inappropriately sought a civil resolution of a matter between opposing parties, whereas the complainant believed that official police action should have been taken in relation to the matter. It is within the legitimate realm of police discretion not to invoke the law in dealing with complaints of minor assaults and other offences. This is particularly so given the breadth and vagueness of the law itself, which means that police "invariably under-enforce the law" (Lustgarten 1986: Ch 1). However, if an aggrieved complainant alleges that police inappropriately advised seeking private redress for a matter which arguably should have been treated as a chargeable offence, they may allege or imply some form of conflict of interest as the motivating factor behind the officer advising civil resolution.

In a case involving a homicide investigation following a shooting death, no charges were laid against anyone in relation to the death, but one of the suspects stated that he felt such remorse over the death that he wanted the deceased's daughter to have one of his restaurants as "some sort of compensation". The senior investigating officer in charge of the investigation advised the wife of the deceased that no charges were to be laid in relation to the death, but he relayed the offer from the suspect to her. Even though no malicious or wrongful motives were attributed to the police officer, he was admonished because he had been involved in discussions relating to possible civil compensation which allowed the inference to be drawn that the suspect may have influenced the result of the criminal investigation (Case 341).

In other circumstances, the provision of advice to members of the public may lead a complainant to conclude that the police officer is 'taking sides'. In such a case, it was alleged that a police officer had failed to prosecute an offender in relation to an alleged assault—the complainant (aged in his thirties) alleged that his father-in-law (an octogenarian) had assaulted him. The attending police officer had concluded that it was probable that the aged man had acted in self-defence, and in the course of discussions at the scene he provided general advice to the old man in relation to seeking an Intervention Order and securing the eviction of the complainant and his family from premises owned by the old man. It was subsequently alleged that the officer had interfered in private family matters by providing this advice but the Internal Investigations Department found that the police officer's action in providing advice in relation to both an eviction and an Intervention Order was entirely appropriate in the circumstances (action in relation to both matters had already been commenced). The complaint was resolved by conciliation (Case 266).

Another case involved a neighbourhood dispute over a dog. A neighbour of the dog owner had become angry during a dispute with the complainant and had broken a window. The attending police officer tried to negotiate settlement in the form of the man agreeing to pay for the damage he had caused. Whilst the complainant agreed at the time, on reflection the next day the complainant felt that this was not satisfactory and sought official action against the neighbour, who he argued had made threats against him and had admitted to wilful damage. However, no action was taken against the man, and the complainant alleged that this was the result of a friendly relationship between the police officer and the neighbour. Following the Internal Investigations Department investigation, charges were in fact laid against the neighbour. The police officer was counselled, because the notes in his book did not reflect what was later agreed to have happened (Case 28).

5 Official Duty and Private Business Conflict of Interest

The single case in this category involved an officer seeking private payment for private work that he effectively should have undertaken in the course of his police duties. The complainant had been a victim of a burglary and the police officer allegedly offered to provide a private guard for the business at a substantial fee. The complainant alleged that no official police investigation was undertaken and that the police officer was effectively seeking private payment for an investigation that should have been conducted as part of police duty (Case 310).

The Internal Investigations Department investigation found that the police officer had not made a crime report in relation to the theft, as required by standard police procedures. The specific matter relating to the alleged offer to provide private security services to the business was regarded as the most serious aspect of the complaint, but the complainant and the police officer offered different versions of the conversation that occurred between them. Following a formal discipline hearing, neither version could be corroborated and this specific charge was found to be not proven.

B *Relationship with Involved Party Delays or Stops Police Processes*

In considering complaints of conflict of interest, the preceding discussion shows that the appropriateness of a failure to act can be determined in a relatively straightforward manner. By contrast, complaints involving allegations that a police officer has delayed or discontinued police processes due to a relationship with an involved party are more complex because in these cases some form of police action has been initiated or police processes have otherwise been commenced. This adds an extra dimension to a claim that the delay or discontinuance of such processes (itself a particular kind of *action* rather than a *failure* to act) is the result of a conflict of interest.

1 *Delays*

In some cases, the claim is that processes have been delayed to the detriment of a party allegedly opposed by the police officer. In one such case, the general claim by the complainant, who was employed by a security company, was that he was being harassed by police. This claim was associated with a delay of several weeks in processing the man's application for a licence to carry a pistol. The police officer concerned accompanied another police officer to the man's home to inspect the security arrangements for his firearms (part of the application for a permit to carry firearms). The alleged conflict of interest behind the delay was that the police officer was biased against the man. The Internal Investigations Department investigation found that there was no evidence of bias but that the delay in processing the man's pistol licence application was unreasonable. The police officer was issued with a caution notice in relation to the need to attend to the correspondence of the station in a proper and timely fashion (Case 81).

In the case discussed above, there *was* found to be an unreasonable delay in police processes, but the delay was not found to be the result of a conflict of interest. In another case, a police officer's actions seemed to be motivated by a conflict of interest as they were apparently designed to delay official processing of an action against a friend. The officer's sister was involved in a car crash and she contacted the police officer who then telephoned a friend who was a tow truck driver. He arrived at the scene in his tow-truck, collected the sister (but not her car) and drove her home. The man's attendance at the scene, even though he did not tow the woman's vehicle, was not in accord with the strict Victorian towing allocations system (Case 233).

The principal concern in this case was in relation to the subsequent actions of the police officer in failing to cooperate with investigators, which may have been deliberately contrived in order to delay processes. The Internal Investigations Department found that the police officer had indeed been reluctant to provide relevant information to the Tow Truck Directorate, which is responsible for prosecutions in relation to the towing allocations system. The Directorate, which was the complainant in this case, alleged that the police officer was uncooperative and refused to provide them with a statement, also alleging that the police officer had withheld evidence in relation to an alleged offence (they believed the tow truck driver had committed an offence by attending). However, the protocols between Victoria Police and the Tow Truck Directorate were found to be insufficiently clear in outlining an obligation for Victoria Police members to assist the prosecution. No further action was taken against the police officer.

Nevertheless, this case file was subsequently reviewed by a senior officer from Task Force Bart who was undertaking investigations into the tow truck industry. This review of the case was subsequent to the closure of the file as an active Internal Investigations Department investigation, and subsequent to the oversight and approval by the Deputy Ombudsman of the case and its handling. The Task Force Bart officer expressed a level of displeasure at the case, its processing, and outcome.

2   Investigation Stopped or Charges Withdrawn

In the cases discussed in this subsection, the allegations revolve around claims that a police officer has actively sought to have police processes against a friend or relative discontinued or to have charges withdrawn. In most of these cases, where the involvement of a police officer is *indirect*, it is difficult to demonstrate two key aspects that are vital to substantiate an allegation. First, that the police officer actively sought to have police processes delayed or discontinued; secondly, that the police officer's intervention actually did have an impact on the outcome.

The conflict of interest in a case in point revolved around an allegation that a police officer had telephoned the officer investigating a case against the police officer's brother and attempted to put pressure on the investigating officer to drop proceedings against the man. The police officer admitted to making the telephone call but denied any attempt to exert influence over the direction of the investigation (Case 87).

The initial Internal Investigations Department investigation found the matter to be unfounded, even though the evidence suggested that the case against the man was proceeding very slowly. In his review of the matter, the Deputy Ombudsman did not agree with this outcome, stating that the police officer's involvement in a matter in which he had a personal interest created a reasonable perception that could bring the Force into disrepute, and that the complaint was a reasonable one. He suggested that the police officer should be counselled for his conduct. The outcome of the case was consequently changed from requiring no further action to counselling the police officer. The investigating officer in relation to the alleged breach of the law by the police officer's brother was also counselled for taking too long with the investigation.

Many of the issues at stake in such situations came to attention in a case involving an allegation that criminal charges against a person, relating to a fracas in a hotel, were withdrawn following a request from an Assistant Commissioner who was a friend of the alleged offender's father. At the request of a member of the charged man's family, a telephone call was made by the police officer to one of the police informants in the matter (that is, one of the arresting officers). This was in the nature of an 'inquiry on behalf of a friend' and the police officer denied he had made any attempt to intimidate or influence the informant (Case 175).

The case against the person was subsequently withdrawn, but was later reinstated after the matter received major local media attention (the man concerned was from a prominent family). Victoria Police reinvestigated the matter and in a subsequent court hearing, the alleged offender pleaded guilty to the charges. The Internal Investigations Department investigated the case and the allegation against the Assistant Commissioner was found to be not substantiated. It was found that the decision to withdraw the charges against the man was taken within the District, and was not influenced by the Assistant Commissioner's inquiry, and had not been taken with reference to the informant who had been contacted by the Assistant Commissioner.[1] There was no evidence that the Assistant Commissioner had any input into the decision to withdraw charges.

Complaints against a police officer in this area can also be an understandable, but unfair manifestation of assumptions people may make about the relationships between police officers and their spouses or associates. In a case providing an example of this, a police officer had a husband with a drinking problem. An anonymous complaint was received alleging that the officer had intervened in more than one case in order to assist her husband have drink driving charges dropped. However, investigation showed that the husband had actually been charged and convicted five times in relation to drink driving offences, and there was no evidence that his wife had been involved in any way in any of these or other matters (Case 106).

C   Police Action Against an Opposing Party

This section discusses conflicts of interest that are alleged where a police officer actively takes some form of police action against a party who is, in some context, opposed to the police officer or family, friends, or associates of the police officer.

A case that illustrates the complexities and difficulties involved in such matters centred on a police officer's wife's best friend. She had been involved in an argument with another woman that had turned into a fight that resulted in charges being laid against the other woman. The charged woman complained that she had been prosecuted only because the first woman was the police officer's wife's friend. The police officer concerned was alleged to have rung the investigating officer several times to inquire about the case, but as a result of the Internal Investigations Department investigation into the matter, the complaint against the police officer was found to be unsubstantiated (Case 62).

However, other circumstances of the case were a cause of concern for the Deputy Ombudsman in oversighting the file. The Deputy Ombudsman's concerns centred on the police officer's conduct subsequent to the charges

---

[1] Subsequent disciplinary action (not included in the case files for this study) was taken against a number of officers including the two who were actually responsible for the decision (deemed inappropriate) to withdraw charges.

being laid against the woman. The matter proceeded to court and the police officer attended the court, while on duty, for all three days while the case against the woman proceeded. The Deputy Ombudsman was particularly concerned at the fact that the police officer sat in on court proceedings even though his duties did not require him to do so.

The Deputy Ombudsman's growing concern over the problem of conflict of interest resulted in a strong objection to the Internal Investigations Department finding in regard to the complaint. He felt that the case represented a clear conflict of interest and asked that the case be reconsidered, also raising evidentiary concerns. Victoria Police management did not acquiesce, however subsequent information for members was published in the Police Gazette in March 1992. Despite this, the police officer continued to deny that his involvement in the case represented any conflict of interest. This matter, and the advice provided in the Victoria Police Gazette item, was later referred to by the Deputy Ombudsman in his Annual Report to the Parliament of Victoria (The Ombudsman 1993).

The Deputy Ombudsman's concern over police officers acting in cases in which they had a conflict of interest continued in subsequent years. In 1995 he made comments in relation to a case in which a man's shooters' licence had been cancelled and his firearms had been seized, following a decision of the Firearms Consultative Committee. The man lodged a complaint asserting that the police officer who had been involved in action to have his licence revoked had acted unfairly. Specifically, he alleged that the police officer had compiled a report that was not properly researched and was based on biased, unsound and vindictive allegations. It was alleged that the police officer had a pre-existing personal relationship with one of the people involved in a series of events that led to the application to revoke the man's shooters' licence. Upon investigation, even though it seemed apparent that many of the man's allegations carried substance, the complaint against him was found to be unsubstantiated (Case 246).

The Deputy Ombudsman expressed particular concerns at this outcome, relating to two main issues: the behaviour of the police officer in terms of possible intimidation of witnesses and his action in being involved in a case in which he had a pre-existing personal relationship with the main witnesses against the man. Concern was also expressed about the fact that the police officer had attended the Firearms Consultative Committee hearing in uniform when it appeared he was not on duty, but was there as a friend of the witness. Despite the seriousness and clarity of these concerns, a senior officer within the

Internal Investigations Department responded to the Deputy Ombudsman by implicitly relying on the integrity of the police officer concerned to carry out his Oath of Office to carry out his duties "without favour or affection". These comments implicitly nullified any concern over the problem of conflict of interest. The senior officer's defence of the police officer was lengthy and detailed, and even offered praise of the police officer's actions, further stating that country police could not operate at all if they were not to pursue inquiries involving any person they knew, "since they know the majority of people in their area". He stated that as an Internal Investigations Department member he had, on an everyday basis, conducted inquiries on behalf of people he knew. He claimed that "[i]f a strict conflict of interest was applied, IID could not operate properly".

This senior IID officer was prepared to rely on the integrity and experience of the police officer, who had more than 15 years' experience, stating that experienced officers are able to deal with areas of conflict of interest. A key problem with this conclusion is that it was based on a fallacious assumption. As evidenced in many of the cases examined for this research (and discussed in Chapter Three), the level of experience of police officers neither mitigates their tendency to become involved in conflict of interest situations, nor their tendency to act in neglect of their duty as a result of a conflict of interest.

This particular matter went for review to the Assistant Commissioner for the Internal Investigations Department. His comments showed perhaps a better appreciation of the problems in the case, and gave some ground to the Deputy Ombudsman, but were still broadly supportive of the position taken by the reviewing senior officer, and he proposed that the matter would be taken no further:

> [I] acknowledge that there are clear-cut conflicts of interest and they should be avoided. Members should also be given some credit to determine what is normal police practice and procedures and what constitutes a conflict of interest that would cause a "reasonable man" to be concerned with the action of the member.

> I also acknowledge that matters can be referred to other members or areas but there should be some evidence of bias, partiality, and direct evidence of a conflict, as opposed to a perception of a conflict merely because a member knows someone or has an association with them ...

This case demonstrates that the problem of conflict of interest has a number of facets, although the reluctance on the part of Victoria Police to even recognise the existence of a conflict of interest in the case is perplexing. Such recognition is the first step in determining appropriate action to ensure that a conflict of interest does not affect the performance of duty.

The remainder of the discussion in this section is divided into two subsections: cases where police action was taken against a party *personally* opposed to the police officer, and cases where police action was taken against a party opposed to family, friends, or associates of the police officer.

1   A Party Personally Opposed to Police Officer

A context that recurs in a number of cases is police officer involvement in some form of action against alleged offenders in motor vehicle and traffic-related matters. The alleged conflicts of interest arise because these traffic matters also involve the police officer that is the subject of the complaint. Traffic-related charges are often the only point of contact that members of the public have with the police, thus conflicts of interest in this area can give rise to an emotional reaction on the part of the driver who is subject to police action. Further, in traffic matters there is considerable discretion in decisions as to whether to issue Infringement Notices, or to lay charges requiring an appearance before a court, or to take no action. These matters therefore provide a context within which conflict of interest breaches can be manifested in a straightforward manner and are clear examples of the types of personal involvement to be avoided by police officers.

The first case of this type provides an insight into a number of important public policy issues considered by the police. The complainant in the case was involved in a traffic incident and subsequent verbal altercation with an off-duty member and his partner (who was driving the vehicle). Both attended at the local police station where the complainant spoke with the duty sergeant to lodge a complaint. After their discussion the complainant believed the matter had been resolved and that no action would be taken against him. However, as a result of a Brief (prepared by the police officer involved in the incident) he was subsequently charged with traffic offences (including many that were trivial) and assault—all of which charges he denied. The important conflict of interest here was that the police officer who alleged he was the victim of the assault and the traffic offences was *also the informant* in the case (Case 16).

The senior officer who investigated the case believed that the police officer had acted correctly in the matter and that no further action should be taken against him, apart from a counselling with regard to failing to provide full particulars to the Officer-in-Charge. However, a reviewing senior officer within the Internal Investigations Department stated that the police officer should be reprimanded for acting as the informant, and for acting in a manner likely to bring discredit to the reputation of the Force. The reviewing officer argued that the sergeant who had been on duty at the station when the charge was laid needed to be interviewed before proceeding against the police officer (in the form of a reprimand). The duty sergeant, when he was interviewed, was of the view that it was an over-reaction by the member to a minor incident. He believed that he had resolved the dispute at the time and, after discussion with both, recommended that the matter should go no further. It also later emerged that the police officer had not disclosed all of the details of the case to the Senior Sergeant who subsequently authorised the Brief for prosecution against the complainant.

The officer responsible for assembling the Brief for prosecution at court raised serious questions regarding the initial police officer's actions. A further review by a senior officer within the Internal Investigations Department concluded that the charges that had been laid against the man were "at best, technical" and that they should not have proceeded. However, he thought that court procedural rules may have meant the proceedings could not be withdrawn, and the Department could not at law direct the police officer concerned to withdraw the charges himself. The police officer had indicated he was not prepared to withdraw the charges. The reviewing senior officer was highly critical of the police officer's actions in refusing to conciliate the case, especially as the complainant was willing to do so, and felt that the case would damage the reputation of the Force. He further stated that the police officer should be admonished.

In the end the complaint was conciliated and the charges were withdrawn. The police officer was counselled. The key issues raised by the Deputy Ombudsman in his oversight of the file related to the issue of the police officer's conflict of interest in the matter and a concern that this could reflect adversely on the Force. The Deputy Ombudsman suggested that even if the police officer had not intervened in initially recommending that no charges be laid, he should not have been the informant in the matter.

Several other conflict of interest complaints arose out of the issuance of Traffic Infringement Notices to drivers of motor vehicles, where the relevant traffic accident or incident also involved an off-duty police officer. These circumstances, where known to the recipient of an Infringement Notice, are perhaps an understandable source of claims about conflict of interest.

In one such case, a police officer was involved in a multiple-vehicle collision in which his wife was a passenger in one of the other vehicles. The police officer nominated himself as the investigating officer and produced his own traffic accident report, but did not disclose that the key 'witness' was his wife. Two Traffic Infringement Notices were issued to one of the other drivers involved. In addition to a complaint about the police officer's involvement, the complainant also alleged that sections of an alleged interview with him at the scene were falsified (Case 311).

The Internal Investigations Department investigating officer found that there was insufficient evidence to support the offences alleged against the driver and recommended withdrawal of the Traffic Infringement Notices. It was further recommended that any further action in relation to the accident be left to civil action by parties. Disciplinary action was taken against the police officer for failure to comply with an instruction from the Chief Commissioner (in relation to his compilation of his own accident report) and improper conduct (in that he investigated an accident his wife was involved in). These charges were substantiated and the police officer was fined.

In another case a motorist had lodged a complaint about a police officer in relation to his actions undertaken after he, whilst off-duty (attired in a Hawaiian shirt and shorts, driving an unmarked vehicle), pulled over a young female probationary driver and berated her for driving without her lights on. According both to the complainant and witnesses in the vehicle with her, the police officer was loud and aggressive, reducing the driver to tears. When, at this time of the interaction with the police officer, the driver's father telephoned her on her mobile telephone, the police officer grabbed the phone and informed the father of what was happening, using disparaging words about the driver. The driver was not charged with any offence at the time, but once the police officer found out that she had lodged a complaint about his behaviour, he later ordered that she should undergo a medical test (under the Road Traffic Act 1986) to establish her fitness to hold a licence (Case 253).

It was alleged that the report he issued requesting a medical test was not submitted in good faith but in order to cover up his wrongdoing, and that the police officer had backdated the report by a month so that it looked like it had been made immediately after the incident in question and before her complaint against him. These aspects of the matter only emerged during the investigation of the original complaint. Investigators had the request for medical examination placed on hold pending the outcome of their inquiries, considering that it was legally unsound to allow the matter to proceed at that time. It was later determined that, in relation to the original complaint, there was no independent witness to the incident and it was therefore not possible to determine the truth or otherwise of the complainant's allegations. Definitive evidence in relation to the dating of the report was not available, and no action was taken against the police officer.

In contexts other than motor vehicle and traffic-related matters a small number of matters involved a police officer taking action against a party to whom he or she was personally opposed. In one case, a police officer had property stolen and reported the theft to police, but subsequently found the person believed to be responsible, arrested him and took him back to the police station. The police officer was present and asked some questions during the interview of the alleged offender. The original Internal Investigations Department investigation cleared the police officer, but the Deputy Ombudsman was not happy with this outcome. There were several exchanges between the office of the Deputy Ombudsman and Victoria Police, but they could not agree on the outcome of the case. The Deputy Ombudsman argued that when a police officer is a victim of crime, he should be treated the same as everyone else, and that a member of the public would not be permitted to do what he had done in this case. He was particularly concerned about the police officer's questioning of the alleged offender. His opinion was that the police officer had obtained an advantage because of his position. The Victoria Police response was that, as arresting officer, the police officer's actions were reasonable, particularly in the country location where police resources (and staff) are limited (Case 68).

Another case involved a police officer whose son did not gain admission to the school he wanted. The police officer visited the offices of the relevant government department to appeal the matter, but the appeal was unsuccessful. He subsequently issued eight Penalty Notices to cars parked outside the government building. As a result of the Internal Investigations Department investigation and the Deputy Ombudsman's oversight, the police officer was required to face charges before the Police Discipline Board under then Regulation 402(a) which prohibited a police officer from acting "in a manner prejudicial to discipline or likely to bring discredit on the reputation of the Force". The basis of the decision to charge the police officer was that he had acted in a manner which was considered to be a vindictive attempt to influence the decision of the government department. It was decided that the eight Penalty Notices issued by the police officer were tainted and they were withdrawn (Case 67).

The police officer had five months earlier been reprimanded by the Police Discipline Board for acting in manner likely to bring discredit to the Force. He had also been reprimanded two years earlier for carrying on a business without approval. At the Police Discipline Board hearing, at which the police officer was represented by the Police Association, the charges were dismissed. Counsel for the police officer submitted that, having detected the offences, the police officer was *duty bound* to issue the Penalty Notices. The Board found that, whilst the police officer may have been considered to have been "unthinking and officious", this in itself was not an offence, and there was no evidence that he was being vindictive (despite evidence that vehicles had regularly been parked in the same location for some years, and had never before been issued with Penalty Notices). He was returned to active duty.

2   *A Party Opposed to Family, Friends, or Associates of Police Officer*

Police officers often find themselves in positions where they may take some form of official action against a party that is in a dispute with their family, friends, or associates. In such circumstances, there is always a conflict of interest in so far as the police officer's decisions in relation to the matter may be affected to the extent that they are not fair and impartial. Even if a police officer is able to recognise the conflict of interest and seek to take a decision that is genuinely unaffected by the relationship, it is likely that the confidence of a 'reasonable' observer in the integrity of the process would be diminished.

Several complaints involved allegations that unreasonable action taken by police officers had benefited the private business or commercial interests of family members or friends. One case involved an ongoing (four-year) dispute between the lessee and owner of a hotel. The owner was the son-in-law of a police officer. On various occasions other police officers had attended the hotel in relation to alleged breaches of the liquor laws. The complainant (lessee) alleged that these actions amounted to organised harassment on behalf of the police officer. The investigation showed that the father-in law had sought advice about the general matter from the police officer in question, but the police officer denied he had a hand in having the matters investigated. However it was agreed that the police officer did report alleged breaches of the law to other police officers who investigated the matter, and he followed up the matter with them (Case 114).

The initial finding was that the complaint was unsubstantiated and that the police officer had not used his position to influence the outcome of the investigation, but an Assistant Commissioner did talk to the police officer after the Deputy Ombudsman suggested a lack of action was unsatisfactory. The Deputy Ombudsman specifically raised concern in relation to the conflict of interest associated with the police officer's involvement in the matter, and public perceptions of conflict of interest, arguing that the complainant's perceptions of a conflict of interest were quite understandable.

In another case also involving family business interests in licensed premises (a nightclub) it was alleged that a police officer took out a prosecution against business competitors. In this case, the police officer was also involved in the family business as a director, and had taken leave without pay to assist in the running of the business. After he returned from this period of leave, the police officer (with other officers) visited the competitor's premises several times, and he subsequently provided evidence against the complainant in relation to various breaches of Liquor Control Act. The evidence from the investigation of the complaint suggested that although there may have been an appearance of conflict of interest, the police officer's visits were in the line of duty, and that there was no suggestion that these premises had been targeted relative to other similar premises in the area. The complaint was found to be unsubstantiated (Case 290).

A case with a quite different element involved the police officer who was involved in assisting a video shop proprietor to collect bad debts. This police officer, in uniform, on-duty and using a marked police vehicle, attended the private residences of persons who had not returned rented videos, demanding that payment be made to the shop. This particular complaint involved a case where the police officer, as part of this process, dramatised his demand by undertaking a pseudo arrest of a person, ostensibly for theft. No record of attendance at the various residences, and no crime reports were ever filled out in relation to the ostensible thefts. Initial investigators recommended a reprimand, and a discipline hearing was scheduled, with charges relating to engaging in conduct likely to bring discredit to the Force, failing to make appropriate entries on official documents, and making an unnecessary arrest. The police officer took stress leave and then resigned prior to any hearing taking place. That the police officer in this case was a senior officer with 25 years service illustrates the fundamental problem raised in Chapter Two in relation to the lack of understanding of conflict of interest, even on the part of very experienced officers (Case 70).

A number of complaints alleged that a police officer had inappropriately laid charges or taken other associated action in relation to criminal investigations against a person who was in a dispute with the police officer's family, friends, or associates. Six cases involved defendants in assault, stalking, child molestation, and theft cases. In each case the complainant alleged that the victims and a police officer were friends, and that this had impacted on their treatment, including the laying of charges against them. In two of the cases, a connection between the police officer and the alleged victim was found to be in evidence, although the allegations that these associations had influenced the investigation were initially found to be unsubstantiated.

In one of these cases, a person was charged with stalking. A police officer became involved in the case even though he was attached to a state-wide squad and in the usual course of his duties would not have been involved in the matter. The original investigating officer found that there was no evidence of corruption in the investigation and stated that the police officer's involvement, whilst imprudent, was consistent with the "customer service requirement of Victoria Police ...". However, the ESD oversighting officer disagreed with these findings, stating that it was imprudent for the police officer to be involved because he had a distinct connection to the neighbour of the complainant (in the stalking case) and his position in the state-wide squad meant that he should not be involved with stalking charges. The police officer was counselled over his involvement in the matter, as was the Officer in Charge of the state-wide squad who had approved his member's involvement (Case 379). This latter point illustrates how supervising officers at an operational level often do not understand the problem of conflict of interest. The next case reiterates this point.

In a theft case, it was alleged that a police officer had used his office to assist a friend of his wife in a civil matter relating to a dispute over payment for repairs made to an auto transmission box. The police officer claimed that he had never met the woman involved in the dispute (the alleged friend of his wife) and that his wife and the woman had an occasional association through their local school canteen. He stated that he had only become initially involved in the matter in order to ascertain if any criminal offence had occurred (as the repairer had retained possession of the transmission box). Once he felt that a criminal offence may have been involved, the police officer passed the matter on to the relevant Criminal Investigation Bureau. The police officer, however, continued to be involved in the case, under the instruction of his supervising officer (Case 368).

Whilst the case against the police officer was found to be unsubstantiated, in his review the Deputy Ombudsman expressed concern that the Officer in

Charge had ignored the police officer's conflict of interest in the matter. A footnote to the case is that as a result of the original investigation, the complainant was eventually charged with auto theft relating to this and other associated matters.

The context of motor vehicle-related incidents also provides several examples of conflict of interest allegations involving associations with an involved party. One case demonstrates how conflicts of interest in such cases can cause problems on a number of levels. A police officer's wife claimed that she was almost run down when crossing the road on foot. She took details of the vehicle and reported them to police. The woman's husband was on administrative duties; he asked his superiors if he could apprehend and arrest the at-fault driver. They said he could not, but he left the station and apprehended the man anyway. Allegations were subsequently made that the police officer in question participated in an interview of the complainant, and that the police officer assaulted the man. In the investigation of the complaint, two other police officers who were present supported the police officer, but the police officer who apprehended the man was admonished; the two police officers who had conducted the interview were counselled for allowing the aggrieved police officer to be present; and two superior officers were counselled for failing to take action when the police officer ignored their direction not to attend to the matter (Case 61).

In another case involving a motor vehicle incident, an accident occurred while one vehicle was attempting to overtake another towing a trailer. The trailer had faulty lights, and the driver turned right whilst being overtaken, thus causing the collision. The overtaking driver was charged with speeding. The complainant alleged that the attending police officer knew the turning driver on a first name basis, and that he (the overtaking driver) had been treated unfairly, given that the trailer lights were not working, the trailer was not registered, and the other driver had failed to signal. As a result of the complaint, the speeding ticket was ordered to be withdrawn, the other driver was booked for failing to signal, and the police officer concerned was counselled for his actions (Case 39).

A woman involved in a motor vehicle collision received a penalty notice for failing to give way. She later lodged a complaint alleging that she only got a penalty notice because the other party's husband was a police officer (the other party mentioned this when the two women were exchanging particulars). The evidence showed that the police officer in question had not had any part in the accident investigation, which was handled by another police officer. His only contact was to advise the investigating police officer that his wife's statement would be faxed so that an accident report could be commenced. The complaint was unsubstantiated (Case 214).

Two other cases illustrate other circumstances in which a police officer took action against a party in dispute with the police officer's family, friends, or associates. In the first, a complainant alleged that three police officers took unreasonable action when they exercised a search warrant against him without good cause. He alleged that this was the result of a longstanding acrimonious relationship between himself and the police. These aspects of the complainant's allegations were found to be not substantiated (Case 232). The second case involved a prisoner who made a complaint that a police officer was friends with his wife, and that this had influenced the manner in which the police had dealt with the proceeds of the thefts for which the man had been convicted. The allegation of a friendship between the police officer and the man's wife was found to be entirely without foundation, but the police officer was nevertheless counselled for giving the property to the wife prior to the completion of the investigation (Case 92).

One final case was particularly interesting and unique. It involved a complainant who alleged that a police officer used his influence to have a friend flown to Melbourne from interstate, and accommodated in Melbourne, at public expense. The person in question was a witness in criminal proceedings against the complainant and his wife, and her travel had been authorised by the Director of Public Prosecutions. The complainant also alleged property damage at his home, but he provided no detail or evidence of this (Case 258).

The complaint was found to be unfounded, but the most interesting aspect of the case was that the complainant was subsequently charged with criminal defamation, partly as a result of making this complaint (which was sent to the Deputy Ombudsman and the state Attorney-General). The complaint had been made whilst the man was in custody on charges (unrelated to this particular matter) of attempting to obtain property by deception in a matter relating to a telephone marketing fraud. He was found to have circulated documents (signed by him) to over 100 people alleging misconduct on the part of four police officers involved in the investigation.

This was the first prosecution in Victoria for criminal defamation in almost 50 years. The prosecutor in the criminal defamation case argued that this was an attempt to discourage police witnesses in the pending criminal matter against the man and his wife. The judge stated that he was not satisfied that an attempt to intimidate witnesses had been proven, but neither did he accept the defendant's argument that he was merely attempting to expose police corruption. The man pleaded guilty to 13 counts, and was fined $9100. The unique aspects of the case led to media publicity in the local and national press.[2]

The case demonstrates the clear imperative to distinguish between vexatious and mistaken complaints. Mistaken complaints are to some degree inevitable, based as they principally are on misperceptions of a situation. Vexatious complaints are not so much based on *appearances* as they are on particular *constructions* of events in an attempt to discredit a police officer.

D *Investigation or Other Processes in Relation to an Associate*

Investigating a fellow police officer with whom one has an association is specifically prohibited under both the *Police Regulation Act* and the Victoria Police *Code of Conduct*. This prohibition is grounded in sound logic: regardless of the outcome of such an investigation, the police officer involved is prone to allegations of conflict of interest if he or she is perceived to have failed to act appropriately against a fellow police officer, delayed or discontinued action against a fellow police officer, or inappropriately taken action against a party opposed to a fellow police officer.

In such cases, *any* involvement of a police officer is likely to be a cause for complaint (whether or not there is a failure to act, a delay or discontinuance of action, or inappropriate taking of action), since the conflict of interest is immediately apparent merely through the police officer's *involvement* in the matter. An additional type of potential problem that was evident in the earlier discussion is also involved here—supervisory issues in relation to the assignment of cases and other police matters to particular police officers.

Several matters involving police officers investigating associated fellow police officers arose in respect of motor vehicle accidents. In the first, following a complaint relating to the issuing of a Penalty Notice, it emerged

---

[2] The wife of the complainant pleaded guilty to four counts, related to her role in assisting the man to distribute the letters. She was released without conviction and was placed on a two-year good behaviour bond. The last prior known case of criminal defamation in Victoria was the famous prosecution of author Frank Hardy, in relation to the contents of his book *Power Without Glory*.

from the Deputy Ombudsman's review of the investigation that the police officers involved in the accident were from the same Traffic Operations Group that investigated the accident. Whilst there was no suggestion that this compromised the investigation in this particular case, in order to ensure both the fact and the perception of impartiality new procedures were put in place to ensure that such a situation could not happen again (Case 51).

The second motor vehicle matter involved quite a different set of circumstances in relation to the investigation of fellow police officers. A complaint arose following official police action against one of the drivers involved in a car accident. No action was to be taken against the other involved driver, who was an off-duty police officer (Case 317).

A particularly interesting aspect of this case related to the conduct of the internal investigation itself. The senior officer who was directed to investigate the matter questioned his suitability for this investigation. He was reluctant to be involved on the basis that his impartiality in such an investigation may come under question because he was at the time serving as relieving Officer in Charge at the same station as the police officer who was the subject of the complaint. (He also stated that the off-duty member concerned (the driver) was located outside the Police District, and that this may create transport, time, and possible protocol difficulties.) The Command level officer who had directed that the investigation be undertaken by the senior officer took his questioning as a refusal to undertake this assigned duty. The police officer questioned whether he could be required to investigate Internal Investigations Department files, in any circumstances. The Command level officer then informed the senior officer that he would be admonished for failing to comply with a lawful instruction, and issued an admonishment notice.

At the same time, the senior officer received the complaint file with instructions that he "action" the file. These instructions came from a Chief Superintendent from whom he had sought informal advice, in relation to the question of his impartiality in the matter. The senior officer requested that the instruction to action the file be reviewed by another Chief Superintendent, but this request was refused. Ultimately, the senior officer conducted the investigation as required, and the admonishment was withdrawn.

The remaining cases in this group involved criminal matters. In the first, a complainant stated that it had become clear to her during a police interview in relation to a matter over which charges were laid against her, that there was a relationship between the police officer interviewing her and a person who she alleged owed her money. She was being interviewed in relation to allegedly making threatening telephone calls to that person. The other person was actually a police officer, although the woman complainant did not know his occupation—she described the relationship as being a "close personal friend". The police officer concerned had complained to a detective about receiving threatening phone calls from the woman, and this matter had been followed up. The woman was charged over the making of the telephone calls (Case 348).

The initial investigating officer stated that the matter was "amicably conciliated and reconciled", recommending no further action be taken, but in his review the Deputy Ombudsman said there was a conflict of interest however the relationship was described. He was concerned that the detective who interviewed the woman had a friendly relationship with the police officer whom the woman had telephoned. The key problem in his view was that the detective's oversighting officer had permitted him to conduct the investigation when as oversighting officer he had a clear duty to arrange for the allegation to be investigated at another station. Victoria Police management did not back down with regard to the specific case, but the conflict of interest problems were recognised at a general level. The Deputy Ombudsman wrote to the complainant advising that although no disciplinary action was appropriate, the Officer in Charge would be spoken to in relation to the avoidance of conflict of interest situations.

Another matter involved an alleged possible attempt by a police officer to protect fellow officers who were facing criminal charges. Two police officers were facing charges for an alleged conspiracy to pervert the course of justice (the charges were ultimately unsuccessful). A third officer (the subject of this complaint) provided information that evidence against the two police officers in question was false, but he refused to divulge the source of this information, despite being directed to do so. The conflict of interest here was that the police officer was associated with the two police officers facing conspiracy charges. In response, it was proposed to take disciplinary action against the police officer for failing to obey a lawful instruction, but in the end he was counselled in relation to the matter (Case 286).

The specific prohibition on involvement in matters involving associated police officers (under the *Police Regulation Act* and the Victoria Police *Code of Conduct*) seems to be relatively effective, in that only nine cases studied involved such complaints. The prohibition clearly has the effect of obviating several possible manifestations of conflicts of interest, but a number of particular problems remain, particularly in regard to supervision and the official allocation of cases to officers.

E *Other Involvement, Investigation, or Intervention in a Case with a Personal Interest*

In addition to the identifiable categories discussed above, several other cases included miscellaneous complaints of involvement, investigation, or intervention in a matter in which the police officer had a personal interest. These cases provide evidence of a range of additional conflicts of interest that police officers may be confronted with.

One case also involved a claim that a police officer who had received a parking fine (in relation to his private vehicle) sought to avoid paying the fine by claiming to the parking officer who issued the ticket that he was an undercover police officer working on surveillance duties. The parking officer endorsed the ticket accordingly, and advised the police officer to submit a Statutory Declaration to support his claim. No such declaration was forthcoming, and inquiries revealed that the police officer was off duty at the relevant time. Several other claims were associated with this case. The police officer was eventually dismissed on the basis of the group of allegations as a whole, with a focus on claims that he made unauthorised public comments about police operations (Case 318).

A further case also involved a police officer attempting to intervene in a case to prevent the laying of charges against a friend. An off-duty probationary officer was with a group of friends (none of whom was a police officer) at a hotel. The men in the group became intoxicated and were involved in a fracas. Police were called to the scene, where one of the men was arrested. As he was being put into the divisional van, the off-duty police officer approached them, revealing his identity (showing his police identification) and vociferously stating that they had no right to arrest his friend. He also went to the police station and argued the matter with a superior officer (Case 65).

There was a recommendation from an oversighting senior officer that the police officer's employment be terminated, although two senior officers who originally investigated the case did not agree that this was an appropriate outcome. The matter was eventually referred to a Deputy Commissioner who decided that the police officer should be counselled and warned that similar conduct in the future would result in termination of his employment (Case 65).

The Deputy Ombudsman, whilst not asking for termination of the employment of the police officer, was concerned at the leniency of this outcome, but accepted the decision made. The Deputy Commissioner explained his reasoning at length, citing significant issues associated with probationers, including costs of training, discipline, and sanctions. He argued that the officer was a trainee and that he had been placed on special assessment until the end of his probation, a measure which would have a greater impact. An associated issue of free admission to nightclubs, arising from the investigation of the case, was also addressed in response to this case.

In other cases, police involvement in a criminal case involving family or friends may be much more active and may be regarded as an attempt to pervert the course of justice. In one such case, the father of a police officer had been the victim of an assault. The police officer, whilst he was on recreation leave, actively became involved in the matter as it was going to trial. The police officer attended the court hearing while his father gave evidence; at the same time, all other witnesses in the trial were excluded from the courtroom while the evidence of the man was given. Later the same evening, the police officer attended the private residence of another witness (his father's former *de facto* spouse) who was yet to give evidence, and discussed with her the evidence that had been given by his father. This was an apparent attempt to ensure consistency between the witness's account and that of his father (Case 15).

This attempt came to light when the witness contacted the police officer who acted as informant in the case, and he advised the Director of Public Prosecutions what had happened. As a result of the police officer's actions, the trial was aborted and the jury discharged. The home of the police officer's father was searched and a number of official Victoria Police documents relating to the case were found, along with matters that suggested the police officer had worked in collusion with his father to ensure consistency between the father's account of the alleged assault and that of the witness.

The investigating officer within the Internal Investigations Department found that the police officer had taken an active interest in the case from the outset, regularly contacting the police officer in charge of the case to check the progress of the matter. Ultimately, criminal charges were laid against the police officer and his father, but the charges were unsuccessful (the charges against the father were dismissed at committal stage).

Following advice from the Deputy Ombudsman and the Assistant to the Police Discipline Board, a subsequent discipline brief was prepared under section 71(2) of the *Police Regulation Act* alleging a breach of section 69(1). The discipline charges related to the police officer's use of information about a matter not related to his duties, and, in particular, his disclosure of this confidential information to a third party. The police officer had partially justified his actions with the suggestion that other members in similar circumstances would have done the same thing and claiming that his actions were well-motivated and intended to assist police inquiries. But good intentions are neither sufficient to justify intervention in official criminal justice procedures and processes or inappropriate intervention or involvement in non-official matters. Even if a police officer's actions are motivated by good intentions—indeed, even if the police officer feels he or she is doing the *right* thing in the circumstances—involvement at any level in a case in which the police officer has some personal interest is always inappropriate.

Another case in which a police officer was accused of inappropriate involvement in a stalking case also illustrates this. It was alleged that the police officer had 'lost' a document and associated materials that had previously been seized from the complainant when he was charged with stalking offences. The material in question consisted of photos and letters, and it emerged that the police officer had returned them to the alleged stalking victim. The crux of the complainant's allegations was that the police officer's actions demonstrated an inappropriate relationship between the police officer and the alleged victim. However the victim stated that she did not know the police officer prior to the case. She was highly praiseworthy of his efforts in the case, even though the charge of stalking (against the complainant) was ultimately not successful (the brief was not authorised). The allegation in relation to the documents returned to the victim was substantiated and the police officer was counselled in relation to the correct procedures and processes for the handling and recording of property (Case 264).

In a further case, a police officer became involved in a family law dispute between a woman and her ex-partner. The man had custody of their child, but the woman was challenging this custody in the Family Court. A close friend of the police officer was now seeing the woman. Through his friend, the police officer became aware that the mother had concerns about the safety of her daughter when the child was in the car with her ex-partner, alleging that he drove while intoxicated. The police officer checked the police database and discovered prior drink driving convictions and he subsequently reported the man to the Traffic Operations Group for allegedly driving in an intoxicated state. Some time later, the man (who was the complainant in this case) was charged with drink driving offences. The police officer also signed an affidavit in support of the woman's Family Court case for custody (Case 343).

The police officer was admonished for his involvement in the matter. He requested a review of the admonishment, disputing that he had acted in an improper manner. He stated that in an earlier incident (an alleged assault on the woman by her ex-spouse) he had advised the woman to contact the Community Policing Squad, but she had not done so because she feared retribution from the man. The incident complained about in this case occurred three months later. The police officer claimed that, pending the custody hearing, the woman had not wanted to make a formal complaint about the man's alleged drink driving herself, and that he was motivated by concern about the safety of a child. He also expressed concern about the possible impact on his career prospects. However, the subsequent review found that the admonishment notice had been appropriately issued in the first instance and that there was no additional evidence to warrant any change in this situation. The Deputy Ombudsman summarised the implications of this case, suggesting that the case contained a useful example of the 'every day' situations in which even where actions may be claimed to be in good faith, a lack of impartiality can cause problems for members.

III   Use of Police Power to Harass

In 29 cases, a central feature of the allegations made was that a police officer had harassed the complainant (or family members of the complainant) in one form or another.[3] These cases all involved allegations that police officers had misused the power and/or authority of their position as police officers to harass the complainant. This was either expressly alleged by the complainant or implied in the terms of the complaint. In many instances, the form of harassment alleged was related to a specific instance or incident, with wider allegations of a pattern of ongoing harassment or harassment with malicious intent implied but often not detailed or evidenced. Nevertheless, the incidents complained about were often relatively minor, invariably involving variations on allegations of rude, aggressive, or intemperate behaviour, or actions motivated by bias, attempts to intimidate, or discrimination.

---

[3] As is clear in case discussions throughout the book, harassment formed a general element of many allegations. Cases discussed in this section were identified as being centred on allegations of the use of police power to harass. Mere use of the word "harassment" in the context of more specific components by a complainant did not yield a coding of the case as involving alleged harassment. The "harassment" coding was used in cases where there was an allegation or implication of *ongoing* harassment *or* harassment with malicious intent. The "harassment/discrimination" coding was used for three cases where it was not possible to infer any other form of conflict of interest on the basis of either the allegation of the facts as evidenced in the case file.

Table 5.3 summarises the outcomes of the complaint cases explicitly alleging harassment. The table shows that only a relatively small proportion of cases (13.8 per cent) result in substantiated findings and a significant majority of cases (69 per cent) result in findings in favour of the police officer. *Prima facie*, these raw figures suggest that the problem of harassment is not a serious one relative to other categories of behaviour related to conflict of interest.

Table 5.3: Findings in Complaints Relating to the Use of Police Power to Harass

| Category of conflict of interest | Determination | | | | | | Total Occurrences | |
| | Finding against police officer (substantiated) | | In-determinate finding[1] | | Finding in favour of police officer[2] | | | |
	N	%	N	%	N	%	N	%
Engagement in harassment	4	15.4	5	19.2	17	65.4	26	100
Harassment/discrimination	0	0.0	0	0.0	3	100	3	100
TOTAL	**4**	**13.8**	**5**	**17.2**	**20**	**69.0**	**29**	**100**

(1) *Indeterminate finding* = Lesser deficiency, Unable to determine, Conciliated, Not proceeded with (resigned prior)

(2) *Finding in favour of police officer* = Withdrawn, No complaint, Not substantiated, Unfounded, Exonerated

However, harassment may form a legitimate and important part of conflict of interest allegations because the types of interests that may be problematic for conflict of interest may include subjective and ideological biases. Such biases may be reflected in the treatment of persons with whom police officers come into contact in the course of their duties. If such treatment is thought to be unreasonable or unfair, this may be regarded as a manifestation of this specific form of conflict of interest. In relation to the harassment complaints discussed in this section, the specific conflicts of interest allegedly underlying or motivating the harassment were often difficult to glean from the case file contents examined. Although complainants may have alleged ongoing or malicious harassment on the part of the police officer, the alleged reasons for this behaviour were often not explicated and it is even possible that a handful of these cases may have been misclassified as conflict of interest cases. Their inclusion in the study may suggest that the coding system used by Victoria

Police is not without flaws, lending some support to a key argument of this book that the understanding of conflict of interest is 'fuzzy'. The small number of cases out of a total pool of some 377 usable cases represents less than 1 per cent of all cases examined and thus suggests that any miscoding represented by these cases does not compromise the overall picture of conflict of interest obtained in this study. For these reasons, this section details only a few cases.

The forms of harassment alleged in a number of cases were all found to be unsubstantiated (although the standard of evidence ranged from very weak to what might be described as insufficient); some were conciliated. These unsubstantiated cases included:

♦ Matters related to motor vehicles or driving, such as declaring a car unroadworthy, checking licence and registration details, or pulling a driver over for alleged minor infringements (seven cases);

♦ Laying of criminal charges or taking other police action (10 cases);

♦ General allegations of rudeness, undue verbal aggression, or similar behaviour (five cases).

The sensitive context of these matters, in terms of the nature of interactions between police and members of the public (including suspects or alleged offenders) may suggest that the motivation for the complaint is not entirely rooted in the actual behaviours of the police officer, but may also be influenced by the negative experiences or outcomes of the complainant in relation to the matter. One case illustrates this particularly well.

In this matter, a licensee of a tavern alleged harassment by police in general and one police officer in particular. It was alleged that the police officers made frequent visits to his premises and unnecessarily questioned patrons and staff. Public Incident Resolution[4] was attempted but the complainant was not satisfied. Yet the records showed that the premises were the subject of a District licensing file, and the evidence suggested that the police officers had not acted in an inappropriate way. A senior officer at the ESD concluded that the complainant may have been using the complaints system to 'muddy the waters' in relation to impending prosecutions relating to

---

[4] Public Incident Resolution is a formal process whereby police can use a conciliatory process in an attempt to resolve minor public complaints, placing responsibility for resolution of such incidents at a local level (Ethical Standards Department 1998: 5).

licence breaches under the Liquor Control Act. Indeed, there was no conflict of interest suggested by the evidence, and the allegation was more in the nature of an inference that a particular police officer was conducting a vendetta against the complainant. No personal, family, pecuniary, or other interest was identified beyond this general notion (Case 385).

Another case involving a complaint from a hotel licensee alleged harassment from a police officer who had sought to have alcohol supplied at cost for the local rifle club, of which the police officer was a member. It was alleged that the refusal of the licensee to continue what the police officer had claimed was an arrangement with the previous licensee had resulted in harassment from the police officer. It was found that this complaint could not be determined on the available evidence (Case 151).

A further case involved unduly rough handling of a man at a railway station, following a report that the man was behaving suspiciously and that he may have been carrying a weapon. The person who reported the matter had left the scene by the time of the arrival of the three police officers who attended. The police officers tackled the "suspicious" man to the ground. It emerged that the man was an elderly visiting academic dignitary who was merely unfamiliar with his surroundings (Case 383).

The complainant, who was the honorary consul for the man's home country, alleged excessive use of force (although the man did not seem to have been injured) and claimed that the man was offered no explanation given at the time as to what was going on. Following the complaint, the police officers concerned offered an apology to the man and attempted to conciliate the matter. However, the injured party and the honorary consul did not accept this as a satisfactory outcome, requesting both a formal apology and the payment of compensation. In response, Victoria Police management offered a written apology and a nominal sum ($25) to cover a medical consultation.[5] No action was taken against the police officers concerned, as it was concluded that their actions were reasonable in the circumstances, given the situation and the information they had received.

---

[5] This offer was described by the honorary consul as "quite offensive" and he threatened legal action for pain, suffering and shock. The file did not contain anything to suggest that any further claim was actually made.

The third matter involved a luncheon conversation between a senior officer and another person. The complainant alleged that she overheard the two people discussing the complainant and her partner in a derogatory manner. The other party to the conversation was a person with whom the complainant and her partner undertook business within the security industry. The complaint alleged that the overheard conversation contained an inference of bias and thus indicated a likely tendency on the part of police to favour other companies (that is, other than their own) in tendering and associated processes that the complainant and her partner may participate in. The complaint, in so far as it alleged bias, was found to be not substantiated (Case 392).

One further complaint of harassment was substantiated *as* harassment. In this case, an officer who had formerly been a local government councillor was found to have harassed a driver who was a foe of the police officer from his ex-council days. The harassment amounted to a deliberate targeting of the driver for roadside checks and similar actions. The initial complaint was found to be substantiated, and the police officer was admonished for acting in a manner prejudicial to the discipline of the Force. The police officer was further counselled for harassment in that he persisted to intercept the motorist, subsequent to the complaint against him being lodged, instead of using an independent member of the Force to conduct any relevant matters (Case 54).

IV Exercise of Improper Influence in Civil Matters

This section discusses a range of cases where a police officer, whilst not taking formal police action, was alleged to have exercised his or her authority, or used his or her position or status as a police officer to exercise improper influence in a civil matter.

In his response to a particular case (discussed below) the Deputy Ombudsman summarised the key issues involved in attempts by a police officer to influence outcomes in relation to civil matters:

> Even a gratuitous reference by a party to a civil dispute that that party is also a member of the police force can give rise to an inference that reference has been made for some purpose connected with the dispute— for example, to add authority to the position adopted in the dispute or statements made during the dispute by a party who is a police member, or to create a certain impression in the arena of the dispute. If in referring to one's occupation as a police member during a civil dispute one were seeking to attain such an end, I think you will agree that one would be improperly exploiting one's membership of the Force for

private purposes ... (Correspondence from Deputy Ombudsman to Internal Investigations Department, Case 64, repeated in Case 10).

The outcomes of the complaint cases examined are summarised in Table 5.4.

Table 5.4: Findings in Complaints Relating to the Exercise of Improper Influence in Civil Matters

Category of conflict of interest	Determination						Total Occurrences	
	Finding against police officer (sub-stantiated)		Indeterminate finding[1]		Finding in favour of police officer[2]			
	N	%	N	%	N	%	N	%
Misuse of authority or position as a police officer in a civil matter, with a personal interest	18	42.9	11	26.2	13	31.0	42	100
Other improper influence in a civil matter, with no personal interest	5	19.2	7	26.9	14	53.8	26	100
TOTAL	23	33.8	18	26.5	27	39.7	68	100

(1) *Indeterminate finding* = Lesser deficiency, Unable to determine, Conciliated, Not proceeded with (resigned prior)

(2) *Finding in favour of police officer* = Withdrawn, No complaint, Not substantiated, Unfounded, Exonerated

The table shows that the key problem area involves cases where it is alleged that a police officer has misused his or her authority or position as a police officer in civil matters in which the police officer has a personal interest (42 cases, with substantiated outcomes in 18 cases—42.9 per cent). The remainder of this section discusses both matters where it was alleged that the police officer had a personal interest, and those where the alleged interests related to family, friends or associates of the police officer.[6]

---

[6] In twenty-six further cases the conflict of interest, as an alleged connection between a police officer and another party to a civil dispute or other civil matter, was not made clear by the complainant (at least, according to the material in the case files). In these cases, there was no

A   *Misuse of Authority or Position/Status in Civil Matters in which a Police Officer has a Personal Interest*

Two areas stand out in the allegations in this area: seeking an advantage in relation to civil matters involving motor vehicles, and seeking some form of advantage in a business transaction or other business matter.

1   *Motor Vehicles*

In several cases it was alleged that a police officer had used his or her authority for personal benefit in the context of matters related to the purchase of, repairs to, or payment for damages to, a motor vehicle.

In one of these cases, a police officer had purchased a motor vehicle by private sale. He was unhappy with the quality of his purchase and in action to obtain the history of the vehicle he contacted the auction group which previously owned the vehicle and had them fax to him, at the police station, details of their transaction with the original owner. He thereby discovered that the previous owner had bought the vehicle as a 'wreck'. The police officer had not been informed of this when he purchased the vehicle and he decided to pursue a refund from the person from whom he bought the vehicle. The original owner lodged a complaint alleging that a number of anonymous calls regarding the vehicle had been made to his private home, and that on one occasion he had found the police officer, the police officer's wife, and a friend of the police officer "snooping" around the rear of his house. It was alleged that the police officer had threatened to have the man charged with an offence in relation to the sale of the vehicle (Case 121).

The original investigating officer found that the allegation of harassment was unfounded and that the complainant had induced the police officer to buy the car by way of a false representation that the vehicle had not been previously involved in a major accident. However an oversighting senior officer did not agree with this conclusion, arguing that having made threats to have the complainant investigated, the police officer had acted in an intimidating manner

---

apparent, alleged, or implied personal, family or acquaintance benefit. These cases merely alleged unwarranted and illegitimate police involvements in civil matters therefore they do not clearly exemplify a conflict of interest and are excluded from this chapter for reasons of brevity.

and had misused his authority. Further, he had misused his position by having the auction group fax him details of their transaction with the previous owner. As a result, the police officer was counselled on these matters. A counselling was regarded as appropriate, given the police officer's relative lack of experience.

In another case, a police officer had car repair work undertaken, but he believed that he had been charged a new-part price for what he believed to be second-hand part. The police officer attended the premises of the part supplier and pretended that he was conducting an official investigation, including producing his police identification. He thus used his authority to obtain details of the original invoice between the supplier and the car repairer, even though this was an entirely private matter. The police officer admitted the claims and apologised for his actions, but he was nevertheless admonished for his actions (Case 64).

In a subsequent matter, a police officer was involved in a dispute over a minor motor vehicle accident. At the scene, the police officer stated that she was a police officer. She attempted to settle as a civil matter, but a settlement could not be reached, and the other driver was subsequently charged with reversing when unsafe. This followed an official report of the matter by the police officer (on the advice of her insurance company). The investigation found that the charges against the other driver were appropriate and the complaint was found to be not substantiated, although the police officer was counselled (Case 10).

In his review of this case, the Deputy Ombudsman repeated concerns he had earlier expressed in relation to an earlier case (Case 64, discussed above).[7] He was concerned that at the scene of the accident the police officer had made gratuitous reference to her occupation as a police officer, arguing that a reasonable interpretation of such a comment would be that it was designed to use a police position in order to exercise influence in relation to a private civil matter.

Another case involved a police officer who, having been beaten to a car parking spot, approached the other driver and became involved in an argument with her. During the argument, the police officer (who was off duty) produced

---

[7] The Deputy Ombudsman referred to Case 64, discussed above, and Case 66, discussed in the next subsection, in his comments on Case 10. His advice from Case 64 was repeated in full.

his police identification. The other driver took this, along with allegedly abusive language, as a threat and intimidation, and lodged a complaint (Case 185).

In response to the complaint, the police officer argued that his use of his identification was an attempt to provide evidence of his status as a police officer in order to demonstrate that he was *not* a threat to the woman. It seemed that this argument from the police officer was initially accepted by investigators who found that whilst his actions may not have been "good manners" they ought not be regarded as improper. However, the oversighting officer disagreed with this conclusion and argued that the police officer should be counselled. Indeed, while the incident itself was regarded as trivial, the police officer's actions were not necessarily regarded in the same way and the oversighting officer was very concerned that an experienced officer (seven years experience) would act in that way. Consequently, it was found that the police officer should not have become involved in the argument in the first place and that, having done so, he should not have identified himself in the way he did. The police officer was counselled about the need to keep a lower profile while off duty.

This case shows that police management are sometimes prepared to deal with even seemingly trivial breaches. The case also demonstrates an understanding of two important implications of even trivial conflict of interest breaches. First, seemingly trivial matters can have a significant impact on public perceptions of policing. Secondly, a police officer's actions in a trivial matter can be indicative either of that police officer's tendency to act in certain ways, or the police officer's lack of understanding of the issues relating to conflict of interest.

2   *Business Transactions or Other Business Dealings*

The conduct of business dealings, including transactions with commercial organisations, produced several cases in which it was alleged that a police officer had misused his or her position or authority to further private interests. The various matters encompassed in these complaints related to: collection of debts, payment for materials, disputes over payment, acceptance of cheques, and matters related to commercial tenancy. Illustrative examples are discussed below.

A police officer was owed a civil debt by a former business partner, and it was alleged that he had used a police facsimile machine to send a letter of demand to the other person. The complaint expressed a concern that the police officer was attempting to use his position to influence the outcome of the dispute. It was also alleged that the police officer had attempted to influence business associates of the complainant, advising them not to do business with him, however in regard to this allegation the complainant refused to provide any particulars of the persons who had allegedly been approached by the police officer. The complainant was advised that the allegations in his complaint had been found to be unfounded, and that his non-cooperation had not assisted in the matter. In relation to the sending of the letter on the police facsimile machine, whilst it was concluded that the machine had indeed been used, there was no specific evidence that it had been the particular police officer who used the machine (Case 381).

In another business transaction, a police officer paid a contractor to have fill removed from his property. The contractor stated that such material was mostly dumped, but on occasion he was able to sell it; if he was able to sell this material, he would let the police officer know. The police officer subsequently heard a rumour to the effect that the contractor did get money for the police officer's removed fill, but had not advised the police officer of this and had not provided him with the proceeds. The police officer confronted the contractor and asked him to accompany him to the premises of the recipient of the fill material. Both denied that there had been any payment for the fill, but the police officer did not accept this denial. He swore, produced his police identification, and threatened both men with police action. Following the lodgement of a complaint by the contractor, the investigation found that the two men had been telling the truth, and that no money had changed hands in the transaction. The complaint was conciliated when the contractor accepted an apology from the police officer (Case 33).

Other cases involved allegations that police officers had attempted to use their positions to influence creditors to accept cheques. In one case, the police officer had a gambling problem and had been bouncing cheques in various places and he subsequently faced 16 charges at a Discipline Hearing. Evidence presented at the hearing included bank records and copies of the cheques that had not been honoured. The police officer cooperated with the internal investigation, admitting three charges. A further three charges were regarded as proven, eight were dismissed as duplicate charges, and two further charges were dismissed. The proven charges all related to acting in a manner unbecoming a member of the Police Force and acting in a manner likely to bring discredit to the Force (Case 123).

In making submission as to sanction, and requesting that no monetary penalty be imposed, the police officer (represented by a trained prosecutor) argued that all the money in question had subsequently been paid in full, that his past work performance was good, that he had regained control of his problem and was prepared to attend Gamblers Anonymous. In addition, he argued that he had accepted advice to transfer to a large station in order to receive better supervision, despite the possible loss of earnings this would entail. In response, the police officer was put on a one year Good Behaviour Bond however he resigned before the one-year period was up.

Another complaint involving a real estate transaction illustrates the manner in which both the complaints system itself and the fact that a person is a police officer can be used against an individual officer. The police officer had sold his house to the complainants and allowed them to move into the house prior to final settlement, whilst awaiting sale of their house. They did not pay rent during this time and did not pay the police officer the full balance of the sale price. The police officer subsequently took action against them and they ignored a legal instruction to quit the residence. They complained to the Internal Investigations Department, alleging that the police officer had returned to the house after the sale and had changed the locks and threatened them. In general the complainants argued that he attempted to use his police position to advantage in relation to a dispute between them, going to great lengths to argue this position (Case 221).

Despite the seriousness of these allegations, they were found to be entirely vexatious and fabricated in an attempt to divert attention from their own attempt to gain an advantage over the police officer. This case illustrates quite starkly how complaints against police cannot be taken at face value. The issues involved can sometimes go beyond mere misperceptions on the part of members of the public.

3   Other Matters

Other complaints related to neighbourhood-based civil disputes or a police officer's alleged use of position to gain information that would otherwise not be obtainable.

In three of the matters relating to noise-related disputes, the police officers concerned were cleared of any wrongdoing, but the bitterness ingrained in the dispute and the nature of the neighbour's ongoing complaints about the police officer, or manner of dealing with the police officer, caused distress for the officer. The police officers concerned suffered a form of harassment from their neighbours, essentially *because* they were police officers. In one of these cases, the police officer had expressed his concern as to the difficulties he had in balancing his police position with that of his status as a normal member of the community in dealing with such situations (Case 245). In the other case, in which two separate complaints were lodged (Cases 182 and 307) the police officers involved eventually moved from their place of residence in order to obviate ongoing difficulties with their neighbour. Here again it seemed that the complainant had used the complaints system in order to 'get at' the police officers in an inappropriate and malicious manner (Case 307).

Another case involved an allegation that a police officer had used his position to obtain information that would otherwise not be available to him, in relation to the medical condition of his mother who was in hospital. The police officer telephoned the hospital seeking to speak to her doctor but when he was advised that the doctor was not at the hospital, the police officer requested the doctor's home telephone number. He later telephoned the doctor at his private residence, late on a Sunday evening and proceeded to ask him about his mother's condition and her treatment. When asked by the doctor, the police officer stated that the hospital had given him the telephone number. The doctor subsequently lodged a complaint alleging that the police officer had used his official position to intimidate the telephonist at the hospital. This was denied by the police officer and the telephonist later admitted that she may have herself jumped to the conclusion that it was official business because he had introduced himself as a police officer. Thus there was insufficient evidence to sustain the complaint, but it was conciliated. The police officer contacted the doctor and apologised for any misunderstanding (Case 25).

B   *Misuse of Authority or Position/Status in Civil Matters for the Benefit of Family, Friends, or Associates*

As in the previous section, areas prominent in this section include cases involving motor vehicles and business transactions or other business matters. In addition, two other key areas involving alleged attempts to gain private advantage were evident from the case files: involvement in disputes over ownership and possession of property, and involvement in disputes of a domestic nature.

Whereas in the previous subsection, the nature of a police officer's alleged interest in a civil matter was reasonably clearly explicable, in the cases discussed in this subsection, relating to the interests of family, friends, or associates of a police officer, the nature of the alleged interests is not so clear. The discussion is organised according to whether a relationship was demonstrated or *specifically* alleged by the complainant, or whether a relationship was merely implied in general terms either in the complaint itself or by the nature of the complaint (for example, alleging bias or favouritism).[8]

1   Motor Vehicles

Several of the cases discussed in the earlier section on official action against an opposing party involved a police officer taking action in relation to motor vehicle incidents in which a family member, friend, or associate was involved. In such circumstances, allegations may also include a claim that a police officer has attempted to influence the outcome of a civil dispute pursuant to the collision—relating to the making of payment for damages caused. An attempt to influence a civil outcome in such cases may thus flow from the police officer's attempted use of *otherwise* legitimate official police action, as considered in the earlier discussion, or a *threat* to take such action, which is considered in this subsection.

(a)   Demonstrated Relationships Between a Police Officer and an Involved Party

The nature of the conflicts of interest in such cases was exemplified in a case that arose in 1989. As a result of a collision, damage was caused to the motor vehicle of a police officer's mother. The police officer identified himself as a police officer to the other driver and stated that if he failed to pay for the damage caused, he could be charged in relation to the incident. The police officer denied the allegations, and as there was no corroborative evidence, the matter was unable to be determined (Case 66).

---

[8] It is not possible to decide whether these cases were appropriately coded by Victoria Police and the Deputy Ombudsman's office as 'conflict of interest'. Certainly, they all involve a claim that a police officer was in some way biased towards one party to a civil dispute, but the precise nature of any alleged or possible relationship is not always clear from the files. The cases nevertheless provide useful examples of situations in which aggrieved members of the public may allege wrongdoing on the part of police officers.

Despite the indeterminate outcome, this case produced changes in the relevant Police Standing Orders following action on the part of the Deputy Ombudsman. He sent the Internal Investigations Department a strongly worded letter outlining a number of problems in this case, and identified six other similar cases where similar problems or "misuse of position" were evident (including Cases 10 and 64, considered earlier in this chapter). As a result, the Internal Investigations Department conducted a study into the problem and found eight other similar cases in the previous 12 months. Subsequent changes to the Standing Orders sought to codify the disciplinary offence involved in such circumstances, including the following:

Improper influence

6.14.   (1)   A member shall not -

    (a) use the fact that he or she is a member for the purpose of improperly obtaining any personal advantage;

    (b) place himself under a pecuniary obligation to a person so that there are reasonable grounds for believing that the person may be able to influence the member in the manner in which the member is to carry out his duties;

    (c) without approval give in his capacity as a member any testimonial of character; or

    (d) use the fact that he is a member for the purpose of improperly influencing voting in an election.

(Victoria Police Standing Orders)

An additional Inspector was allocated to the Internal Investigations Department to act as a full-time training officer on ethics, complaint reduction, and complaint investigation, and to promote active communication to members that this type of activity is unethical.

Other cases examined for this research involved allegations that a police officer had used an official position in an attempt to coerce another party to pay damages to a family member or friend of the police officer. For example, in one case, following damage to the motor vehicle of a police officer's girlfriend, a civil dispute over the question of liability arose. The police officer accompanied his girlfriend in attending the private residence of the other driver. The other driver was not at home at the time and it was alleged that the police officer left a message with children at the house stating that he was a police officer and that their mother risked losing her licence if she failed to pay damages. The complainant alleged that her children had been intimidated (Case 63).

Initially, the Internal Investigations Department could not identify the police officer involved, and the matter was not pursued. However, on oversight the Deputy Ombudsman would not accept this outcome. He served a subpoena on the girlfriend of the police officer (the driver seeking damages) requiring that she reveal the police officer's name. The police officer was thus identified, and he was subsequently counselled on two matters: for revealing that he was a police officer in the context of a civil dispute; and for not identifying himself to the Internal Investigations Department when he knew they wished to speak to him.

Quite different circumstances were involved in another case that arose when a friend of a police officer was involved in a motor vehicle accident. The police officer in question attended the scene and issued his friend with a Penalty Notice. Whilst this act in itself would tend to suggest that the police officer's attitude was one of detached independence, when there was a subsequent dispute between the two drivers over the matter of liability, the police officer became involved. The other driver sent the police officer's friend a number of letters of demand. In response, and at the request of his friend, the police officer (a senior officer at his station) wrote to the other driver to the effect that he should cease 'harassing' the woman driver or he could be charged with offences under the Post and Telecommunications Act. The driver then lodged a complaint against the police officer for allegedly attempting to influence the outcome of a civil matter. The complaint included an allegation that, whilst he had acted appropriately in issuing her with a Penalty Notice, the police officer had been "all too friendly" with the woman driver at the scene of the incident, and that this demonstrated a close relationship that led to the sending of the letter (Case 118).

The investigating officer found that the police officer had known the woman, but he was said to know almost everyone in the country town location. The police officer had argued that he saw no reason to be artificially officious in issuing a Penalty Notice to someone known. The sending of the letter was deemed to be inappropriate, but the matter was ultimately conciliated.

(b) *Alleged, Assumed, or Implied Relationships Between a Police Officer and a Party to the Civil Matter*

The cases discussed in this subsection involved an alleged, assumed, or implied relationship between a police officer and one of the parties involved in the civil matter.

The first case involved an assumed relationship between two police officers and one driver in a motor vehicle incident. The police officers involved in this case visited the other driver to obtain details in order to assist the insurance claim of the first driver (whose vehicle had been reversed into). The complainant assumed that the police officers were illegitimately assisting the other driver in relation to a civil claim. Inquiries confirmed that neither police officer had any knowledge of either driver prior to the incident, and thus had no interest in assisting either way. The complaint was found to be not substantiated as the provision of the information for insurance purposes was in accordance with the law and the police officers' actions were accepted as legitimate—it is an offence to refuse to provide details in the case of motor vehicle accidents (Case 131).

Another case related to a police officer's involvement in a civil dispute relating to payment for auto repairs—here, the police officer was alleged to have intervened on the side of the repairer by telephoning the complainant with regard to payment of a debt owed to the repairer. The complainant alleged that the police officer was misusing his position to assist the auto repairer in relation to a private matter, but the police officer stated that he had only telephoned the complainant in order to ascertain if a criminal offence of deception had been committed. The Deputy Ombudsman was concerned to ascertain whether there was any association between the police officer and the auto repairer. His office contacted the repairer and found that he had simply contacted his local police and reported the matter. Thus, it was concluded that the police officer had legitimately followed up on a matter reported by a member of the public, and the complainant had only *assumed* a conflict of interest existed (Case 209).

In another case the police officers who attended a broken window incident arranged a civil resolution of the matter. Subsequently, the complainant alleged that he had been badly assaulted, yet no official action had been taken against the alleged assailant. He alleged that the police took no action because the other party was a friend of one of the police officers. Upon investigation of the complaint, the evidence showed that the youths involved in the incident were not known to the police. These aspects of the allegation were found to be unsubstantiated or unfounded. However, the complainant also alleged that the police had no right to become involved in the civil matter relating to settlement for the window repair costs. This aspect of the complaint was found to be substantiated and a Performance Improvement Notice was issued to the police (effectively, a counselling) (Case 386).

In this matter, even though the police officers concerned were simply trying to act as facilitators, and there was no evidence that they acted with improper motives, it was concluded that it was possible to perceive a conflict of interest flowing from inappropriate and active involvement in seeking to resolve a civil matter.

2   *Business Transactions or Other Business Dealings*

These cases involve civil disputes in relation to private business activity where a police officer is alleged to have used his or her police position or authority to further the private business interests of family, friends, or associates in relation to such disputes.

(a)   *Demonstrated Relationships Between a Police Officer and an Involved Party*

Three of the seemingly most overt uses of police position to advance a private business interest involved a police officer attempting to exert influence over a person to pay money that was allegedly owed to a businessperson-friend of the police officer.

One of these cases received particular attention within the ESD up to the Assistant Commissioner level. The case involved a police officer who had a friend who was a washing machine repairer. The police officer had travelled in a marked police car to the house of a customer who the repairer claimed owed him money (the actual amount due was in dispute), and left an official card at the house. The man responded by telephoning the police officer at his station, whereupon he was told to pay the amount claimed, or it would become a police matter (Case 256).

The police officer himself lived near the repairer and interacted socially with him, but he was stationed some distance away. This fact was important in relation to any possible defence for the police officer because although the repairer had sought the police officer's assistance, even if it had been a police matter it could not have been regarded as part of the remit of the particular police officer. The investigating senior officer stated that whilst there could have been some plausibility in making the inquiry at the request of the repairer, the police officer should have instructed the repairer to go to the *local* police. A counselling was recommended, but on review a senior District officer wanted to increase the penalty because the police officer had intentionally used his official position and implied possible criminal action against the complainant in order to assist a friend to recover a civil debt. He suggested that the circumstances were serious enough to consider laying formal charges against the police officer in relation to the 'Limits of Duty' instructions in the Operating Procedures Manual (provision 1.3.1) which stated that police members must be careful not to become involved in matters of a civil nature. It was recommended that the file be referred to the Discipline Advisory Unit (DAU) for advice, but a Command level officer with carriage of the case indicated that he would issue an admonishment and not seek further advice from the DAU.

The Deputy Ombudsman was prepared to accept this outcome, as was an ESD Superintendent, but the Assistant Commissioner for the ESD was not satisfied. He stated that greater accountability was required and he did not approve the admonishment notice, requiring instead that a Discipline Brief be prepared. The police officer was subsequently charged with conduct likely to bring the Force into disrepute and improper conduct, was found guilty, and was fined $200.

Despite the apparent clarity of the situation to others, the police officer concerned could not see the inherent conflict of interest that was involved in the matter (or at least, would not admit to this). This case is a good example of how an undeveloped or inadequate understanding of conflict of interest can lead a police officer to abuse his or her position. It also underlines the importance of a rigorous process of monitoring and oversight of investigations within police organisations.

In another case, it was initially accepted that the police officer concerned had a genuine understanding that he was acting within his official duties. However, the initial investigator and a reviewing officer regarded this as a mitigation of the conflict of interest issues involved: it was proposed that no action be taken against the police officer, ostensibly because *he believed he had done nothing wrong*. Thus, the lack of understanding of conflict of interest extended to those charged with investigating and reviewing his actions.

The details of the case were that the police officer telephoned a motor vehicle repairer, on behalf of his brother-in-law, demanding the return of a vehicle that the repairer was holding while awaiting settlement of a disputed account that the repairer had presented to the brother-in-law for 'storage' of the vehicle. There were conflicting accounts as to the details of the interaction between the police officer and the repairer, and the internal investigation concluded that it could not be said that the police officer had done anything wrong and that he had genuinely believed that he was correctly discharging his duty (Case 71).

Another Inspector reviewed this initial finding, and agreed with the conclusion. However, the Deputy Ombudsman was not satisfied with this outcome, because:

- the police officer was not on duty at the time he made the call;

- the matter was not properly investigated (the word of the police officer's brother-in-law was accepted); and,

- even if the police officer genuinely believed that it was possible that the repairer may have committed an offence, he should have referred his brother-in-law to his local police station (where he would most likely have been advised that the matter was a civil one).

The Deputy Ombudsman's concerns centred on the conflict of interest in the case and he reiterated concerns about police officers investigating cases where friends are involved. Although this advice in relation to the conflicts of interest in the case was clear, the Internal Investigations Department did not accept the Deputy Ombudsman's advice. A Chief Superintendent wrote that the Deputy Ombudsman should be informed that no action would be taken against the police officer, but that he would be advised not to involve himself in situations where allegations may be made that he was not impartial. This outcome seems inexplicable, given the outcomes and understandings demonstrated in other cases. Here, the problems were threefold:

1. the conflict of interest that was central to this case was downplayed;

2. the involvement of the police officer in the matter in which he had an indirect but explicit personal interest was accepted as legitimate; and

3. the essentially civil nature of the dispute was not made an issue.

These problems all point to an inadequate understanding of the problem of conflict of interest and its implications.

In another case, a police officer assisted in a landlord–tenant dispute, by undertaking a check using the Victoria Police computer-based database known as the Law Enforcement Assistance Program (LEAP), to obtain details on a problem tenant of his father. He discovered that there were two outstanding police warrants on the tenant, and telephoned him threatening to activate these warrants if he failed to pay rent that was owing.[9] As a result of the investigation of the alleged threat against the tenant, the complaint could not be corroborated, and it was originally proposed that it be concluded that the police officer had not acted in an improper manner. However, on review the Deputy Ombudsman suggested that this action was not satisfactory, arguing that the police officer had acted improperly in checking on the complainant through the LEAP system. In response to these representations, the police officer was counselled for accessing the LEAP database in relation to a civil matter (Case 176).

These cases are illustrative of the range of *business-related* circumstances in which police officers may become embroiled. Without a solid understanding of the issue of conflict of interest and the need for a clear separation between the private interests and public duties of a police officer, there is a heightened potential both for the misuse of authority in influencing civil matters and the generation of public perceptions that authority has been misused in this way.

(b) *Alleged, Assumed, or Implied Relationships Between a Police Officer and a Party to a Civil Matter*

If a police officer is seen to have used his or her authority in relation to the settlement of a civil dispute, it is not at all unlikely that an aggrieved party to the dispute will suspect (and allege) that the police officer 'must have had' a personal interest in the matter. This research found a small number of cases in this category; one is discussed here.

In this case two evictees alleged that two police officers must have had a personal interest in relation to an eviction in which the officers assisted the owner. The police officers had attended a commercial premises and informed the occupiers (who had been evicted) that they would have to leave. But the matter was entirely a civil situation, as there were no court orders in relation to

---

[9] One question that arose during the investigation related to the police officer's failure to act on the warrants (in line with his duty), given that he had information on the whereabouts of the person named therein.

the eviction and it thus relied on the cooperation of the occupiers. In addition, while police were in attendance, a melee broke out, and one of the police officers struck one of the occupiers with his torch. As a result of the internal investigation of the complaint, two police officers were counselled on the need to maintain independence in civil incidents. Nevertheless, the complainant and a number of other people were subsequently charged with criminal offences (Case 40).

There was no direct allegation that the police officer had a personal interest in the matter, but the perception that they had taken one side in relation to a civil dispute led the complainant to imply that the police officer had a personal interest in the matter.

3   Disputes Over Ownership and Possession of Property

Civil disputes over the ownership and possession of property provide another avenue where police officers may find themselves embroiled in allegations that they have used their authority to pursue personal interests, or to favour one side to such disputes. Many of the cases in this group involve police officers being seen to have assisted a person recover property from a former place of residence or other location.

(a)   Demonstrated Relationships Between a Police Officer and an Involved Party

Two cases involved a police officer assisting a friend to recover property. In the case discussed here, the recovery of the property was legitimate, but the police officer's involvement in the matter was not.

This case involved a police officer who assisted a friend to recover possessions from a prior place of residence. The police officer's friend had a court order to retrieve his possessions, but when the Sheriff had previously visited the flat to assist the recovery, it was claimed by the then-occupant that the other previous occupant had moved out and had taken all of the possessions in question with him. Subsequently, the police officer and his friend attended the flat where, it was alleged, he had used his police identification and an official demeanour, to gain access to the premises. The police officer denied having used his police identification, and the matter came down to the word of the police officer against that of the complainant. However, the complainant indicated that he was prepared to have the matter resolved by conciliation, and this was done, although the police officer was also counselled regarding the need for discretion in such matters (Case 24).

The Deputy Ombudsman was not satisfied with this outcome, being particularly concerned that a counselling may not have reflected the seriousness of the matter. He argued that counselling is a "training matter" and that this offence was clearly a disciplinary offence. He also asked for a clarification of the difference between an admonishment and disciplinary measures, and asked why an "administrative admonishment" was not given. The Assistant Commissioner at the Internal Investigations Department responded to the Deputy Ombudsman's concerns, advising that currently there was no such sanction as an "administrative admonishment" but that he proposed asking a Chief Superintendent to "personally admonish" the police officer. The Deputy Ombudsman agreed with the proposal.

(b)   *Alleged, Assumed, or Implied Relationships Between a Police Officer and a Party to a Civil Matter*

In these cases, though there was not a demonstrated personal interest in the matter on the part of the police officer, his or her involvement led an aggrieved party to assume that such an interest must exist. For example, police officers accompanied a woman as she attended her former residence, following a relationship break-up, to recover items of property. Their attendance was legitimate on the grounds of keeping the peace. The complainant, however, alleged that his ex *de facto* spouse took items from the home that were not hers, and that the police officers had effectively allowed her to steal these items. He claimed that they forced him to stay in his bedroom while the woman took the items. In response, the police officers claimed that the man had agreed to allow the woman to remove all of the items of property in question. It was agreed that at one stage the man had became argumentative and the police officers asked him to move into another room for a short time (consistent with their duty to prevent a breach of the peace), but he still had full view of what the woman was doing. The complaint was unsubstantiated and the complainant agreed that the matter could not be taken any further. He further agreed that the matter should have been regarded as settled by conciliation. Nevertheless, the police officers were informally counselled in relation to the need to clearly establish that both parties were in agreement when dealing with such cases, or to leave the matter to civil litigation (Case 215).

Another case followed from the lodgement of a complaint of sexual assault against the former *de facto* partner of the complainant. There was a current Intervention Order against the man, and in executing the Order, the police officers who attended the scene required him to leave the premises and accompany them to the police station. As he was being loaded into the divisional van, the woman removed items of property from their (former) joint residence. As a result, it was later alleged that the police officers had in fact assisted the woman to remove possessions that she was not entitled to take. However, evidence suggested that the police officers had no role as alleged, and one of the police officers in fact had advised the woman that she should not take anything from the premises that did not belong to her. It was found that the police had acted appropriately, and the complaint was unsubstantiated (Case 127).

Even though police attendance in relation to such matters may be justified on the basis of preventing a breach of the peace, if a police officer does anything other than merely be in attendance, complaints alleging personal motivations in such actions may arise.

4   Domestic Disputes

Several matters involved allegations that a police officer had improperly used his or her position to assist one party in a domestic dispute. The issues involved in such cases can never be clear-cut because police do have a duty to prevent possible offences and to investigate alleged criminal offences, and thus may legitimately be in attendance in situations where domestic disputes are involved.

(a)   Demonstrated Relationships Between a Police Officer and an Involved Party

Most cases in this area involved an alleged, assumed, or implied relationship between a police officer and a party to the civil matter, rather than a demonstrated relationship, although in three neighbourhood-related cases, and two other cases, the police officer concerned did have a direct interest in the matter.

One illustrative example of neighbourhood-related cases involved a noisy dog. It was alleged that a police officer had attempted to facilitate civil settlement of a dispute between neighbours of the police officer's partner. The police officer stayed at the house occasionally, so the barking affected him as well as his partner. In response to the complaint, he agreed that in a dispute with the neighbour he had stated that he was a police officer, but only to contextualise the problems he had with the dog barking. The complaint was found to be unfounded (Case 4).

Another complaint involving an allegation that a police officer had intervened in a family domestic dispute, threatening to use police powers, was conciliated (Case 1). In a further case it was alleged that a police officer had abused his position to help one side of a family in a dispute over a deceased estate. Whilst the police officer was found to be a friend of one side of the family, all aspects of the complaint were unsubstantiated (Case 179).

(b) *Alleged, Assumed, or Implied Relationships Between a Police Officer and a Party to the Civil Matter*

There were six cases involving an alleged, assumed, or implied relationship between a police officer and a party to a civil matter. Three of these cases involved Intervention Orders, and three involved disputed custody of a child. This discussion uses one example of each of these types of cases.

One complaint arose from a police officer's involvement in the granting of an Intervention Order against the complainant. The complainant had been very aggressive during a domestic dispute with his wife, and police were called. He did not strike the woman, but he was subsequently charged with assaulting the police officer who attended the scene. The police officer was the informant in the subsequent granting of an Intervention Order against the complainant (in relation to the woman, not the police officer). The complainant alleged that this was an improper interference in domestic matters, but police Operating Procedures *required* the police officer to seek an Intervention Order in such circumstances (Case 309).

The second example involved an allegation that a police officer had favoured one party to a custody dispute. The woman had taken her eldest child from the residence of her ex-husband's parents. The man had physical custody of the child but there were no extant court orders in relation to custody. The father was not in attendance at the time, as he was temporarily interstate. The woman had requested police attendance in case there was trouble (Case 8).

Advice received from the Government Solicitor suggested that the police should not have acted in the manner in which they did in attending the premises having only heard the mother's version of the matter. Of itself, this tended to indicate that the mother had been favoured by police. Advice from the Government Solicitor also suggested that the woman had used the police to intimidate the grandparents into surrendering the child, with the mere presence of police possibly overcoming any unwillingness on the part of the child to leave. The Solicitor clearly stated that it is not for the police to decide custody or access in such cases, nor to assert what is in the best interests of the child. Despite this advice the Victoria Police internal investigation exonerated the police officers concerned, presumably on the basis that their actions were not taken maliciously, and they in fact had no personal interest in the case (thus there was no conflict of interest involved).

V   Discussion

Where a conflict of interest is manifested in a use or abuse of police powers and authority, the breach of duty thus entailed impacts on a function at the heart of policing: the disinterested application of the unique power and authority accorded to the police. The number of occurrences (215 in total) in the three categories of conflict of interest discussed in this chapter represents over 40% of all conflicts of interest identified in this research.

The overall substantiation rate across the three categories is approximately 31 per cent—slightly lower than the overall substantiation rate for all conflict of interest complaint cases in the 10-year period (at almost 38 per cent), but a substantiation rate over 30 per cent still suggests that the conflicts of interest discussed in this chapter have a significant impact on a core area of performance of police duties where disinterestedness is vital. The total number of complaints involving this type of allegation also suggests that public perceptions of conflict of interest, or associated misconduct, have implications for the general level of community trust in policing.

A   *Inappropriate Intervention, Involvement, or Action in Police Investigations and Processes*

These cases involve very public aspects of policing inasmuch as they often implicate members of the public in offences, whether of a minor or serious nature. As such, these cases involve scenarios where members of the public come into formal contact with policing. Where an action or outcome is not to the liking of an aggrieved party, it is in such circumstances that complaints are perhaps more likely to arise.

Complaints of conflict of interest can arise from perceptions that may not necessarily be justified by the actual circumstances. Members of the public may see police officers acting in ways that are taken to imply familiarity with a victim or alleged offender, and they may then assume that the actions taken or outcomes are a result of the assumed familiarity. These cases therefore illustrate the challenge for police officers in maintaining professional detachment whilst treating people in a manner which does not alienate them or make tense situations worse.

Illustrating these points is the fact that many of the alleged conflicts of interest related to motor vehicle accidents and related matters. This suggests three factors: the sensitivity with which members of the public view traffic matters; the high visibility of policing in these areas; and the apparently easy opportunity provided by such instances for police officers to act at variance with their duty in a conflict of interest situation. One other strong theme that emerged in the group of cases examined in the subsection on *failure to act due to a relationship with an involved party* involved cases where a police officer sought *civil resolution* of a matter but a complainant felt official police action should have been taken.

It must be stressed that an adequate mode of dealing with the problems of conflict of interest discussed in this chapter must start with a clear conception of the problem. It is clear that this is not always evidenced. For example, the police officers involved in Cases 62 and 246, discussed at the start of the section on *police action against an opposing party*, failed to even recognise the existence of a conflict of interest, before, during, or after the complaint cases concerned. Subsequently, police management and Internal Investigations Department officers (of various ranks) also failed to clearly distinguish between issues associated with a conflict of interest, on the one hand, and an associated breach of duty, on the other. On both counts, these failures suggest a significant lack of understanding of key issues central to matters of conflict of interest.

B   Use of Police Power to Harass

Three areas dominated the conflict of interest complaints that alleged some form of harassment by a police officer:

♦   Matters related to motor vehicles;

♦   Laying of criminal charges or taking other police action; and

♦   General allegations of rudeness or undue verbal aggression.

Overwhelmingly, allegations of harassment resulted in indeterminate findings or findings in favour of the police officer, indicating that such allegations may often be without factual foundation or that they are particularly difficult to substantiate. For many people, motor vehicle or criminal matters represent their only form of contact or interaction with police and when the outcomes of such contacts are negative for the person/s concerned, they may perceive that the police officer's actions have been unreasonable. Of course, this is not to ignore the possibility that there is substance to these sorts of allegations and that the key factor in their non-substantiation relates to the sorts of evidentiary problems referred to earlier, but there was no pattern of evidence in the case files examined to suggest that this was the case.

Individual police officers need to be aware of the possible roots of public dissatisfaction with policing, and take care to ensure that their behaviour cannot be perceived to be a result of a prevailing negative attitude towards specific people (or types of people) they deal with in the course of their official duties. Police management also need to recognise that the difficulty in substantiating such allegations is not necessarily an indication that they are without foundation.

C   Exercise of Improper Influence in Civil Matters

Over 13 per cent of all conflict of interest occurrences in this study alleged some form of improper influence in civil matters, either to advance a police officer's personal interests, or the interests of family, friends, or associates. A common element in many of the cases considered is that it was alleged that a police officer had attempted to influence some other person to do something that they otherwise might not do, and that in so doing had advanced the private interests of some party.

Two particular contextual themes emerge from the discussion: many of the cases involved matters relating to motor vehicles; and attempts to improperly exercise influence in relation to business transactions or other business dealings, advancing either a police officer's interests or those of family, friends, or associates. These contexts provide significant opportunities for police officers to advance their personal interests, or those of family, friends, or associates. A small number of additional cases involved civil matters associated with neighbourhood-type disputes.

Two other important issues emerge from the discussion of these conflicts of interest especially in the cases involving the advancement of interests of *family, friends, or associates* of a police officer. The first issue is the frequency with which police officers, and sometimes, police investigators or police management, do not recognise that a conflict of interest is involved in a particular situation, and fail to clearly distinguish between a conflict of interest and a conflict of interest *breach*. Some cases exhibited a tendency to excuse the former on the basis of a lack of evidence of the latter. In the field of day-to-day police work, recognition of conflicts of interest must be the first step in dealing with the problem. In particular, an important step in avoiding conflict of interest breaches is to develop an awareness of the sort of circumstances in which conflicts of interest are evident (or may be perceived), and to avoid involvement in such situations. The cases show that police managers also need to be aware of these issues in terms of their assignment (or approval) of duty to subordinate officers.

This limited or partial understanding of conflict of interest has been a consistent concern of the Deputy Ombudsman during the period of study, and the oversight of the Deputy Ombudsman has provided an important source prompting closer attention to issues related to conflict of interest.

The second key issue is that in many of the complaint cases, the nature of the conflict of interest involved was more in the form of *allegation, assumption, or implication*, rather than evidencing an *actual* relationship between the police officer and the party allegedly favoured, particularly in allegations that a police officer had improperly attempted to influence the course of domestic disputes. Dealing with this issue requires, once again, a clear understanding of what conflicts of interest involve. Whilst neglects of duty or other forms of 'bad policing' may emerge whether or not there is a conflict of interest, in situations where there is a demonstrated conflict of interest, the motivations and actions of a police officer must be subject to particular scrutiny.

Appropriate disciplinary, training and management actions also differ in these circumstances. Where poor policing is evident in the *absence* of a conflict of interest, the question arises as to what are or are not appropriate forms of police action in particular circumstances, including what is the appropriate application of police discretion. The issues in cases where a conflict of interest is evident encompass, but go beyond, these questions. They relate to the implications of allowing one's personal interests (or those of family, friends, or associates) to influence one's actions. In cases where a conflict of interest is evident, explicit attention to these private interests may obviate some forms of 'bad policing'. Thus, the avoidance of action in situations where a conflict of interest pertains is an important part of good policing, although not a guarantor of it.

In dealing both with improper uses of influence in civil matters, and the management of political optics in cases where such influence might be perceived, the discussion here shows how an awareness of both the existence of conflicts of interest in such cases and the appropriate forms of action in such cases (including no action or involvement), are essential to the integrity of policing.

CHAPTER SIX

The Public Realm:
Use and Abuse of Police Resources

I   Introduction

As with any section of the public sector, care must be taken to ensure that police resources are not misused or misappropriated for private purposes. A conflict of interest is manifested when a police officer seeks to advance a personal interest through the use of any police resources. Whatever the circumstances, where police officers utilise police resources for private ends there is a conflict between their private interests and the public duty to utilise official resources only for official purposes. The private use of police information, police property, or other police resources may also breach specific regulatory and operational provisions, such as the requirement to keep police information confidential.

A number of activities involving the alleged misuse of police resources are outlined in this chapter. These include inappropriate access to, and disclosure of, police information; various uses of a police officer's official identity (as a police officer) for private purposes; and the misuse of resources such as police vehicles and fuel, police time and police personnel. Many of the complaint cases examined involve the misuse of police property in more than one of the ways identified here.

The chapter discusses two categories of problems in relation to the use and abuse of police resources. The area of *misuse of confidential police information* is the largest category, comprising 61 per cent of the conflicts of interest involving use and abuse of police resources. The discussion in this area is broken down into two areas: access to, and use of, police information for private purposes; and disclosure of police information to outside parties. Various forms of *misuse of other police resources* comprised the remaining 39 per cent of the conflicts of interest in this area. Of these, the main identifiable area is the misuse of police identity for private purposes.

II   Misuse of Confidential Information

The impartiality of a police officer can be said to have been compromised if confidential police information is used for the private benefit of the police officer or another person (Royal Canadian Mounted Police External Review Committee 1991: 64–66). In general, the leaking of official information for non-official purposes involves commercial interest prevailing over public ethics, and private interest prevailing over public duty, including the duty to keep particular kinds of information confidential (see Independent Commission Against Corruption 1992a). Research undertaken for the British Home Office by Miller (2003: 7–8) suggested that "the picture of corruption [in England and Wales] is dominated by the leaking of information to those outside the organisation" (p 8); other forms of inappropriate use of police information were also found to be significant in terms of less serious police misconduct.

Table 6.1 summarises the findings in this study for complaints alleging misuse of confidential police information. The table shows that inappropriate disclosure of police information was the category that yielded the greatest number of complaints, with 39 complaints in total, 15 of which were substantiated (38 per cent). Allegations of inappropriate access to police information were involved in 19 complaint cases, 14 of which were substantiated (73.7 per cent). For the 58 complaint cases in the two groups combined, there was an overall substantiation rate of 50 per cent.

A   Police Information Accessed and Used for Private Purposes

1   General Considerations

The need for operational police to have access to official records has long been recognised as an important tool in modern policing and police officers necessarily have access to a range of formal records in the course of their usual duties. These include both paper and computerised records, various police databases, paper files, and other documents. Various verbal sources of information can also be formally or informally obtained by a police officer.

Table 6.1: Complaints of Misuse of Confidential Police Information

Category of conflict of interest	Determination						Total Occurrences	
	Finding against police officer (substantiated)		Indeterminate finding[1]		Finding in favour of police officer[2]			
	N	%	N	%	N	%	N	%
Access to, and personal use of, police information	14	73.7	1	5.3	4	21.0	19	100
Disclosure of police information to outside parties	15	38.5	7	17.9	17	43.6	39	100
TOTAL	29	50.0	8	13.8	21	36.2	58	100

(1) *Indeterminate finding* = Lesser deficiency, Unable to determine, Conciliated, Not proceeded with (resigned prior)

(2) *Finding in favour of police officer* = Withdrawn, No complaint, Not substantiated, Unfounded, Exonerated

The increased focus on intelligence-led policing methods (Miller 2003: 13) and on the use of information technology (Chan *et al.* 2001) enhances both the amount of information available and the opportunities for access to such data. Despite the confidentiality that is attached to police information in computerised databases, it is a simple matter for a police officer to gain data access. Thus, developments in information and communication technologies may have made the perpetration of ethical breaches easier because formerly bureaucratic processes have been replaced by technology accessible to all police officers. However, this same technology also provides the possibility of tracking and monitoring the access that police officers gain to such information.

The Victoria Police computer-based database known as the Law Enforcement Assistance Program (LEAP) provides police officers with online access to data and information relating to crime reports and associated dealings between police and victims, offenders and members of the public. Information contained within the LEAP system is confidential and is intended solely for official police use. Release of the information to others is prohibited. The Victoria Police Administrative Procedures Manual specifies the confidentiality that must be attached to any information that becomes available to members in the course of their police duty (paragraph 7.1.2). In addition, the LEAP system access screen clearly states that information contained in the system is confidential and must not be disclosed to unauthorised persons (discussed in Case 289). These clear provisions in regard to data access and use mean that when a police officer accesses LEAP data for private purposes, whether the motivation is personal curiosity, the pursuit of personal advantage, or disclosing or otherwise providing such information to a third party, this action represents a conflict of interest *breach*.

The Victorian Ombudsman noted in 1993 that the lack of an effective tracking system prior to that time resulted in a limited capacity to identify *which* officer had accessed *what* items of information on the database and *when* this had occurred. This limitation had the effect of frustrating many investigations of this particular type of conflict of interest breach. He noted that measures ensuring better auditing of use of the database had improved matters, and that other measures such as swipe cards and fingerprinting could further enhance the security of the system. He expressed the hope that:

> [T]he adoption of these measures will dissuade members from abusing their access to confidential information by improperly releasing it and will enhance the likelihood that any members engaging in such activity in future will not do so without being detected (The Ombudsman 1993: 12).

Subsequently, quite comprehensive processes were put in place for tracking users of the LEAP data system, including the use of access codes that leave an audit trail so that details of access to the system can later be checked. It was thought that, on the basis of these security and integrity controls, police internal investigators may rely on the LEAP database access log as an important source of evidence in cases where inappropriate access to and use or disclosure of police data was alleged. However, the 2001 Annual Report of the Ombudsman reveals that the problem of inappropriate access to and disclosure of police information continued, some eight years after this expressed optimism. Whilst the audit trail discussed above has been successful in enabling ready identification of system users, and of proof of their access, the debate about the legitimacy or otherwise of their actions now centres around their *justification*. The Ombudsman's Report notes that when interviewed:

> [M]embers have commonly justified their access by reference to some police duty - for example, to avoid forming a possible undesirable personal association; to ascertain from car registration details seen in the vicinity of a person's home if the member or his family were under

possible surveillance or to ascertain whether there were outstanding warrants against a family member. (The Ombudsman 2001: 20)

Further, as noted by the New South Wales Independent Commission Against Corruption (1992a: 13, 108–109), the use of access codes alone does not represent a high level of security, since police officers invariably know, or can guess, the access codes of colleagues. This complicates detection and enforcement measures.

The case files examined for this book appeared to indicate that, towards the end of the study period, merely *accessing* database information was considered to constitute a lesser offence. This situation changed dramatically several years later following a public scandal in which claims surfaced in the media and the Victorian State Parliament that a number of police officers had accessed and leaked the police files of candidates contesting a forthcoming Victorian state election. The scandal resulted in significant pressure being placed on both Victoria Police and the office of the Victorian Ombudsman to confirm or deny the reports. Chief Commissioner Nixon established an internal task force to review the use of the police data system (see Victoria Police 2003; Silvester and Baker 2003). The initial response from Victoria Police was to suggest that "tougher penalties" (including dismissal from the Force) would be introduced for unauthorised and improper use of police information, and that audit and accountability procedures would be tightened up (Victoria Police 2003), however two years later the Office of Police Integrity indicated that many of the problems that had previously been identified in relation to unauthorised or improper police access to information persisted with the LEAP system under the ostensibly tougher access protocols (Director - Police Integrity 2005a: 2).

2   Cases Involving Police Information Access and Use

Three sources of police information that could be accessed and used for private purposes were identified in the complaint case files examined. The first source involved the use of *police databases* to obtain personal details of members of the public, whether for personal interest or curiosity, or for some other more specific purpose. The second source involved a small number of cases involving allegations that police officers had used information gleaned from sources other than a police database, in the course of their police duties. The third source of information identified involved allegations that police officers actively used police channels to obtain information that was not required for police work specifically for private purposes.

(a) *Using Police Databases to Obtain Personal Details*

The use of police databases for the purposes of obtaining personal details of citizens for personal curiosity or for use in relation to private interests is the classic "domestic" use of police information (Miller 2003: 13). Based on the complaint case files examined for this book, seven areas of domestic use of police information were identified. Examples of each area are discussed here to illustrate the relevant issues.

First, a police officer accessed the patrol database to obtain personal details of a person with whom he had private commercial dealings, in an attempt to gain a *personal advantage* in those dealings. In his private capacity, the police officer had been contacted a number of times by a major finance company in relation to his monies owing on a vehicle. The finance company employee lodged a complaint alleging that the police officer had used abusive language and threatened the complainant by indicating he knew his licence details and home address. The police officer admitted obtaining the personal details of the complainant from the database and to using bad language during a telephone conversation with the complainant. He was reprimanded for acting in a manner likely to bring discredit to the reputation of the Force (Case 69).

The second area of domestic use involves a police officer using police information for private business dealings. In this example, it was alleged that a police officer used police information to assist him in the conduct of authorised private business activity. The police officer, whilst on duty (on his way to work), conducted an ostensibly 'random' licence check of a driver. On the basis of the licence details and subsequently obtained LEAP data about the driver, the police officer telephoned the man and asked if he was interested in a work-from-home networking business opportunity, and he also mailed promotional material to the man. As a result of the investigation of the man's complaint, the police officer was admonished and fined and his permission to engage in outside employment was revoked. Both his interactions with the complainant and his use of police information in order to assist his private business interests were regarded as serious ethical breaches (Case 236).

The third area of domestic use of information involves seeking to gain a private advantage for a *friend or family member* by obtaining police information in relation to people with whom that person has private commercial dealings. In one case a police officer undertook a LEAP check to obtain the personal details of a problem tenant who occupied a property owned by the police officer's father. The police officer discovered outstanding warrants in relation to the tenant and he telephoned the man and allegedly threatened to activate the warrants if he failed to pay the outstanding monies to the landlord. Although the specific nature of the alleged threat could not be corroborated, the police officer was counselled in relation to accessing to the LEAP system for private purposes (Case 176).

The fourth area of domestic use of information involves a police officer seeking to gain a *personal advantage* in private, non-commercial matters. In one case in this area it was alleged that a female police officer had used police databases for the purposes of tracking her ex-husband in relation to problems concerning maintenance payments. In this case, it was found that the police officer had indeed obtained the information about the man, but there was no evidence of her having accessed the data from police systems, and the police officer refused to name her source (Case 120).

The fifth area of domestic use of information revolves around attempts to obtain information for use in private family matters, particularly family law disputes. One case illustrates how, even when it is substantiated that a police officer has accessed a database for private purposes, mitigating circumstances may be taken into account by police management. The police officer concerned had undertaken LEAP database checks on his sister's ex-husband and some of his associates. He justified his actions as being concerned to make sure that the woman's welfare was not threatened (she had expressed fears for her safety). Following the database checks, which revealed no cause for concern, he told his sister she had nothing to worry about in relation to the matter. He did not disclose the content of any LEAP data to her. The official finding in the matter was that the complaint was not substantiated, even though the police officer *had* accessed the database for private purposes. The original investigating officer felt that his limited access and non-disclosure of specific information mitigated his actions. The office of the Deputy Ombudsman, however, demurred. Whilst agreeing that the police officer had not supplied the content of confidential information to his sister, the Assistant Ombudsman argued that accessing the information was inappropriate and asked that the case be reconsidered (Case 372).

Victoria Police continued to support the police officer, arguing that if the LEAP information accessed by the police officer had revealed any threat to the woman, "he would have immediately passed it on to the CIB", and that the information was not passed on to any party. The conflict of interest was implicitly recognised, but only informally and lightly dealt with: "Perhaps he could have mentioned these inquiries to a supervisor and sought advice ... This is an isolated incident ...".

This management of the case reveals a failure to clearly separate a conflict of interest from a conflict of interest breach. Even though the police officer did not disclose information to an outside party, his conflict of interest in the matter was clear, and his actions in inappropriately accessing the LEAP database were motivated by that conflict of interest.

The sixth area of domestic use of police information involves officers seeking to use police information in association with intimate personal relationships in attempts to facilitate such relationships. Several such uses were evident in the complaint case files. Two such cases (Case 19 and 113) were included in the section on *personal relationships* in Chapter Four. In another example, a police officer accessed the LEAP database to obtain the telephone number of a former girlfriend. This matter was substantiated and the police officer was cautioned (Case 223).

The final area of domestic use of information involves police officers who access personal details of members of the public on the basis of 'professional curiosity'. In a case illustrating how such curiosity may easily be misinterpreted, the complainant at first thought she was being stalked by a male who regularly caught the same train as she did. In one conversation with the man, he indicated that he knew her private details, including that she had not changed her address with VicRoads (the motor vehicle licensing and registration authority). He did not reveal how he knew this information. Following this incident, the woman's husband attended the train and abused the man. The woman raised her concerns with the police, and during their investigation of the matter it was discovered that the man in question was a police officer. The file was thus forwarded to the ESD for investigation. The complaint of stalking was found to be unfounded. In relation to alleged misuse of police information, the complaint was not substantiated, as it was deemed to be an acceptable access to information on the basis of 'professional curiosity', and there was no disclosure of the information to any third-party (Case 268).

This inexplicable outcome, given the other cases examined in this section, is perhaps partly as a result of two factors. First, during the investigation the woman stated that she and her husband may have overreacted to the conversations with the man; secondly, all parties confirmed that there had had been no other contact. The police officer stated that he had only accessed the information out of concern for the woman's welfare, on the basis of aspects of a conversation with her. On these aspects of the case, it was found that a complaint of improper conduct against the police officer was substantiated because his actions were immature and childish even though there was no malicious intent or nefarious motive. The police officer offered an apology to the complainant, and he was counselled and issued with a Performance Improvement Notice.

These seven areas of domestic use of information span wider than the characterisation of being used for 'personal interest', such as "running checks on friends and neighbours, or cars they were thinking of buying" (Miller 2003: 13).

Access to information in these circumstances is inappropriate because it breaches protocols on access to police information. More seriously, it may be a precursor to a more serious breach of duty in so far as it indicates a police officer's propensity to use his or her position as a police officer to advance personal interests.

(b) *Private Use of Information Gleaned in the Course of Police Duties*

In addition to actively obtaining confidential police information from police databases, police officers may turn information gleaned in the course of their duties to private purposes. Two cases in the complaint files involved allegations that a police officer had attempted to obtain a private benefit from the use of information obtained in the course of the officer's police duties. In each of these cases, the alleged private benefit was related to unapproved private business activities. The first case (Case 310) was discussed in Chapter Five (in the section on *failure to act*), and the discussion is not repeated here. The second case concerned an allegation that a police member had the intention of using information obtained in the course of his duties to assist in the setting up of a private business. The case involved concerns that a police officer intended to privately use information obtained in the course of his duties when he attended a privately run police preparatory education course. The complaint came from the provider of the course, who noted that the member had taken copious notes and was concerned that the member might be planning to set up a competing business. As the matter transpired, the police officer did indeed lodge a request for leave without pay to set up a private business offering police preparatory courses, citing the "poor" existing availability of programs (Case 234).

This matter was taken particularly seriously by Victoria Police management. It was found that the member was planning to develop his own private course for people interested in a police career. His request for leave without pay was denied, as activity he was planning to undertake during the proposed leave would present a conflict of interest, particularly in relation to his use and possible disclosure of information relating to his official duties, or obtained in the course of those duties.

(c) Using Police Channels to Obtain Information for Private Purposes

In some cases information obtained by the police officer and subsequently used for private purposes is not even incidentally required for police work. In these cases, and except for the police officer's pursuit of personal interest (that is, a conflict of interest), the information would not otherwise have been obtained.

For example a police officer in an attempt to facilitate a personal relationship, used his position to obtain personal information from Australia Post about the operator of a telephone sex service. He also used the police database to obtain further personal particulars relating to the woman who operated the service. In attempting to establish a sexual relationship, he also allegedly told the women he could obtain criminal histories on other people for her in return for money or sexual favours. The police officer admitted the substance of the allegations, and ultimately resigned prior to the activation of a recommendation that he be dismissed (Case 11).

B   Disclosure of Police Information to Outside Parties

1   Background

During the period under study, the Deputy Ombudsman expressed his concern over the release of confidential police information to outside parties:

> One of the types of complaint which occurs most frequently and has one of the highest substantiation rates concerns the improper release by police of confidential information to people unauthorised to have access to that information ... (The Ombudsman 1993: 11)

The Deputy Ombudsman reported that during 1991–1993, 78 such complaints were investigated, and 25 of these (32 per cent) were found to be substantiated. In the present study, over a 10-year period some 39 complaints included an allegation that a police officer had disclosed police information to outside parties, and of these 38.5 per cent were found to be substantiated (as summarised in Table 6.1). The disclosures identified by the Deputy Ombudsman included "purposeful, mischievous 'leaks'" of several kinds of information, including names of people charged, criminal histories, police intelligence, police photographs and vehicle registration details (The Ombudsman 1993: 11). Apart from the damaging effects of a breach in confidentiality, such disclosures may also lead to future reluctance on the part of those who supply information to police.

The leaking of police information to criminals and others has been identified as a particular problem in New South Wales. A report from the New South Wales Independent Commission Against Corruption (1994b) expressed concern in relation to the security over particularly sensitive types of police information. The problem was linked to a longstanding illicit trade in government information that had previously been the subject of a major inquiry (Independent Commission Against Corruption 1992a, 1992b, 1992c). This earlier inquiry had found that "Information from a variety of State and Commonwealth government sources ... has been freely and regularly exchanged for many years" (Independent Commission Against Corruption 1992a: 5). Thirty-seven serving New South Wales police officers were found to have been involved in a corrupt trade in government information, including the provision of licence records and criminal histories to outside parties. The immediate recipients of such information were often found to be private inquiry agents, many of whom were former police officers. Private inquiry agents, in particular, were said to have formed a "vast information network" through their contacts with former colleagues (Independent Commission Against Corruption 1992a: 14).

The Independent Commission Against Corruption also found that not all of the police officers who were involved in leaking official information realised that they were doing wrong:

> Some were motivated by a naive belief that private investigators and the police are always working towards the one end. Many were simply responding to misguided notions of mateship (Independent Commission Against Corruption 1992a: 15).

Such notions of friendship and mateship may be equally misguided in situations where a police officer is asked by a friend, relative or acquaintance to make unofficial inquiries on their behalf. Even though disclosures in such circumstances may generally be regarded as low-level leaks, police officers can be caught in a conflict of interest between loyalty to family or friends and their obligation to keep confidential those matters coming to their attention as a member of Victoria Police. Effective management lies in the responses that police make to these requests and in recognising that this area presents a problem that police officers may reasonably expect to have to confront.

The disclosure of information represents a more serious matter than simply accessing it, as disclosure represents a breach of police regulations. In relation to written police material, Regulation 402(x), specifically stated that it was prohibited to "without proper authority show to any person outside the Force any document or material under the control of the Chief Commissioner". Passing on information verbally may also result in an admonishment or disciplinary charge relating to improper conduct (Police Regulation Act s 69(1)(e)). However, in relation to the issue of sanctions, the standard of evidence required to support a breach of regulations or of the Police Regulation Act is quite high, and many cases result only in counselling.

2   Cases Involving Disclosure of Police Information

The case files examined reveal that, at the very least, it is usually imprudent for an officer to make enquiries on behalf of someone with whom they have a connection. In more serious cases, such information may be used for personal ends by parties other than the officer, with or without the knowledge of the officer.

Most disclosures of police information involved low-level leaks, and most involved leaks of information from the police database. Drawing on and extending Miller's (2003) categories of information compromise, six types of information disclosure were found: low-level leaks; leaks in the context of a business or commercial matter; leaks in the context of criminal investigations, legal, or associated matters; leaks to the media; trading in police information for the purposes of financial or commercial benefit; and inadvertent leaks. Examples of each category are discussed below.

(a)   Low-level Leaks

Low-level leaks are an extension of the category of "domestic" use of information, as discussed in the preceding section on access to police information. Whilst they may seem relatively innocuous, the conflicts of interest involved are nevertheless often quite clear, yet not necessarily recognised either by the police officers themselves or investigating and oversighting officers.

A case dating from the first part of 1998 exemplified the complexity of matters involving the alleged use or misuse of police information. This case reveals that even at that time the understanding within Victoria Police of issues about conflict of interest was limited in some important respects, in particular, the distinction between a conflict of interest and a conflict of interest breach.

In this case, a police officer's brother (who was a landlord and an ex-police officer) asked the police officer to check the criminal history of tenants with whom he was involved in a dispute. The tenants were subsequently evicted, and they lodged a complaint alleging that the police officer had improperly passed police information to his brother. Upon investigation, the database access logs showed that the police officer had indeed checked the criminal history of the tenants, but the police officer denied passing any information on to his brother. He claimed that he was making an inquiry on behalf of his brother to see if a complaint to the local police had been acted upon. The brother also denied receiving any police information (Case 365).

The investigating officer recommended that the police officer be charged with a disciplinary offence, based on the conclusion that, on the balance of probabilities, the disclosure did occur. However, the manager of the DAU within the ESD was concerned that there was no direct corroboration of the disclosure, since both brothers denied it and he concluded that there was insufficient evidence. This resolution of the case generated a significant degree of interchange between the office of the Ombudsman and Victoria Police, with the Ombudsman taking a strong line arguing for tougher treatment and a more severe outcome. However, Victoria Police management went to significant lengths to avoid such an outcome.

The Deputy Ombudsman, although conceding that the data access of the police officer was not unlawful, remained unsatisfied. His concerns centred on the police officer's conflict of interest in the matter, and even though he agreed that the evidence was inadequate he could not understand why the investigation of the police officer's conduct had been completed without reference to the Force's "conflict of interest policy". The reply from a senior officer within the ESD defended the earlier decision on the basis of a claim that the Force effectively had *no* binding policy in this matter, but that a policy for the future was in the process of development. However, the Deputy Ombudsman remained unsatisfied with the Victoria Police response, suggesting that the police officer be counselled on the nature of conflict of interest, particularly in relation to the possible criticisms and ramifications when a lack of independence could be perceived in the action for which he was using his position as a member of the police force. Finally, the police officer was formally counselled in relation to the matter, although the actual complaint of disclosure was found to be not substantiated.

What was particularly interesting about this case was that the Victoria Police view of the police officer's actions seemed to revolve around the issue of the lack of sufficient evidence to prove that the police officer had actually disclosed police information to his brother, a matter on which Victoria Police and the Deputy Ombudsman agreed. However, the Deputy Ombudsman's concerns revolved around the issue of conflict of interest, and the Deputy Ombudsman was of the opinion that a conflict of interest was evidenced by the police officer's own admissions (and the database log record) that he had accessed police information in order to follow-up an inquiry from his brother. The key contrast with the Victoria Police position was that, as there was no apparent conflict of interest breach—that is, a neglect of duty flowing from a conflict of interest—this somehow negated or lessened the inherent conflict of interest.

(b) *Business or Commercial Leaks*

At what might be thought of as the high end of low-level leaks are leaks in which the party to whom the police officer discloses police information is motivated by a quite specific type of business or commercial interest. Although Miller (2003) does not make a distinction between leaks in this context and other low-level leaks, given the sensitive circumstances in which such information may subsequently be used for private purposes, the distinction is warranted in terms of better understanding the nature of the conflicts of interest involved. One case is used to briefly illustrate some of the issues.

In this case, a police officer's wife worked as a process server. A complaint alleged that the police officer regularly used the police database to obtain information for his wife's process serving work. It was alleged that the police officer surreptitiously got other officers to look up the information for him, so that database audits could not be traced to him. The matter was settled as "unable to determine", on the basis of insufficient evidence (Case 380).

This case shows that although the police database logs provide a good source of evidence in relation to such matters, this is not always conclusive, and does not always result in a definitive resolution of a complaint.

(c) *Criminal Investigations, Legal, or Associated Matters*

Leaks of police information in the context of criminal investigations, legal, or associated matters are more than low-level leaks because of the nature of the information disclosed and the context within which it may be used. There is considerable potential for damage to be caused to individuals, whether information about them that is released is accurate or not. This potential for damage reiterates the importance of police officers being aware of their duties both *not* to release confidential information, and not to allow personal interests to interfere in their professional actions and decisions in relation to the disclosure of official information. More recently in Victoria there has been considerable disquiet surrounding leaks of police information, including the identities of police informers and other key operational matters, to criminals. Some of these leaks have compromised major drug investigations, prosecutions, and, in once instance, were believed to have resulted in the murders of a police informer and his wife (see Director - Police Integrity 2005c).

Three cases from the case files exemplify key issues and some of the situations that arise in this area.

Case 45 is particularly revealing as it shows the very limited range of effective sanctions available to police management in dealing with such cases, and it illustrates the lengthy process (30 months from complaint to final resolution: 1990–1992) that is often involved in the investigation, review, oversight, and ultimate resolution of conflict of interest complaints. In this case, the police officer was alleged to have released a statement taken by another police officer to the solicitor of the police officer's wife, who worked as a process server. The statement was the result of an interview with the complainant conducted by a second police officer the day after an altercation between the woman and the complainant (at which the police officer complained against was also present; he was also present when the police interview was conducted). No criminal charges were lodged against the man, but a photocopy of the pages of the interview was provided to the wife's solicitors after she had decided to take legal action alleging civil assault against the complainant in relation to the incident. The police officer admitted that he had provided the statement to the solicitor as it "was important in these proceedings".

Whilst various aspects of the complaint relating to assault, illegal search, and improper action against the man were found to be not substantiated, in relation to the allegation of disclosure, the complaint was substantiated. This finding was on the basis of the fact that the provision of the statement was in clear breach of Regulation 402(x), which prohibited a police officer from showing police documents to people outside the Force. A counselling was recommended, but on further review within the Internal Affairs Department, a senior reviewing officer found that the police officer was in fact in a "serious conflict of interest" situation relating to all aspects of the case, and it was directed that the police officer be admonished both in relation to the release of information and improper involvement in the case. The relevant reviewing officer and District Commander agreed with these findings.

However, in a letter to the Ombudsman some months later, Victoria Police informed the Ombudsman that the police officer concerned had lodged a grievance (effectively, an appeal) against the admonishment notification and that: "The Assistant Commissioner has authorised an admonishment to be reduced to counselling." The Ombudsman indicated that he did not disagree. The reasoning for this decision was based mainly on an argument that the available evidence was not of a sufficient standard to support an admonishment. It was also noted that a counselling was not to be regarded as a punitive measure, but advice and guidance designed to improve a police officer's future performance of duty.

The matter may have rested there but the complainant, on being notified in writing of the change from an admonishment to a counselling, would not agree to nor accept this reduction in sanction. He questioned the assertions made about the standard of available evidence, given that the police officer had admitted supplying the other police officer's written police notebook statement to the solicitors acting for the police officer's wife, and that as a consequence the police officer had been found guilty of improper conduct. He requested that his complaint be handed to the Deputy Ombudsman (Police Complaints). As a result of his review the Deputy Ombudsman stated that he disagreed with the legal advice Victoria Police had received and he thought that the police officer's behaviour was improper. He nevertheless stated that he accepted that acting according to legal advice was reasonable but he asked for further clarification.

In legal clarification of the issue it was concluded that the police officer showed no propensity to bring discredit upon himself or the police force, and the following advice was provided:

The main issue of concern regarding [the police officer] appears to be that counselling is not appropriate when he has made full admissions ...

... In my opinion, for actions to be regarded as improper they must breach a rule of conduct or law.

In these circumstances there is no breach of law or of the rules of conduct. The general rules on this subject relate specifically to information that must be kept secret as a matter of duty. The secrecy aspect clearly relates to information that would breach security or affect the success of an operation.

The Deputy Ombudsman had little choice but to accept the counselling outcome in the matter. This eventual outcome placed a strict limitation on the range of sanctions effectively available to Victoria Police management in cases involving a breach of Regulation 402(x). It also clarified the nature of counselling, emphasising its remedial and training characteristics rather than its use as a sanction. Thus, it would follow that attention to counselling as part of a suite of remedial and training techniques, rather than a one-off event, would seem to be required on the part of police management. However, there was little evidence in the case files that in practice counselling is regarded as anything more than a one-off measure.

This case also demonstrates the strong role of the Deputy Ombudsman in oversighting complaint files, and his relatively well-tuned understanding of relevant conflict of interest issues. Often, the Deputy Ombudsman had a clear view of conflict of interest issues whereas police management were more focused on disciplinary breaches (conflict of interest breaches).

Some cases in this group involved allegations that police officers had provided information about the *criminal history* of certain people to third parties. It may be suggested that at the time of this study the consequences of such breaches were not taken as seriously as the case discussed above, as they related to past criminal matters rather than pending matters. Given the legal reasoning in Case 45, above, it would be surprising if the release of criminal histories of individuals during the period under review would have breached the security and sensitivity test suggested in that case, or that disclosures would be regarded as *intended* to bring the Force into disrepute. It would therefore be expected that sanctions more serious than a counselling would only be the result of quite serious breaches in such circumstances.

One case involved what was claimed to be accidental leaks of the criminal history of individuals. The complainant was in the midst of a civil dispute with his neighbour, who was the father of a police officer. The father disclosed to a number of other people details of the complainant's criminal history. The complainant assumed that this information had come from the man's daughter (the police officer). Investigations revealed that she had printed out the man's criminal history from the LEAP system, and had taken the printout to her home, but the father said he took it from her home without her knowledge. The matter was conciliated at the local level, but the investigating officer nevertheless recommended that the police officer be counselled. This outcome was approved by the relevant Internal Affairs Department senior officers, but in his oversight of the matter the Deputy Ombudsman stated that he felt an admonishment would be more appropriate. He related his concerns to the wider problem of release of confidential information and suggested that the police officer be interviewed about why she accessed the complainant's record (Case 115).

The police officer was interviewed as suggested. She denied any improper intent and denied intentionally providing the information to her father. The police officer's father was also interviewed. It was concluded that the police officer could not provide a valid reason for printing the file, and that it was not required for any ongoing matter that she was investigating.

The final resolution of this complaint revolved around the issue of the standard of proof required to sustain a disciplinary outcome greater than a counselling. In later correspondence between different sections of the Internal Investigations Department it was reiterated that the police officer had not erred in accessing the file, but that the provision of the information to her father was a different matter. It was also concluded that the police officer's defence in relation to this aspect of the allegation was not credible. Further advice was sought on the suitability of an admonishment. Surprisingly, given the legal advice discussed earlier (which was provided in January 1992; the processing of the complaint in Case 115 commenced the same year) it was concluded in this case that admonishment was warranted in the circumstances, because "the evidential burden is now not as severe as it once was for admonishment". Although the file did not detail this, a change in policy seemed evident.

This outcome and the reasoning outlined above also clearly suggests that the key problem in the area of misuse of confidential police information is held not to be accessing information for private purposes, but what is done with the information once it is accessed.

A severe outcome resulted from a case where a police officer who was having an affair with a married woman provided the woman with information about the criminal history of her father. In this matter, which involved a number of associated allegations, the police officer was found to have acted in a matter likely to bring the Force into disrepute, and he was fined. This outcome suggests that where there is blatant use of confidential information for illicit personal ends or in the context of an apparent exploitation of the position of a police officer for sexual favours police management are prepared to seek strong disciplinary action, including fines (Case 247).

(d) Leaks to the Media

Particularly in high profile cases, the release to the media of confidential police information may directly impact on police sources (Miller 2003: 13). On the other hand, the release of police information to the media and other parties outside the organisation may form an important public accountability function, often referred to as "whistleblowing" (The Ombudsman 1998b).

Only two cases, both in the mid-1990s, included specific allegations involving the release of police information to the media: one is discussed here for illustrative purposes.[1] This case involved several complainants who had been charged with various criminal offences, including fraud. When the charges were withdrawn prior to going to trial, the complainants alleged various forms of harassment, including an allegation that police had maliciously released details of their arrest to local television and other news media. The investigation of this matter found that the police officers in question had not engaged in any form of harassment, or undue release of information to the media (Case 124).

(e) Trading in Police Information for Financial or Commercial Benefit

In its report on a major investigation, the New South Wales Independent Commission Against Corruption (1992a) identified greed as a major contributing factor to a growing trade in government information. This was said to represent a triumph of private interest over public duty. In relation to

---

[1] Given the statement by the Deputy Ombudsman during the period that there were a *number of complaints* that related to leaks to the media (The Ombudsman 1993; The Deputy Ombudsman (Police Complaints) 1993), it seems likely that most cases involving leaks to the media were not coded as conflict of interest cases.

policing, the key concern outlined by Miller (2003) in relation to the release of information to the media was that these often involved the making of payments to police officers for information provided to journalists.

No such instances of payment for release of information to journalists were included in the case files examined, nor were there cases that suggested a level of trade in police information of the type disclosed by the New South Wales Independent Commission Against Corruption in the early 1990s (Independent Commission Against Corruption 1992a: 14). However, alleged payment for the disclosure of police information in other contexts was an element in four complaints in the study.

In the most extreme of these cases, police information and other police resources were effectively used as stock-in-trade by two police officers who were privately paid (in cash and kind) to travel interstate and conduct unofficial inquiries (although purported to be official) in order to locate the estranged wife of a friend. Part of what the police officers traded on in this private venture was their access to police information and police sources that would otherwise not be available to a member of the public. They were charged with various disciplinary offences, were found guilty, and were fined and transferred (one resigned) (Case 300).

(f)   *Inadvertent Leaks*

In Cases 86 and 115, discussed above, the police officers against whom allegations were made had claimed that the disclosure of information was inadvertent or accidental. These claims were not accepted in those cases, but in other cases, it has been accepted that disclosure of police information to outside parties have been inadvertent or unintentional. In general, even where there is no apparent *personal* connection on the part of the police officer either to the reason for disclosing the information in question or in terms of benefit from its private use, it may be assumed by a complainant that inadvertent leaks are the result of a conflict of interest.

In one case illustrating this problem, a complainant was a member of one of the local emergency services who had been arrested for being drunk and disorderly (the arrest involved injury to some police officers). The arresting officer rang the complainant's emergency service employer and disclosed information about the arrest. Subsequently, the complainant was asked to resign or told he would be dismissed from his employment. At the time there were guidelines in existence as to which organisations/employers had to be notified of the arrest of a person under certain circumstances, but the complainant's organisation was *not* one of them. Thus, even though the evidence suggested that the police officer had not acted with malicious intent, and that she believed she was acting appropriately, the complaint was found to be substantiated. The police officer was counselled for disclosing information to the offender's employer. Her supervising police officer was also counselled for failing to properly supervise and for providing incorrect advice in relation to the disclosure (he failed to check the Police Manual prior to giving the police officer advice to telephone the complainant's employer). Even though the complainant was charged and convicted of a criminal offence in relation to the assault, the resolution of the conflict of interest complaint seemed to rest heavily on the material result of the police officer's disclosure of what was then otherwise confidential police information—the man lost his employment (Case 74).

III   Misuse of Other Police Resources

Table 6.2 summarises the findings in the complaints alleging misuse of other police resources for private purposes. Complaints alleging misuse of police identity resulted in substantiated outcomes in 12 cases (80 per cent), while other private use of police resources resulted in substantiated outcomes in eight cases (36.4 per cent).

A   *Misuse of Police Identity*

A conflict of interest is apparent when a police officer uses his or her identity as a police officer to directly gain a private advantage or to give a level of imprimatur to private activities. In so doing, the police officer may apply a level of pressure to other parties in transactions and other interactions, or may be perceived to have attempted to do so. At all times where the identity of an individual as a member of the Force is used or otherwise known, police officers are required to act in a manner appropriate to the status of a member of the Force.

Table 6.2: Findings in Complaints of Misuse of Other Police Resources

Category of conflict of interest	Determination							
	Finding against police officer (substantiated)		In-determinate finding[1]		Finding in favour of police officer[2]		Total Occurrences	
	N	%	N	%	N	%	N	%
Misuse of police identity	12	80.0	1	6.7	2	13.3	15	100
Other private use of police resources	8	36.4	4	18.2	10	45.4	22	100
TOTAL	20	54.1	5	13.5	12	32.4	37	100

(1) *Indeterminate finding* = Lesser deficiency, Unable to determine, Conciliated, Not proceeded with (resigned prior)

(2) *Finding in favour of police officer* = Withdrawn, No complaint, Not substantiated, Unfounded, Exonerated

Police management concerns over the use of the police identity in this way are most frequently related to the disciplinary offence of engaging in conduct that is likely to bring the Force into disrepute or diminishing public confidence in it (Police Regulation Act s 69(1)(e)). If a police officer allows any other person to use items of police property or equipment, that person may also be subject to provisions of the criminal law in regard to impersonation and other matters. He or she may also be subject to action under s 97 of the Police Regulation Act.

The case files demonstrate a variety of ways in which it may be alleged that a police officer has used police identity in an attempt to gain a private advantage. The official identity (and, possibly, authority) of a Victoria Police officer is most obviously indicated through the production of police identification ('the badge'). The wearing of the police uniform (or parts thereof), visible use of marked police vehicles, use of official police letterhead, or use of police fax machine identification in the context of private activities may also be seen as an attempt to use a police officer's identity as a member of the Police Force for private advantage. Examples of each of these circumstances are discussed in the subsections below.

1   Official Identification ('the Badge')

In private commercial dealings where a police officer is acting in the role of a customer, the police identity may be used to gain some form of advantage. In one complaint, a Victorian police officer was intercepted in New South Wales (off duty) for speeding. He attempted to use his position and badge to avoid a radar infringement notice. He was charged with engaging in conduct that is likely to bring the Force into disrepute (under the Police Regulation Act s 69(1)(e)), and was reprimanded and fined (Case 321).

The *manner* in which a police officer uses identification as a police officer is also a potential source of problems. In relation to a substantiated allegation that, on being asked to leave the hotel, a police officer became abusive and swore at hotel staff and had to be forcibly removed, the police officer was told that he had engaged in conduct likely to bring the Force into disrepute and that he was reasonably expected to understand that when a police officer's identity as a member of the Force is known, members of the public will judge his actions in light of the Force's reputation.

This case demonstrates that problems may arise even where a police officer does not attempt to use his or her identity directly (although, as discussed in the next subsection, this police officer had used his police identification to gain free admission to the hotel). When that identity is known, a police officer must be careful to ensure that actions are not interpreted in such a way that implies he or she is attempting to use that identity to gain a private advantage.

2   'Lending' Identification

The 'lending' of police identification to others to enable them to obtain offers normally available to police is regarded very seriously by Victoria Police management. Such a use opens up the illegitimate user of the police identification to possible charges of impersonating a police officer and of attempting to gain a financial advantage by deception. The police officer may also be liable to police disciplinary charges of failing to comply with a standing order or instruction of the Chief Commissioner, under s 69(1)(b) of the Police Regulation Act, because Chief Commissioner's instructions regarding the use of police equipment are held to apply to police identification, deemed to be "police equipment".

One case illustrates the seriousness of these matters. A young police officer with less than two years experience was out with friends. He lent a friend his police identification in order to impress some girls at a hotel bar. The police officer was initially uncooperative with the investigation, but he later admitted that he had been untruthful and that he had loaned his police identification to the other person. The police officer's friend was charged with impersonating a police officer and the police officer himself was to be charged with two aiding and abetting offences. He was charged with disciplinary offences, but resigned prior to the disciplinary hearing (Case 37).

3   Uniform and Marked Vehicles

Where a police officer conducts private activity whilst dressed in police uniform, allegations may be made that he or she is either attempting to convey an impression that the activity has official Victoria Police approval, or to apply unspoken and subtle pressure on other parties to take part in transactions or proposed transactions.

Police identity in the form of uniform may be misused in the course of attending civic or social meetings, such as a school council (Case 228), but the conflict seems even clearer where the allegation involves the conduct of private business activity whilst in uniform (Cases 122, 26), especially where a police officer becomes involved in disputes. The other party to a dispute may lodge a complaint if they either feel the police identity has been used to pressure them or to forestall action (Case 79). Even the signing and passing of private cheques relating to private activities whilst dressed in police uniform (or in the context of telling creditors one is a police officer) may apply pressure on creditors to accept what might otherwise be regarded as doubtful cheques (Case 72).

4   Letterhead and Facsimiles

The use of police letterhead or faxes (especially where a Victoria Police coversheet is used as part of a facsimile transmission) for non-official purposes can also identify an individual as a member of the Force. This gives rise to problems because it creates the appearance of private activities and actions having official imprimatur.

In one case, when a member used a police facsimile machine and fax cover sheet for a transmission relating to a private civil matter, the recipient (who complained) felt intimidated. The member was counselled (Case 168).

Even if the police officer has official permission to use the facsimile machine, does not use police stationery (cover sheet), and pays the cost of use, complaints may arise. Such circumstances were evident in a case in relation to involvement in private business activity. Here, approval had been given by a senior police officer and a fax was sent to other police stations offering discounted flowers from the police officer's wife's florist business. An anonymous complaint was received over the use of police resources for personal gain (Case 394). The specific circumstances of the case, particularly that permission had been given, led to a finding that the allegation was unfounded, but a subsequent District Instruction clarified Force policy:

> The use of official police facsimile machines for a member's private business has the potential to cause embarrassment to the police force and to other members. In accordance with current Force and District policy on the use of police telephones and mobile telephones, members are not to use official facsimile machines to transmit information relating to a member's private business.

The use of police letterhead in an *official* capacity can also give rise to complaints. One such complaint resulted from an annual police–business liaison event conducted by police at a local restaurant. Subsequently, a 'standard-form' letter from the police social club was sent to the restaurant owner to thank him for his support (he had provided discounted food and service). All participating businesses were thanked in the same manner. It was intended as private thanks, but the restaurant owner displayed the letter in the restaurant. A complainant argued that the display of the letter conveyed the impression that Victoria Police recommended the restaurant. The matter was regarded as a misunderstanding, and was conciliated and the letter removed (Case 105).

B   *Other Use of Police Resources*

Whilst some private uses of police resources, such as making a private telephone call from a police station, or driving a police vehicle between a police officer's place of residence and their station (with authorisation) seem quite innocuous, members of the public may see such matters differently. In addition, the case files show that identifiable conflicts of interest may arise if a police officer seeks to further private interests by using the equipment and accoutrements of a police officer, and police time and personnel.

1   Telephones

In most cases, the use of the telephone is a minor matter, incidental to more significant aspects of a complaint. However, in instances where a complainant infers or alleges that a police officer has attempted to use his or her official influence in a private matter, the use of a police telephone may itself be commented on in the course of an investigation. Illustrating this issue is a case where a police officer made a telephone call from a police station in relation to a dispute over a private business transaction. It was claimed that the police officer had attempted to misuse his authority in a civil matter, but it was accepted that the police officer had not attempted to use his position to influence the outcome of the dispute. However, the oversighting superintendent suggested that the police officer probably should not have made the telephone call in question from the police station, this act itself connecting Victoria Police to the dispute. The police officer explained his action by stating that his wife was very upset about the matter and he did not want her to be involved or to be contacted by the other party at home, and this explanation was accepted (Case 7).

2   Vehicles and Fuel

In the ordinary course of their police duties, individual police officers have access to the use of police vehicles (and fuel), making the appropriation of these police resources for non-official or private ends a relatively easy matter logistically. If police vehicles are used in the context of unauthorised outside employment arrangements, this may be seen both as a breach of outside employment provisions and a misappropriation of police resources. Thus, whilst outside employment can give rise to potential conflicts of interest, the problem is magnified when the police officer uses police vehicles to assist in the work.

The use of police vehicles, particularly marked vehicles, is an obvious source of visible activity on the part of members of the police force that may give rise to a range of complaints. Even in the absence of conflicts of interest, police officers should be cognisant of public perceptions of their actions and activities. For example, police are generally well-known and highly visible in country town settings. This level of familiarity with individual police officers may give rise to complaints where there is no conflict of interest at all.

Notwithstanding the above comment, in a case where a (married) police officer, whilst on duty in uniform in a small town, used a marked police vehicle to visit a woman with whom he was engaged in an affair, the police officer was found to have engaged in conduct likely to bring the Force into disrepute because, among other concerns it became known in the local community that his visits in a marked police vehicle were on duty and not in response to duty-related matters (Case 247).

In other cases, there may be evidence suggesting vexatious motives on the part of the complainant. For example, one anonymous general complaint about police use of vehicles alleged that numerous officers used police vehicles "as they like" and that members of the Police Force would daily take vehicles to and from their homes. The complainant put the matter in the context of media reports of vehicle and staff shortages. In commenting to the Ombudsman on this, Victoria Police explained that off duty personnel who are available for duty may garage police vehicles at their private homes. Also, sworn and unsworn members may use marked police vehicles to travel to meetings, undertake training, attend court, and conduct other official duties. Such uses were stated to be in accordance with Force and District policy and it was suggested that perceptions of misuse were affected by a lack of knowledge of District operational requirements. The Ombudsman agreed with a proposal to continue with existing policy (Case 201).

Even uses of vehicles within the Police Force itself may give rise to complaints. Where several police used a police bus to go on a ski trip organised by a Command level officer, who said the activity was a "team building exercise", an internal complaint was lodged, suggesting that this amounted to a private recreational activity. The investigation of the complaint found that the motivations behind the trip were commendable, but perhaps not enough thought had gone into whether it was appropriate in all the circumstances, and it was recommended that the police officer be informally counselled (Case 5).

Where the public are witness to seemingly innocent, innocuous or humorous misuse of police resources without particular private gain, concern will arise as to the likelihood of bringing the Force into disrepute. Two male police officers on Divisional Van patrol were approached by a group of young women who requested their assistance to play a practical joke on their friend who was going to enter the Airforce. They were giving him a send-off at a local restaurant. They had a civilian friend dressed in police uniform items (not official uniform) and he got into the back of the van. The police officers drove to the restaurant, parked out the front, flashed their lights and sounded the siren. One of the women led her friends out of the restaurant, the male civilian inside the police van was then let out and he proceeded to disrobe down to his underwear. He then climbed back into the van and it drove away. The pseudo-strip show had happened in front of other restaurant patrons and members of the public, one of whom lodged a complaint. The initial investigation and internal police review regarded the matter as a mistake in judgment on the part of the young police officers, and recommended a counselling, but on review and recommendation from the Deputy Ombudsman (Police Complaints), the penalty was increased to a caution notice (Case 297).

3   *Equipment and Accoutrements of a Police Officer*

Like the use of the uniform and the badge, the use of police equipment and other paraphernalia is regarded particularly seriously by Victoria Police management. Illustrating this is a case involving an allegation of the use of a police hat in a table-top dancing act at a bar. Two on duty uniformed police officers were in attendance. They made a case that they had legitimate police business at the bar, and this was accepted (although the length of the visit seemed questionable), and the specific allegation about the use of the police hat was unprovable on the evidence available. However the two police officers were admonished and counselled on charges relating to failing to officially account for why they were there—there were inaccuracies in the police officers' official police records (Case 391).

More serious was a case that involved allegations relating to the use of a police firearm to assist in the resolution of a contentious civil matter. A police officer went to his brother's commercial premises in order to assist in settlement of a civil dispute at the factory (the brother was the dispossessed occupier of the factory). At the factory, the police officer (a detective) did not display his identification, but was not wearing a jacket, thus his firearm was on display and was taken as a possible attempt to intimidate people at the factory. Other people in the factory were worried about the presence of the weapon and called the police. The investigating officer found that the police officer was unaware that other people were on the premises (the complainant and others had concealed themselves), so he had not necessarily displayed his firearm in a deliberate attempt to intimidate others (Case 203).

The Deputy Ombudsman was especially concerned about the carrying of a firearm in the context of private family business, arguing that the police officer was *not* in any meaningful sense on duty (he had told his superior officer that he had to pick up his son). The Internal Affairs Department accepted the Deputy Ombudsman's points and the final letter to the complainant reflected these concerns. The police officer was admonished on three separate counts: improperly displaying a firearm, improper involvement in a civil dispute, and misleading his superiors as to his reasons for absence from the station.

4   *On-duty Time and Police Personnel*

On-duty police time can be used for private purposes in the context of outside employment and private business activities, other organised activities, or for general private affairs. The case files indicate that police management view the appropriation of police on-duty time for private purposes as a serious matter. The seriousness seems to be exacerbated where multiple police personnel are involved, particularly where junior or subordinate officers are asked to undertake private tasks for senior officers. The case files illustrate the types of circumstances where the files indicate the use of police on duty time and/or police personnel for private purposes. One case is discussed here (the ranks of the relevant police officers are pertinent in this discussion).

In this case, a senior officer used a police vehicle along with police manpower to pick up building materials from a public location and transport them to his private address. The activity was conducted entirely in police time and involved a Detective Inspector (the owner of the property) who asked a Senior Sergeant (officer in charge) to get two other officers (another Senior Sergeant and a Senior Constable) to accompany him on the task. The police officers involved had an average of 23.5 years of service in the Police Force (Detective Inspector—23 years, Detective Senior Sergeant—35 years, Detective Senior Sergeant—24 years, and Senior Constable—12 years). All of the police officers involved admitted their involvement. The Inspector was admonished and the other officers were cautioned or counselled (Case 320).

The Inspector made full and frank admissions, and accepted the admonishment. The Senior Sergeant who recruited the other Senior Sergeant and the Senior Constable to assist in the task stated in interview that his reasons for assisting the Detective Inspector related simply to the fact that his senior officer had asked him to do something that was not in itself criminal and that he then did it because the senior officer asked him. An admonishment notice was prepared against this Senior Sergeant, but it did not proceed following a decision of the Assistant Commissioner on the advice of the DAU, which noted he had an "unblemished record" of 30 years, and that the officer had clearly learned from the experience. Counselling was considered adequate. At interview, the other Senior Sergeant involved made a number of points that indicated he did not appreciate the seriousness of the matter, including a denial that there was anything improper in getting the Senior Constable to assist in the job and a suggestion that a young member would not feel obliged to do the work for a superior. He was issued with a formal caution.

IV   Summary and Discussion

The analysis in this chapter demonstrates that the conflicts of interest inherent in the misuse of police information and other police resources are not just matters of perception, but are very real. If a police officer appropriates any police resources for private ends, the private interests of the officer have been placed ahead of the general duty to use police resources only for official purposes. In cases involving the misuse of police information—the most common form of conflict of interest in this area—there is a related breach of specific regulatory previsions. In addition, the analysis in this chapter shows that the private use of a range of other police resources may give rise to conflict of interest breaches at least as serious as those relating to the misuse of information.

A   *General Problems Relating to Context*

Two general *contextual* problems in relation to misuse of police resources can be identified from the complaint case files in this chapter. The first involves the misuse of police resources in the context of outside or secondary employment or the conduct of private business. The use of police information, vehicles and specialist items of police equipment in this context represent particularly problematic areas of complaint in this category.

The second general problem relates to cases involving the use of police resources in the furtherance of activities or relationships that were in themselves regarded as problematic, such as problematic sexual relationships or relationships with criminals and informers. In a number of cases, the alleged disciplinary breach of a police officer included misuse of police resources in facilitating, furthering, or otherwise conducting such relationships.

The involvement of police officers in problematic relationships is itself a matter for concern and outside employment arrangements also give rise to a range of concerns, as discussed in Chapter Four. The unauthorised use of police information and other resources in these contexts magnifies the problem of conflict of interest in such matters. Indeed, the breach of duty exemplified by the private use of police resources signifies the problematic nature of the conflict of interest inherent in such private activities and relationships. For individual police officers and police management, these observations reinforce the importance of awareness of the nature of conflicts of interest.

B   Misuse of Confidential Police Information

While much of the discussion in the extant literature focuses on the private use of information obtained from *police databases*, the analysis in this study shows that police officers may also use a range of information obtained in the ordinary course of duty, or they may actively use their position to obtain information. A significant implication of recognising these multiple sources of information is that it is not possible to rely on database security, access logs, and audits as the sole means to mitigate against the unauthorised use of information. Wider preventive and detective measures are clearly required. The diversity of possible information sources and the general difficulties in ensuring that electronically accessed police data is not used for non-official purposes, reiterate the point made by the New South Wales Independent Commission Against Corruption (1994b: 9) that the attitude of individuals is as much a factor in the security of official information as policies, procedures, and systemic security measures.

In relation to the *disclosure* of confidential police information, the problems are much broader than the primary concern reflected in Miller's (2003) report on police corruption in England and Wales, being the leaking of information to criminals. Although this study does not undermine Miller's concerns in that leaks to criminals would not necessarily be coded by Victoria Police as conflict of interest cases, this chapter shows that there are a wide range of other uses of confidential police information that give rise to conflict of interest problems.

Low-level leaks may cause relatively little damage but they can reduce public trust in the disinterested performance of the policing. Leaks motivated by a desire to advance the private interests of a third party, such as information that is used in landlord–tenant or other civil disputes, may cause greater damage to the reputation of the police force. Leaks of police information in the context of private business matters presents a situation in which an outside party receiving the information may unfairly gain. It is difficult to see how such matters would not lead to a diminution in public confidence and trust in policing.

Leaks in the context of criminal investigations or legal or associated matters (not to criminals) are more serious again, and have the potential to severely damage public trust in policing. The opportunity to use one's position to offer unofficial assistance to another party should sound a clear warning bell to a police officer that the private realm may be intervening in the performance of public duty. Unauthorised leaks of police information to the media did not figure prominently in the case files examined.

The cases where a police officer was alleged to be engaging in some form of trade in police information for the purposes of financial or commercial benefit illustrate the extreme end of the problem of disclosure of confidential police information. Where evidence supported such allegations, Victoria Police management took appropriately severe action against the police officers concerned.

The final group of cases involved inadvertent leaks. In these cases, although Victoria Police management were generally sympathetic to the officers involved, where there was likely damage to the public trust, action was taken against them.

Several cases also illustrated how the effective operation of internal review processes within Victoria Police can lead to clearer and more sound outcomes but perhaps more important was the significant role of the Deputy Ombudsman in the resolution of conflict of interest cases. Often, questions asked by the Deputy Ombudsman were instrumental in changing the eventual outcomes of cases or in producing clarification of the reasons behind decisions. The importance of the oversight role of the Deputy Ombudsman should not be underestimated in this context.

C   Misuse of Other Police Resources

In addition to the misuse of confidential police information, the analysis in the chapter shows how conflicts of interest may be manifested in the use of a range of other police resources. Most prominent is the attempted use of police identity in order to gain some private advantage. The case files show that a police officer's status as a member of Victoria Police can be signified through the use of official identification ('flashing the badge'), wearing police uniform or parts thereof, use of a marked police vehicle, or use of police facsimile machines.

Use of police identity in any of these ways is doubly problematic because there may also be an implicit attempt to use the authority that comes with that identity to influence a third party to do something that they otherwise may not do. These attempts to gain private advantage almost always represent a conflict of interest breach under the provisions of the *Police Regulation Act* relating to engagement in conduct likely to bring the Force into disrepute or diminish public confidence in the Force. If police officers seek to privately use their police identity to escape or evade fines, or to bring a form of 'private justice' in relation to a matter, the conflicts of interest involved are similar but the disciplinary breach is more serious. The practice of 'lending' police identification to others exacerbates the problem because it leads to a quite specific breach of standing order instructions that require a police officer to retain possession of all items of police equipment.

The contexts in which private advantage may be sought through the use of various police resources are numerous. They include civic and social engagements, commercial or business matters, the conduct of secondary employment, and personal relationships. Much of the case analysis suggests that in many cases individual police officers fail to understand the problems that may flow from even seemingly minor uses of police resources.

Apart from matters of serious misappropriation (or, in the extreme, theft), police management tend to treat as most serious those matters where the actions of a police officer have the potential to damage the reputation of the Force or diminish public confidence in it. Thus, as with the private use of the police identity, police management have a clear and justifiable interest in regulating the private behaviour of individual police officers, and calling officers to account for actions within the private realm that have the potential to damage the Force in a general sense.

D   *Dealing with the Problem*

A key issue to flow from the analysis in this chapter is the need to clearly separate conflicts of interest from conflict of interest breaches. Whether a police officer's *actions* have been affected by private interests is a question to be asked in determining whether there has been a conflict of interest *breach*, but recognition of the existence of a conflict of interest itself does not require a breach of duty to have occurred (other than a general duty to avoid conflicts of interest). The case analysis showed how Victoria Police management often did not make this clear distinction, especially relating to alleged disclosure of police information.

The absence of a determinate policy on conflict of interest right up until early 1998, despite conflict of interest issues being brought to the attention of Victoria Police management by the Deputy Ombudsman over a long period of time, seems to have exacerbated this perceptual difficulty. A clearer distinction in practice between the private interests and the 'public' behaviours of police officers is necessary to effectively deal with this problem.

CHAPTER SEVEN

Conclusions and Reflections:
Conflict of Interest, Police Ethics and
Accountability

I   Introduction

The conflict of interest complaints case files examined for this book show a wide array of concerns for complainants and police management over the 10-year period covered by the study. Conflicts of interest encompass many aspects of the policing role but also include many interactions between police and the public which are outside the domain of standard operational policing. Integrity across all of these areas is vital to police ethics, to the delivery of just policing, and to the development and maintenance of public trust in the police, which is itself essential to the effective performance of the policing function (see Graham 2006). The analysis throughout the book shows that there is a need for a clearer understanding of the nature of the problem and related concerns with the operation and oversight of police accountability and governance.

This chapter summarises the key findings from the research and places these into a context of wider concerns about police ethics and accountability. The primary purposes of this study have been to clearly define conflict of interest, develop understanding of the various dimensions of the problem in policing, and provide insights into how the problem is dealt with in practice. Wider principles and appropriate forms of accountability dealt with in this chapter are important in determining possible future means of dealing with the problem of conflict of interest. It is hoped that police organisations will take up this challenge.

II   Defining the Problem and its Dimensions

A   *Definitions*

Chapter Two examined the concepts of real, potential, and apparent conflict of interest, and concluded that this tripartite distinction, commonly used in the literature, suffers significant shortcomings, most notably that the notion of conflict of interest is often confused with the breaches of duty which may flow from conflicts of interest. In order to transcend this confusion, three distinct elements of the conflict of interest problematic were developed:

1. Conflict of interest: a direct or indirect conflict between a person's private interests and official duties; such a conflict can exist whether or not the person acts in a manner designed to further those private interests;

2. Conflict of interest breach: a neglect of duty that results from a conflict of interest; includes attempts to further private interests in the course of conducting oneself in an official capacity, and breaches of the duty to remain impartial and disinterested in relation to the performance of official functions;

3. Apparent conflict of interest: a situation where it is possible to perceive that a conflict of interest exists, although there is insufficient immediate evidence to determine the matter (for example, insufficient knowledge of whether a police officer *actually* knows a particular person); upon the collection of evidence apparent conflicts of interest may be resolvable into one or both of the first two categories; apparent conflicts of interest may themselves be regarded as problematic in terms of public perceptions.

Conflicts of interest may be latent or actual. An *actual* conflict of interest relates to present actions or decisions that are to be taken in a situation of conflict of interest, while a *latent* conflict of interest relates to a situation where such actions or decisions are within the realm of present duties but there is no such present action or decision to be taken. This distinction between latency and actuality of a conflict of interest does not alter the nature of the underlying problem, which is the potential of a private interest to impact on the performance of official duties.

The focus in other studies and analyses on distinguishing between real, potential, and apparent conflicts of interest (e.g. Parker 1987) can lead to a situation where a conflict of interest is not regarded as 'real' until it is manifested in a neglect of duty. The clear conceptual and analytical distinction between *having* a conflict of interest and engaging in a conflict of interest *breach* is an important point underlying the analysis in this book. Nevertheless, as a practical matter, the existence of a conflict of interest may become evident only at or after the point where a breach (neglect of duty) occurs, or after allegations relating to conflicts of interest are made. Although conflicts of interest and conflict of interest breaches can be clearly distinguished conceptually, in practice it is not always possible to deal with conflicts of interest separately from associated conflict of interest breaches.

Case file analysis throughout the book demonstrates the problem with traditional conceptions of conflict of interest as not being 'real' until they are manifested in a neglect of duty. Debates around whether a conflict of interest is 'real, potential or apparent' often result in confused understandings and a failure deal with conflict of interest itself as a problem, whether or not there are consequent breaches of duty.

B   *Dimensions of the Problem*

The dimensions of conflict of interest were clarified throughout the book by considering the situations in which conflicts of interest that are manifested in the public and private realms. The analysis showed how a complex mix of interests, relationships, involvements, actions, and activities in the private realm may clash with the duties and obligations of officials in the public realm. Several findings about the nature of the problem stand out:

1.   Non-financial interests were the focus of a large majority of complaints against police officers (three-quarters of all police officers complained against);

2.   Non-financial interests were the focus of a clear majority of complaints against police officers for each year of the study;

3.   Almost one-quarter of complaints involved indirect/external interests, including family, friends, or associates of the police officer;

4.　　　In relation to complaints involving allegations that a police officer had furthered direct or indirect private *financial* interests, money or money equivalents were involved in almost half of the complaints; and

5.　　　A range of other financial interests were also important, including free or reduced price/better quality goods or services, private and unpaid use of police resources, and advantage in relation to private business or secondary employment arrangements.

Four further overarching points can be made. First, an effective understanding of the problem requires a clear explication of the sources of conflict of interest in the private realm and the manifestations of the problem in the public realm. An analytical distinction between the private and public realms is of assistance because even though conflicts of interest can arise in either realm, conflict of interest breaches that occur in the public realm are often related to a number of identifiable circumstances that arise in the private realm. Issues of regulation and accountability are different for the two realms. Obligations associated with public duty are easier to articulate and regulate in the form of police orders and regulations whereas regulations that impinge on the private involvements, activities, and relationships of police officers are potentially more contentious as they go beyond the official realm of public work and obligation. Similarly, it may be appropriate to use different strategies and processes for ensuring accountability for actions in the private and public realms.

Secondly, a range of breaches of duty may be directly or indirectly related to conflicts of interest. The identification and classification in this study of the types of breach that are empirically related to conflicts of interest shows how the problem impacts across the span of areas of core police activity—police power and authority and police resources—as well as traditionally understood problem areas such as secondary employment.

Thirdly, individual police officers and police managers often have a limited understanding of the problem of conflict of interest and its relationship to neglects of duty. When individual police officers offer justifications suggesting ignorance of conflict of interest issues, this may reflect poor understanding or may represent disingenuousness and a preparedness to consciously flout regulations in the pursuit of private gain. However, this study shows how the lack of understanding of the nature and implications of conflict of interest extends to senior ranks, and in some cases to internal investigators and police management. Case analyses showed that police internal investigators and police management may minimise the effect of ethical transgressions (in terms of outcome or sanction applied) if no conflict of interest *breach* is apparent, or if conferral of a private benefit to the police officer is not immediately obvious. That investigators and oversighting officers often interpreted such circumstances as *not* involving conflicts of interest provides evidential support for a misunderstanding of the distinction between conflicts of interest and conflict of interest breaches.

Judgmental confusion may result from a failure to realise that the main regulatory focus is to prevent *upstream* failures or breaches. Conflicts of interest encumber the actions and decisions of police officers. Prevention and avoidance of conflicts of interest (the ethical problem) should preclude both associated breaches of duty and the negative impact on public perceptions that conflicts of interest give rise to. This recognises that the key ethical problem involves police officers being officially *involved* in matters in which they have a private interest, not necessarily the particular action or decision itself. A failure to recognise the manner in which private interests may impact on performance of duty, and/or may be seen to do so, is problematic because the mere fact of a private interest taints official actions in such circumstances. If a conflict of interest breach occurs, the ethical problem extends to police misconduct and, in serious matters, corruption. The recent development by Victoria Police of a Best Practice DVD and Training Kit on conflict of interest represents a welcome step in attempting to raise awareness of this problem and its dimensions.

This leads to the fourth point. This relates to the question of holding police officers to account for appearances or perceptions as well as actual breaches of duty. Because of the erosion of trust in public institutions and public office that flows from perceptions of conflicts of interest, regulation further aims to obviate *perceptions* of partiality, bias or private benefit.

III   Conflict of Interest and Police Ethics

The exposure of police corruption in various jurisdictions has damaged the reputation of police forces in Australia and elsewhere. It has also led to a number of high-profile public inquiries that have spawned flurries of more or less *ad hoc* reform attempts, but such reforms are often fleeting and temporary. An additional source of damage of a systemic nature may occur on a daily basis through a range of conflicts of interest and associated lapses in police integrity. The impact on the ethics of policing may be crucial.

Even relatively minor conflicts of interest may provide fertile ground for serious police misconduct and a variety of forms of unethical activity can be seen to have their roots in conflicts of interest. Identification and analysis of conflict of interest as being causally related to a range of behaviours lying on the continuum between minor misconduct and corruption provides an important avenue for dealing with the problems because awareness of conflicts of interest may assist in identifying precursors of corruption, but tendencies to conflate conflict of interest problems with police corruption and police misconduct more generally may detract from the ability to deal with the problems appropriately.

Clear understanding of *conflicts* as central to the capacity of a private interest to affect the performance of public duty means that it is possible to clearly distinguish between conflict of interest and corruption. Clarity about various forms of problematic conduct is important in understanding specific motivational and behavioural roots, and it is also important that the range of *interests* that now come within the ambit of the concept are appropriately identified.

A   *Governing Conflict of Interest: The Practice*

The Organisation for Economic Cooperation and Development (OECD 2000) has emphasised the need for development of more rigorous and effective regulatory frameworks in "core functions of the state and areas where citizens are fully dependent on public services" (p 13). This is especially the case in sensitive areas such as policing, where there is a high degree of risk of conflict of interest. Regulation of conflicts of interest is justified both in the broader public interest and in light of the social responsibility that attaches to official public roles (Wueste 1994). By accepting roles in public institutions, individuals who occupy such roles are obliged to serve the public interest. There is now little debate that police officers are regarded by the public as key public office holders (Graham 2006).

1   *Evidence from this Study*

Case analyses throughout this book provide insights into existing disciplinary mechanisms within Victoria Police and portray the heavily regulated nature of policing as an occupation. The expectations and requirements of individual police officers are enunciated in legislation, regulation, and various formal directives from police management. These regulatory strictures by which police

253

are controlled contrast sharply with populist portrayals of police as 'out of control' or a 'law unto themselves'. The principal function of the discipline system relates to the maintenance and enforcement of standards of conduct, ostensibly to protect the reputation of the organisation and to maintain public trust in policing. Nevertheless, it cannot be ignored that the operation of the system has a punitive element, and police officers often vigorously seek to avoid both the discipline system itself and the enforcement of departmental rules and regulations.

The case analyses lead to several significant findings relating to the government of conflict of interest complaints. First, and perhaps of most concern, was the extent of involvement of senior police ranks and officers with lengthy service records, including officers with responsibilities in management and supervision. Generating cultural change within policing is particularly challenging if senior ranks are key transgressors and if police managers themselves do not have an adequate grasp of the problem and the challenges. The under-representation of female police officers in conflict of interest complaints may provide a signal that change is possible, but it also reinforces the challenge of changing police culture, given the traditionally masculine nature of police organisations.

The second key finding was that almost one-quarter of all complaints were lodged directly with the office of the Ombudsman, illustrating the importance of this avenue for complaints. The results underline the importance of an independent authority to which members of the public can turn when they have concerns about police conduct. Such an independent authority is an important part of the police complaints system. The Deputy Ombudsman was able to perform a valuable role albeit that he was limited in terms of resources and certain constraints and limits on the powers of his office. For example, there was no power to conduct inquiries or investigations on the own motion of the Ombudsman, and the Ombudsman was at all times required to keep the Chief Commissioner of Police fully informed about his activities. The creation of the Office of Police Integrity in 2004 represents a significant enhancement in review, oversight, and independent investigation of police misconduct and associated systematic police policies and procedures.

Thirdly, in the overwhelming majority of cases, complaints were dealt with without recourse to formal disciplinary procedures in the form of a Discipline Hearing. Fourthly, and very importantly, this study found a high substantiation rate of 38.5 per cent overall, indicating the scale and extent of the problem of conflict of interest. In terms of the pattern of findings over the 10-

year period covered by this study, there was no evidence to suggest that the substantiation rate was affected either by the number of complaints each year (with a large rise in the years 1994–1996) or the organisational changes that led to the establishment of the ESD.

The fifth finding in relation to the operation of the discipline system was the prevalence of counselling outcomes. Whilst a counselling is not formally regarded as a disciplinary sanction, and may therefore be regarded as a 'soft' outcome, the case analyses showed that many individual police officers regard counselling both as punitive and as detrimental to their service records and career prospects. This resistance to counselling may negatively impact on the ostensible developmental intent behind counselling and may inhibit the development of a better understanding of the problem of conflict of interest.

At the higher end of the spectrum of sanctions it is of concern to note that 15 per cent of police officers against whom there were adverse outcomes resigned or were dismissed. This is indicative of the seriousness of the conflict of interest breaches that were involved in these cases, thus reinforcing the gravity of the problem in terms of its capacity to negatively impact on policing practice.

The sixth key finding relates to internal and external reviews of initial recommendations from internal investigations. Four sources of challenge and review were considered: internal oversight, the lodgement of grievances by aggrieved police officers, involvement by the Police Association, and external review and oversight by the Deputy Ombudsman (Police Complaints). For the first of these, analyses revealed that in one-quarter of all cases, there was some form of challenge to the initially recommended determination and/or sanction, and more than half of these challenges resulted in a change to the determination and/or sanction. This finding is significant as it indicates, first, some propensity by oversight officers within Victoria Police to critically evaluate and reconsider initial findings; second, a degree of willingness to change those findings when further analysis and consideration merited a change; and third, an important capacity for self-policing within the internal investigations structure itself. This presents a more complex picture than that encompassed by simplistic notions of 'rubber-stamping' within the organisation.

By contrast, in relation to the small proportion of matters (5.6 per cent) where a police officer lodged a grievance seeking a review of determination of sanction, less than 40 per cent of these matters resulted in a change to determination or sanction, indicating that the grievance procedure, whilst an important element of procedural fairness, has a limited impact on outcomes overall. The cases in which the Police Association became involved tended to be those that resulted in adverse findings and eventually in more serious sanctions, such as dismissal, resignation, fines, or reprimands.

The final source of challenge and review was in the form of the external oversight of the Deputy Ombudsman (Police Complaints), whose statutory responsibility it was, for the duration of the period under study, to oversee the investigation of all public complaints against police. The Deputy Ombudsman also had an informal arrangement with Victoria Police to oversight internally generated complaints (this arrangement was given statutory authority in 1997). The oversight of the Deputy Ombudsman included a capacity to comment and seek revision in relation to individual cases and in respect of general policy and procedural matters. Whilst recommendations from the Deputy Ombudsman were not binding on Victoria Police, the evidence showed them to be very persuasive and, on the whole, treated with respect and seriousness by Victoria Police.

The findings of this study showed that the Deputy Ombudsman commented on matters relating to particular investigations in just over 15 per cent of all cases and where he requested revisiting or broadening aspects of an investigation, Victoria Police acceded to this request. In more than half of the 6.9 per cent of cases where the Deputy Ombudsman specifically argued for a change in determination or sanction, Victoria Police agreed. It is therefore possible to conclude that the oversight of the Deputy Ombudsman was useful within the overall constraints of the resources that his office could devote to these matters at the time, often resulting in substantive changes in investigation and/or outcome. As noted above, recent developments in this area are positive, with the establishment and allocation of considerable financial resources to the Office of Police Integrity.

Overall, the receptiveness to review and challenge indicated by these findings in relation to the internal review processes within Victoria Police and the Deputy Ombudsman's oversight, is to be encouraged. The Deputy Ombudsman's contributions were valuable and the evidence suggests that they contributed to an enhanced understanding of the problem on the part of police management. The responses of Victoria Police management were often positive and productive but there were a number of instances, evidenced through the book, where for inexplicable reasons police investigators and management insisted that a particular police officer not be treated harshly for what seemed to be clear ethical transgressions.

2   General Conclusions

Without concluding as to their efficacy in particular cases, these findings in relation to the operation of the discipline system, taken together, suggest that the various elements of the system are able to deal with many elements of appropriate governance for the problem of conflict of interest, to the extent that it is the subject of formal complaints about police officer conduct. However, the approach adopted remains a reactive model of accountability that invariably requires an allegation of a conflict of interest breach to bring matters to the attention of Victoria Police and the evidence suggests that there is often a limited understanding of the nature and implications of the problem on the part of both police officers and police managers. This is associated with two major difficulties: (i) the basis of the system is in prophylactic regulation; and (ii) attempts to regulate the private lives and private interests of police officers may be both difficult and limited in their effectiveness.

The prophylactic approach obviates the contestability of subjective definitions of conflict where it is required to show that a person's mental state in relation to the performance of official duty actually was impaired by a private interest. Judgments about such matters are problematic because they are, in the final analysis, personal ones. Prophylaxis allows the regulation and enforcement of conflicts to deal with directly observable states, rather than interpretations of perceived mental states. Thus, prophylactic regulation does not directly tackle specific breaches of duty but the *antecedents* of such breaches. For conflicts of interest, elimination of either the *conflict* or the *interest* is regarded as an effective preventive mechanism. Central to the effectiveness of conflict of interest regulation is an understanding of the need to avoid conflicts of interest—both for their potential to be manifested in actual breaches of duty and in negative public perceptions about police. Prevention of misconduct is the most obvious strategy to maintain organisational legitimacy, but whatever preventive approaches are taken they must be coupled with effective mechanisms for dealing with misconduct when it does occur.

In relation to the second difficulty, regulation that prohibits certain relationships, involvements, actions, and activities can be limited in its effectiveness if it is perceived that the prohibitions are an unnecessary and unwarranted intrusion into the private lives of police officers or an implicit attack on their integrity and trustworthiness. However, the analysis in this study showed how a number of specifically identifiable relationships and involvements which police officers engage in during their private off-duty time can give rise to problematic conflicts of interest. Effectively dealing with the problem of conflict of interest requires an understanding of the problematic causal association between the particular types of relationships and involvements and possible neglects of police duty.

Some private involvements and associations can be subject to a blanket prohibition by police discipline codes; for example, consorting and fraternising with known criminals. Outside or secondary employment in specified industries such as gaming, prostitution, and licensed premises may also be subject to general prohibition, because these areas raise fundamental conflicts of interest for police officers, in that they are required to closely monitor the conduct of these regulated areas of business activity. However, regulating private relationships, involvements, and associations is far more difficult than regulating the on-duty behaviour of police officers, and does not always provide an adequate solution. Questions also arise as to the appropriate limits to the control that a police force can exercise over the right to association of citizens who just happen to be police officers.

The answer to this problem seems to lie in a recognition that both liberty and privacy are fundamental to notions of freedom and self-regarding conduct, but they are not applicable to all people in an undifferentiated way (Kleinig 1996). Public officials such as police, who are expected to foster public confidence in their role and power, may not exercise the same liberties or engage in the same forms of conduct as others. Thus, in dealing with the problem of conflict of interest, a level of official involvement in the private lives and private interests of police officers is a necessary and accepted part of police effectiveness.

3   Problems of Accountability

The nature of daily police work complicates attempts to enforce accountability in relation to conflicts of interest. Whilst fighting crime may fit media and governmental images of policing (see Reiner 2000), numerous studies indicate a great deal of police work does not specifically concern law enforcement. For example, in Britain it has been estimated that the social service role of police accounts for in excess of 75 per cent of police time (Loveday 1995, 1994). In Australia it has been estimated that police spend over 80 per cent of their time on tasks other than crime control (Moore 1992). Much police activity involves the provision of an emergency service for problems which may require no legal solution, or for which there is no such solution. As the analysis in this book has shown, it is in this day-to-day operational realm that many conflict of interest transgressions occur.

A perceived need to exercise greater control over the use of police discretion along with an assumption of *lack of* control over the police, may lead to greater use of legal regulation in attempts to further circumscribe the powers exercisable by the police, but officers are already subject to an extensive regulatory environment that structures their exercise of discretion (see Dixon 1999b: 46). More rules cannot be seen as an *alternative* to discretion, since the nature of policing means that significant amounts of discretion are inevitable, particularly at the 'street level', and in practical terms, it is impossible to regulate police with precise rules (Dixon 1997: 303). Even if it were possible to design extensive systems of formal rules to 'control' conflict of interest, the elimination of discretion may be counterproductive because discretion and accountability are mutually reliant. The responsibilities implicit in accountability *necessarily* entail discretion (see Uhr 1993: 4).

A particular challenge for accountability in policing relates to the need to balance discretion with the need for regulation and accountability both of and within police organisations. Internalisation of responsibility underlies meaningful accountability, thus formal regulation must be considered in a broader context of accountability.

B   *Governing Conflict of Interest: Possibilities for Accountability*

1   *Accountability: Concepts and Practices*

Accountability cannot be reduced to a mere technical or procedural exercise, as its practice is "shot through with values and assumptions ..." (Day and Klein 1987: 52). It must be contextualised by considering how it is actually played out in practice but the practical processes of accountability should be recognised as being comprised of a "messy ... series of flows, circuits, connections, disconnections, selections, favourings, accounts, holding to account and attempts at analysis" (Neyland and Woolgar 2002: 272).

It follows that systems of accountability for conduct should look beyond individual pathologies to consider organisational work patterns, culture, and other systemic and contextual factors relating to conflict of interest. Formal, institutionalised police training and individualised on-the-job socialisation work together to generate police cultural norms, and these may be at least as important as the formal regulatory framework (Chan 2001). Indeed, rules may be regarded as most effective if they are internalised as norms of ethical conduct and reflected in the subjective sense of responsibility which police officers hold. Accountability is itself closely related to the question of *responsibility* in that one may be held accountable for those things for which one is responsible and, conversely, responsibility is granted on condition of accountability.

2   Police Accountability

Within an organisation such as Victoria Police, the accountability of police officers is operationalised via a formal discipline system through which individual officers are accountable for their actions. Simplistically, the 'expected' performance of police officers may be enunciated in legislation, regulation, and organisational directives that provide the regulatory framework within which police operate.

Despite the extent of regulation and control of police, it is problematic that the police system remains rooted in a traditional hierarchical system of accountability. The components of the regulatory framework are enforced and reinforced through a 'subordinate and obedient' model of control that is based in the power of those occupying superior positions in the hierarchy to direct and call-to-account those lower in the hierarchy, often through the threat or possibility of formal sanctions (Marshall 1978; Reiner 1995, 1996; Chan 1999b). Enforcement is based on detection and punishment of transgression.

The hierarchical control on which police disciplinary systems are typically premised is near impossible unless organisations are composed of docile functionaries with strictly limited possibilities for discretion (see Bovens 1998: 148). This is a situation that clearly does not pertain within policing. Hierarchical approaches to accountability may also generate resistance to control-from-above, which may itself become rooted in organisational culture. Research has suggested that cultural resistance to being 'called to account' is ingrained in policing, and it has been claimed that organisational culture may excuse and encourage abuses of power (Bayley 1995). If a police discipline system is individualistic and punitive in orientation, it is only natural that those called to account will "try to protect themselves" in the face of calls to account (Crank 1998: 236). Traditional processes of accountability are thereby often frustrated through the proffering of accounts that are designed to obscure rather than inform (Chan 1999b).

In addition to generating resistance, excessive rule making as a control mechanism may encourage pragmatism and instrumentalism on the part of police officers. Detailed rules and laws may come to be seen as signposts around which to navigate (with some more able to navigate than others) as police officers seek to push the boundaries and "trawl the margins" (HM Inspectorate of Constabulary 1999: 3–4). Further, the low likelihood of sanctions being applied in any particular circumstance may overwhelm consideration of a rule's purpose at the street level (Dixon 1997: 303–304). Thus, even seemingly strict systems of rules may effectively encourage those subject to the rules to seek out loopholes and exceptions in order to get around specific prohibitions.

In short, police accountability is not just a function of rules and external controls; it is equally a co-product of internalised role perceptions and commitments on the part of the individual (Thomas 1998). Therefore, effective systems of rules should encourage police officers, individually and collectively, to take responsibility for their decisions and actions (Dixon 1999c).

3   Key Elements of Accountability

(a)   Trust

Some degree of trust is an essential and unavoidable part of policing because trust is always coupled with discretion (see Fox 1974). This form of trust relates to the extent to which individuals expect others to be constrained by the duties and requirements attached to their roles (Misztal 1996: 226) without coercing appropriate exercise of discretion (Braithwaite and Makkai 1994: 2). Trust forestalls the need to monitor and evaluate the behaviour of others (Bigley and Pearce 1998: 413), although it must be recognised that trust itself creates vulnerability to breaches of trust through misconduct on the part of the trusted. The possibility of monitoring is important but continuous monitoring defeats its purpose if it signals distrust and thereby destroys trust (see Dixon 1999b: 61; Braithwaite and Makkai 1994).

Hierarchical accountability may obviate relationships of intra-organisational trust (see Thomas 1998: esp. 373), particularly if the focus is on obedience to authority and the threat of sanctions, because these may be taken as signals of distrust that disrupt trust itself (see Seal and Vincent-Jones 1997). Signals of distrust weaken the moral incentive for police officers to *go beyond* mere rule compliance in both action and account-giving. When distrust is overtly signalled an actor may feel morally self-justified in being untrustworthy.

While regulatory structures are necessary in order to structure the police use of discretion by providing both standards for conduct and accountability mechanisms, it is important to avoid "the suggestion that employees are somehow inherently untrustworthy" (Royal Canadian Mounted Police External Review Committee 1991: 18). Rules and codes must therefore be both "aspirational and admonitory", aiding and encouraging voluntary ethical conduct and avoiding "unnecessary accusatory implications" (pp 18–19).

(b) *Active and Passive Responsibility/Accountability*

Responsibility and associated systems of accountability may be operationalised in a passive or active sense (Bovens 1998). Although the two forms are analytically distinct, they are mutually reliant in effective systems of accountability, although excessive reliance on passive accountability may have the effect of displacing active accountability.

Passive responsibility accords with a traditional sense of accountability-as-answerability and is typified by hierarchical modes of accountability, such as those that are dominant in policing. It is rooted in an individualistic conception of responsibility and passive accountability is often instigated when an account-giver is called to account in relation to a perceived breach of organisational norms, values, or rules. Thus, passive accountability in action is often about the attribution of blame and judgment towards an offender or accused.

In policing, the formal and informal systems of discipline and enforcement are centred on extensive, structured and formal processes that typify passive forms of responsibility. They recognise conflicts of interest and other forms of misconduct as manifested in particular actions of police officers; these actions come to attention through the complaints and discipline system for dealing with police misconduct.

The key problems with passive accountability are that it is centred on obedience to norms and rules and it generally encourages a defensive posture on the part of account-givers: individual accounts tend to be designed to change, mitigate, or modify the assessments of others and "... to recast the pejorative significance of action, or one's responsibility for it, and thereby transform others' negative evaluations" (Buttny 1993: 1). This engenders the sort of cultural resistance to accountability referred to earlier. In general, it is likely that senior, more experienced officers are more able to navigate around the rules and to construct accounts that have the effect of obviating meaningful accountability. As shown in Chapter Three, this group of officers is over-represented in conflict of interest complaints, thus making a regulatory focus on passive accountability especially problematic.

The reliance on passive accountability in the traditional rule-based police discipline system may succeed in catching and punishing some offenders, but is unlikely to be effective in preventing future deviance. Reliance on prescriptive rules may also risk diminishing the personal sense of ethical responsibility held by individual police officers. Changing the rules by which police are governed is not sufficient because the key to the effectiveness of rule change and reform activities are their indirect effects, including on training, supervision, and police culture (Dixon 1997: Ch. 7; Walker 1993). But more than this, effectively dealing with the problem of conflict of interest in more than a reactive sense requires active responsibility to be developed.

Active responsibility is centred on a notion of responsibility as virtue, drawing on loyalty and conscience (Bovens 1998: Chs. 3, 9). This form of responsibility centres on building answerability to self, with associated responsibilities towards other individuals, groups, and organisations. Active responsibility may be realised in the absence or ignorance of particular rules and structures that enforce passive accountability. The focus for active responsibility is less on reacting to past wrongdoings and more on the prevention of future unwanted situations and events.

In policing, the potential for active responsibility springs from discretion that provides the opportunity for responsible behaviour (even as it may also provide an opportunity for misconduct). Active responsibility develops *proactive* accountability because it involves taking responsibility for right and good conduct, prior to the event. It may be that the manifestation of conflicts of interest in breaches of official duty are most effectively addressed through the development of active responsibility in police officers, which can only happen if officers see their responsibilities (and official duties) as lying beyond mere adherence to the formal rules and structures.

Although they are distinct forms, active and passive responsibility are mutually reliant because active responsibility is partly created, explicated, adjusted, or discarded through the processes of passive responsibility, particularly as it is the latter that defines the boundaries within which responsibility is given (Uhr 1993: 3–5). Active responsibility must be an option for action if the sanctions of passive accountability are to be both possible and acceptable. Individuals will not easily accept the idea of bearing responsibility unless the possibilities of behaving responsibly are at their disposal (Bovens 1998: 27). Approaches aimed at nurturing active responsibility may have a role to play in generating trust within accountability relationships and active responsibility may be nurtured in a climate of trust, for where trust is extended, actors will often return the trust with voluntary compliance with fair rules (Braithwaite and Makkai 1994).

Trust is an important, but somewhat fragile, component of active responsibility, but when it is abused, passive accountability processes must come into play. At other times, they should be "in the background" (Braithwaite 1999; Braithwaite and Makkai 1994) so that active responsibility can be nurtured. It follows that passive responsibility cannot be discarded in favour of active responsibility, since the passive form may stimulate the active form by providing explicit norms and guides to conduct. It has been recommended that systems of accountability must first adopt *persuasion*, seeking voluntary ethical compliance rather than obedience to rules. Based on the outcome of strategies based on persuasion, adaptive regulatory strategies should respond to the mode of compliance or evasion adopted by the account-giver (see Dixon 1997: 308; Ayres and Braithwaite 1992; Braithwaite 2002, 1999). Sanctions, in the form of punishment, are not a *necessary* component of this, although the act of calling-to-account is (Bovens 1998: 39–40, 60–64). Even when passive accountability processes are implemented, there is the option of developing active accountability as an outcome of such processes.

In general, formal systems will tend towards the operation of passive responsibility, while informal systems—most notably, police cultures and sub-cultures—may be particularly significant in the development and maintenance of active responsibility. This means that, whilst it is important to get the regulatory framework right in dealing with conflict of interest, in the intermediate and longer term the focus must move beyond formal, rule-bound approaches in order to "win over and work in conjunction with internal disciplinary and self-controlling processes" (Dixon 1999c).

Central to active responsibility, like ethical conduct generally, is the development and nurturing of integrity and trust in and within policing because in the final analysis conflict of interest is both a breach of the trust that the community places in police officers, and a breach of the necessary trust that police officers must have among themselves in order to be effective in their various roles. Looking outward, it has been noted that strong organisational ethical cultures in the public sector drive both increased public trust and improved serviced delivery and performance (Graham 2006).

(c)   *Enhancing Public Trust*

Mere changes in the processes and institutions of accountability are not sufficient to make police more accountable, although such changes may serve an important symbolic and signalling function by sending messages about accountability and responsibility to police officers, and they may play a public relations role by persuading the public that misconduct is effectively dealt with. Although prevention of misconduct is the most obvious strategy to maintain organisational legitimacy, whatever active accountability approaches are taken, they must be coupled with effective mechanisms for dealing with misconduct when it does occur. Vigorous passive accountability and enforcement are needed "both to symbolise police subordination to law and democracy, and to ensure that internal disciplinary and management processes operate effectively" (Reiner 2000: 174).

Regulation of conflicts of interest is underpinned by the concepts of public interest and public trust, the promotion of impartiality and integrity in public life, and prevention of abuse of official positions (Young 1998). Public trust in policing relies on a belief in the integrity of both individual police officers and police organisations as a whole and therefore relies on effective systems of passive responsibility as well as active responsibility on the part of police officers. Public confidence therefore requires that internal mechanisms are complemented by, and themselves made accountable to, passive forms of accountability (Royal Commission into Commercial Activities of the Government and Other Matters 1992). Although the importance of active responsibility and trust is recognised, ongoing public trust is, in part, underwritten by the existence of a system that deals with misconduct reactively when it is discovered—that is, passive accountability.

In short, for reasons both of effectiveness in operation and public confidence in the system, a 'double-track' strategy is needed to combine active and passive elements (Mollen 1994; Goldsmith 1991a; Dixon 1997; Lewis 1999). Effective channels for public complaints and avenues for investigating them need to be available for expressing dissatisfaction about the actions of individual police officers and about police policy and tactics more generally (Reiner 2000: 169).

The use of civilian oversight and external review is also an important element of police accountability and legitimacy (Lewis 1999; Goldsmith 1991a; Beattie Repetti 1997; Bayley 1991), and it is recognised that internal police systems for maintaining standards need to be "supported by independent scrutiny" (Nolan *et al.* 1995: 3). These external forms of accountability can act both as a check on internal accountability processes, and a reassurance to the public. As the case analyses in this book demonstrate, processes of independent external review conducted by the office of the Ombudsman (now, by the Office of Police Integrity) are an important part of the Victoria Police discipline system. Social trust relies on the systematic working of institutions of trust that can themselves be trusted.

4   *Making Accountability Effective*

Traditional rule structures in policing are collections of prohibitions. Because these are oriented towards dealing with problematic events after they have occurred and attributing blame and judgment to an offender or accused, they do not necessarily motivate people to act ethically. As case analyses throughout the book show, extant regulatory prohibitions are, on the whole, adequate to deal with conflict of interest, but many police officers still have great difficulty in clearly recognising appropriate limits on conduct and how these limits contribute to the maintenance of both police integrity and public trust in policing. In particular, many police officers fail to appreciate the capacity for a range of private interests and involvements to impact on their performance of public duty.

Whilst conflict of interest regulation can attempt to limit some opportunities for misconduct, and to obviate some motivations that are also precursors to misconduct, there is a need for special attention to issues of active accountability in the domain of conflict of interest. All accountability systems will fail in some respect at some times, so no system of regulation or accountability can *eliminate* the problems of conflict of interest, nor can it guarantee trustworthiness. But in dealing with the problem of conflict of interest, the police complaints and discipline system, and oversight of it, should be seen as an important mechanism for providing feedback to police and as a basis for organisational learning about the nature of the problems faced.

An essential component to complement a formal system of passive (rule-based) accountability is the encouragement of a sense of active, personal responsibility and accountability that seeks to develop, activate, and draw upon the conscience and the talents of those to be regulated. Rules, codes, and regulations should provide a basis for passive accountability and a framework for consideration of active accountability, recognising that accountability is as much about confirming appropriate practice as it is about punishing deviance. But if attempts to increase accountability are excessively focused on the imposition of formal rule-based controls, this may ultimately risk a loss of responsibility on the part of the regulated (Braithwaite 1999), in part because this "bypasses the issue of moral responsibility which lies at the heart of corruption" (Miller 1998: 51).

Effective accountability for conflict of interest rests on a recognition and development of the links between accountability, integrity, and trust. A direct rationale for prophylactic regulation arises from recognising that conflicts of interest, if acted upon, represent a breach of the trust that is central to police legitimacy and the policing function. Regulation can both reduce the possibility of conflict of interest breaches, and, combined with an effective system of external oversight of internal police processes, provide a source of institutionally based trust upon which the public can rely. Formal processes and institutions of accountability may also serve an important symbolic and signalling function by sending messages about accountability and responsibility to police officers (see Bayley 1996: 151).

Accountability for conflict of interest may be an important element in preventing upstream police misconduct and corruption, but for this to succeed, integrity and trust must be integrated into the professional working identity of police officers and become a part of the visible and internalised role of the police in society (c.f. Kaptein 1998). To achieve this, regulatory strategies should nurture understanding, competence and responsibility, not just passive obedience to rules. Processes to develop and strengthen active accountability should be encouraged, focusing less on prescription and proscription and more on understanding the nature of the problem of conflict of interest and its links to ethical misconduct.

References

Adams D (1996). "Calls for police inquiry continue." *The Age*, February 3: A4.

Ayling J and P Grabosky (2006). "When police go shopping." *Policing: An International Journal of Police Strategies and Management* 29(4): 665–690.

Ayres I and J Braithwaite (1992). *Responsive Regulation: Transcending the Deregulation Debate*. New York, Oxford University Press.

Bailey K D (1994). *Methods of Social Research*. New York, The Free Press.

Baker M (1985). *Cops: Their Lives in Their Own Words*. New York, Simon and Schuster.

Bayley D (1995). Getting Serious about Police Brutality. *Accountability for Criminal Justice*. P C Stenning. Toronto, University of Toronto Press: 93–109.

Bayley D H (1991). Preface. *Complaints Against the Police: The Trend to External Review*. A J Goldsmith. Oxford, Clarendon Press: v–xi.

Bayley D H (1996). Accountability and control of police: Lessons for Britain. *Policing. Volume II: Controlling the Controllers: Police Discretion and Accountability*. R Reiner. Andershot, Dartmouth: 146–162.

Beattie Repetti C-A (1997). The Politics of Civilian Review: Police Accountability in Washington , D.C. and New York City, 1948–1974. *Columbian School of Arts and Sciences*. Washington, George Washington University.

Bellingham T (2000). "Police culture and the need for change." *The Police Journal* 73(1): 31–41.

Bigley G A and J L Pearce (1998). "Straining for shared meaning in organizational science: Problems of trust and distrust." *Academy of Management Review* 23(3): 405–421.

Billingsley R, T Nimitz, and P Bean, Eds. (2001). *Informers: Policing, Policy, Practice*. Cullompton, Willan.

Boatright J R (2000). Trade secrets and conflict of interest. *Ethics and the Conduct of Business*. Upper Saddle River, New Jersey, Prentice-Hall: 128–158.

Bolen J (1990). The police culture – Implications for the reform process. *Corruption and Reform: The Fitzgerald Vision*. S Prasser, R Wear, and J Nethercote. St Lucia, Queensland, University of Queensland Press.

Bovens M (1998). *The Quest for Responsibility: Accountability and Citizenship in Complex Organisations*. Cambridge, Cambridge University Press.

Braithwaite J (1999). "Accountability and governance under the new regulatory state." *Australian Journal of Public Administration* 58(1): 90–94.

Braithwaite J (2002). *Restorative Justice and Responsive Regulation*. New York, Oxford University Press.

Braithwaite J and T Makkai (1994). "Trust and compliance." *Policing and Society* 4(1): 1–12.

Brodeur J (1995). Undercover policing in Canada: A study of its consequences. *Undercover: Police Surveillance in Comparative Perspective*. G T Marx and C Fijnaut. The Hague, Kluwer Law International.

Buttny R (1993). *Social Accountability in Communication*. London, Sage.

Carson T L (1994). "Conflicts of interest." *Journal of Business Ethics* 13(5): 387–404.

Chan J (1996). "Changing police culture." *British Journal of Criminology* 36(1): 109–134.

Chan J (1997). *Changing Police Culture: Policing in a Multicultural Society*. Cambridge, Cambridge University Press.

Chan J (1999a). Police culture. *A Culture of Corruption: Changing an Australian police service*. D Dixon. Sydney, Hawkins Press: 98–137.

Chan J (2000). Backstage Punishment: Police violence, occupational culture and criminal justice. *Violence and Police Culture*. T Coady, S James, S Miller, and M O'Keefe. Melbourne, Melbourne University Press: 85–108.

Chan J (2001). "Negotiating the field: New observations on the making of police officers." *Australian and New Zealand Journal of Criminology* 34(2): 114–133.

Chan J, D Brereton, M Legosz, and S Doran (2001). *E-policing: The Impact of Information Technology on Police Practices*. Brisbane, Queensland Criminal Justice Commission.

Chan J B L (1999b). "Governing police practice: Limits of the new accountability." *British Journal of Sociology* 50(2): 251–270.

Coady T, S James, S Miller, and M O'Keefe, Eds. (2000). *Violence and Police Culture*. Ethics in Public Life. Melbourne, Melbourne University Press.

Comrie N (1995). For Attention of Members - Re: Conflicts of Interest. *Switched Message Print*. Melbourne, Victoria Police: November 10 @ 17:58.

Conroy P (1996). "The night they busted Tasty." *The Age*, May 21: A11.

Crank J P (1998). *Understanding Police Culture*. Cincinnati, Anderson.

Crime and Misconduct Commission (undated). Conflicts of interest, Queensland. Accessed March 10 2003.

Criminal Justice Commission (1995). Ethical Conduct and Discipline in the Queensland Police Service: The Views of Recruits, First Year Constables and Experienced Officers. Brisbane, Criminal Justice Commission.

Criminal Justice Commission (1996). Gender and Ethics in Policing. Brisbane, Criminal Justice Commission.

Criminal Justice Commission (1997). Reducing Police–Civilian Conflict: An Analysis of Assault Complaints Against Queensland Police. Brisbane, Criminal Justice Commission.

Davids C (1998). "Shaping public perceptions of police integrity: Conflict of interest scenarios in fictional interpretations of policing." *Current Issues in Criminal Justice* 9(3): 241-261.

Davids C (2005). Police Misconduct, Regulation, and Accountability: Conflict of Interest Complaints Against Victoria Police Officers 1988–1998. *Faculty of Law*. Sydney, University of New South Wales.

Davids C (2006). "Conflict of interest and the private lives of police officers: Friendships, civic and political activities." *Journal of Policing, Intelligence and Counter-Terrorism* 1: 14–35.

Davids C and L Hancock (1998). "Policing, accountability and citizenship in the market state." *Australian and New Zealand Journal of Criminology* 31(1): 38-68.

Davis K C (1976). The Inquiry - the subject, objectives background, and method. *Discretionary Justice in Europe and America*. K C Davis. Chicago, University of Illinois Press: 203.

Davis M (1982). "Conflict of interest." *Business and Professional Ethics Journal* 1(4): 17–32.

Davis M (1992). "Codes of ethics, professions, and conflict of interest: A case study of an emerging profession, clinical engineering." *Professional Ethics* 1(1&2): 179–195.

Day P and R Klein (1987). *Accountabilities: Five Public Services*. London and New York, Tavistock.

Devery C and T Trevallion (2001). "Conflict of interest." *Policing Issues and Practice Journal*(April/July/October): 16–21.

Director—Police Integrity (2005a). Investigation into Victoria Police's Management of the Law Enforcement Assistance Program (LEAP). Melbourne, Office of Police Integrity.

Director—Police Integrity (2005b). Office of Police Integrity Annual Report. Melbourne, Office of Police Integity.

Director—Police Integrity (2005c). Report on the Leak of a Sensitive Victoria Police Information Report. Melbourne, Office of Police Integrity.

Director—Police Integrity (2006). Office of Police Integrity Annual Report 2005-06. Melbourne, Office of Police Integity.

Dixon D (1997). *Law in Policing: Legal Regulation and Police Practices*. Oxford, Oxford University Press.

Dixon D, Ed. (1999a). *A Culture of Corruption: Changing an Australian police service*. Institute of Criminology Monograph Series. Sydney, Hawkins Press.

Dixon D (1999b). Issues in the legal regulation of policing. *A Culture of Corruption: Changing an Australian police service*. D Dixon. Sydney, Hawkins Press: 36–68.

Dixon D (1999c). The normative structure of policing. *A Culture of Corruption: Changing an Australian police service*. D Dixon. Sydney, Hawkins Press: 69–97.

Dixon D (2004). Police governance and official inquiry. *Crime, Truth and Justice: Official Inquiry, Discourse, Knowledge*. G Gilligan and J Pratt. Devon, Willan.

Elliston F A and M Feldberg, Eds. (1985). *Moral Issues in Police Work*. Totowa, New Jersey, Rowman & Allanheld.

Ethical Standards Department (1998). 1997–1998 Annual Report. Melbourne, Victoria Police.

Feldberg M (1985). Gratuities, corruption and the democratic ethos of policing: The case of the free cup of coffee. *Moral Issues in Police Work*. F A Elliston and M Feldberg. Totowa, New Jersey, Rowman & Allanheld: 267–276.

Fielding N (1991). *The Police and Social Conflict: Rhetoric and Reality*. London, The Athalone Press.

Findlay M (1993). "The ambiguity of accountability: Relationships of corruption and control." *Australian Quarterly* 65(2): 73–83.

Finnane M (1994). *Police and Government: Histories of Policing in Australia*. Melbourne, Oxford University Press.

Fitzgerald G E (1989). Report of a Commission of Inquiry Pursuant to Orders in Council. Brisbane, Commission of Inquiry into Possible Illegal Activities and Associated Police Misconduct.

Fox A (1974). *Beyond Contract: Work, Power and Trust Relations*. London, Faber and Faber.

Goldsmith A (1990). "Taking police culture seriously: Police discretion and the limits of law." *Policing and Society* 1: 91–114.

Goldsmith A J, Ed. (1991a). *Complaints Against the Police: The Trend to External Review*. Oxford, Clarendon Press.

Goldsmith A J (1991b). External review and self-regulation: Police accountability and the dialectic of complaints procedures. *Complaints Against the Police: The Trend to External Review*. A J Goldsmith. Oxford, Clarendon Press: 13–61.

Goldstein H (1990). *Problem-oriented Policing*. New York, McGraw-Hill.

Goldstein J (1960). "Police discretion not to invoke the criminal process: Low-visibility decisions in the administration of justice." *Yale Law Journal* 69(4): 543–594.

Gould L A (1997). "Can an old dog be taught new tricks? Teaching cultural diversity to police officers." *Policing: An International Journal of Police Strategies and Management* 20(2): 339–356.

Graham A (2006). "Standards in public life—The challenge of enhancing public trust." *Public Money and Management* 26(1): 3–5.

Grano J D (1985). "Prophylactic rules in criminal procedure: a question of article iii legitimacy." *Northwestern University Law Review* 80(1): 100–164.

Haldane R (1986). *The People's Force: A history of the Victoria Police*. Melbourne, Melbourne University Press.

Hickman M J, A R Piquero, and J R Greene (2000). "Discretion and gender disproportionality in police disciplinary systems." *Policing: An*

International Journal of Police Strategies and Management 23(1): 105–116.

HM Inspectorate of Constabulary (1999). Police Integrity, England, Wales and Northern Ireland: Securing and maintaining public confidence. London, Home Office Communication Directorate/HMIC.

Huon G F, B L Hesketh, M G Frank, K M McConkey, and G M McGrath (1995). Perceptions of Ethical Dilemmas: Ethics and policing—Study 1. Payneham, South Australia, National Police Research Unit.

Independent Commission Against Corruption (1992a). Report on Unauthorised Release of Government Information: Volume I. Sydney, Independent Commission Against Corruption.

Independent Commission Against Corruption (1992b). Report on Unauthorised Release of Government Information: Volume II. Sydney, Independent Commission Against Corruption.

Independent Commission Against Corruption (1992c). Report on Unauthorised Release of Government Information: Volume III. Sydney, Independent Commission Against Corruption.

Independent Commission Against Corruption (1994a). Investigation into the Relationship Between Police and Criminals: Second Report. Sydney, Independent Commission Against Corruption.

Independent Commission Against Corruption (1994b). Report on Investigation into Matters Relating to Police and Confidential Information. Sydney, Independent Commission Against Corruption.

Independent Commission Against Corruption (1997). Under Careful Consideration: Key Issues for Local Government. Sydney, Independent Commission Against Corruption.

Independent Commission on Policing for Northern Ireland (1999). A New Beginning: Policing in Northern Ireland. The Report of the Independent Commission on Policing for Northern Ireland. London, HMSO.

Integrity Commissioner (2002a). Conflict of interest in the public sector. Brisbane, Office of the Integrity Commissioner, Queensland Government.

Integrity Commissioner (2002b). What is a conflict of interest?, Queensland Government. Accessed March 10 2003.

Internal Investigations Department (1996). 1995 / 1996 I.I.D. Annual Report. Melbourne, Victoria Police.

Kappeler V E, R D Sluder, and G P Alpert (1998). *Forces of Deviance: Understanding the dark side of policing.* Prospect Heights, Illinois, Waveland Press.

Kaptein H (1998). Against professional ethics. *Public Sector Ethics: Finding and Implementing Values.* C Sampford, N Preston, and C-A Bois. Sydney and London, Federation Press/Routledge: 26–36.

Kennedy G A (2004a). Royal Commission Into Whether There Has Been Corrupt or Criminal Conduct By Any Western Australian Police Officer. Final Report: Volume I. Perth, Royal Commission Into Whether There Has Been Corrupt or Criminal Conduct By Any Western Australian Police Officer.

Kennedy G A (2004b). Royal Commission Into Whether There Has Been Corrupt or Criminal Conduct By Any Western Australian Police Officer. Final Report: Volume II. Perth, Royal Commission Into Whether There Has Been Corrupt or Criminal Conduct By Any Western Australian Police Officer.

Kernaghan K and J W Langford (1990). *The Responsible Public Servant.* Halifax, Nova Scotia, The Institute for Research on Public Policy and The Institute of Public Administration of Canada.

Kingsley J-P (1996). Conflict of Interest as Part of Political Ethics: The Canadian Federal Government Experience. *Teaching Ethics.* R M Thomas. London, HMSO. One: Government Ethics: 105–120.

Kleinig J (1996). *The Ethics of Policing.* Cambridge, Cambridge University Press.

Knapp W (1972). Commission Report. New York, New York City Commission to Investigate Allegations of Police Corruption and the Anti-Corruption Procedures of the Police Department.

Lersch K M and T Mieczkowski (1996). "Who are the problem-prone officers? An analysis of citizen complaints." *American Journal of Police* XV(3): 23-44.

Lewis C (1997). Civilian Oversight of Complaints Against Police: External relationships and their impact on effectiveness. *Faculty of Commerce and Administration.* Brisbane, Griffith University.

Lewis C (1999). *Complaints Against Police: The politics of reform.* Sydney, Hawkins Press.

Lewis C (2000). The Politics of Civilian Oversight: Serious commitment or lip service? *Civilian Oversight of Policing: Governance, Democracy and*

Human Rights. A J Goldsmith and C Lewis. Portland, Oregon, Hart: 20–40.

Lipsky M (1976). Toward a theory of street-level bureaucracy. *Theoretical Perspectives on Urban Politics*. W D Hawley. Englewood Cliffs, Prentice Hall: 196–213.

Loveday B (1994). "Ducking and diving—Formulating a policy for police and criminal justice in the 1990s." *Public Money and Management* 14: 25–30.

Loveday B (1995). "Contemporary challenges to police management in England and Wales: Developing strategies for effective service delivery." *Policing and Society* 5: 281–302.

Lustgarten L (1986). *The Governance of Police*. London, Sweet & Maxwell.

Lyall K and J Walker (1998). "Law and disorder." *The Weekend Australian*, April 18–19: 18.

Macintyre S and T Prenzler (1999). "The influence of gratuities and personal relationships on police use of discretion." *Policing and Society* 9: 181-201.

Macklin R (1983). Conflicts of interest. *Ethical Theory and Business*. T L Beauchamp and N E Bowie. Englewood Cliffs, New Jersey, Prentice-Hall: 240–246.

Manning P K and B Cullum-Swan (1994). Narrative, content, and semiotic analysis. *Handbook of Qualitative Research*. N K Denzin and Y S Lincoln. Thousand Oaks, California, Sage: 463–477.

Manning P K and L J Redlinger (1977). Invitational edges. *Thinking About Police*. C B Klockars. New York, McGraw Hill.

Marshall G (1978). Police accountability revisited. *Policy and Politics: Essays in honour of Norman Chester*. D Butler and A H Halsey. London, Macmillan: 51–65.

McCulloch J (1997). "Behind the headlines." *Alternative Law Journal* 22(5): 133–137.

McGuire J M (1983). Conflict of interest: Whose interest? And what conflict? *Ethical Theory and Business*. T L Beauchamp and N E Bowie. Englewood Cliffs, New Jersey, Prentice-Hall: 231–240.

Miller J (2003). Police Corruption in England and Wales: An assessment of current evidence. London, Home Office.

Miller S (1998). Authority, discretion and accountability: The case of policing. *Public Sector Ethics: Finding and Implementing Values.* C Sampford, N Preston, and C-A Bois. Sydney and London, Federation Press/Routledge: 37–52.

Miller S, J Blackler, and A Alexandra (1997). *Police Ethics.* St Leonards, NSW, Allen & Unwin.

Misztal B A (1996). *Trust in Modern Societies: The Search for the Bases of Social Order.* Cambridge, Polity.

Mollen M (1994). Commission Report. New York, Commission to Investigate Allegations of Police Corruption and the Anti-Corruption Procedures of the Police Department.

Moore D (1992). Measuring police productivity. *Policing in Australia: Old Issues, New Perspectives.* P Moir and H Eijkman. South Melbourne, Macmillan.

Moss I (1995). Confidential Information and Police. Sydney, NSW Ombudsman.

Moss I (1996). Annual Report 1995 – 1996. Sydney, NSW Ombudsman.

Moss I (1997a). Conflict of Interest. Sydney, NSW Ombudsman.

Moss I (1997b). Conflict of Interest & Police: A service-wide problem. Sydney, NSW Ombudsman.

Newburn T (1999). Understanding and Preventing Police Corruption: Lessons from the Literature. London, Home Office—Research, Development and Statistics Directorate.

Neyland D and S Woolgar (2002). "Accountability in action?: The case of a database purchasing decision." *British Journal of Sociology* 53(2): 259–274.

Neyroud P and A Beckley (2001). *Policing, Ethics and Human Rights.* Cullompton, Devon, Willan.

Nolan M (1996). "The values of public life." *The Age,* August 8: A11.

Nolan M, C Boulton, A King, T King, P Shore, Thomson of Monifieth, W Utting, A Warburton, and D Warwick (1995). Standards in Public Life: First Report of the Committee on Standards in Public Life. London, HMSO.

OECD (2000). *Trust in Government: Ethics Measures in OECD Countries.* Paris, Organisation for Economic Co-Operation and Development.

Owen A (1997). Public sector ethics: some practical implications. *Accountability and Corruption: Public sector ethics*. G L Clark, E P Jonson, and W Caldow. St Leonards NSW, Allen & Unwin: 36–52.

Palmer M (1992). Controlling corruption. *Policing Australia: Old Issues New Perspectives*. P Moir and H Eijkman. Melbourne, Macmillan: 102–131.

Parker W D (1987). Commission of Inquiry into the Facts of Allegations of Conflict of Interest Concerning the Honourable Sinclair M. Stephens. Ottawa, Ministry for Supply and Services.

Preston N, C Sampford, and C Connors (2002). *Encouraging Ethics and Challenging Corruption: Reforming Governance in Public Institutions*. Sydney, Federation Press.

Queensland Police Service (undated). *Code of Conduct*. Brisbane, Queensland Police Service.

Reiner R (1992). *The Politics of the Police*. Hemel Hempstead, England, Harvester Wheatsheaf.

Reiner R (1995). Counting the Coppers: Antinomies of accountability in policing. *Accountability for Criminal Justice*. P C Stenning. Toronto, University of Toronto Press: 74–92.

Reiner R (1996). Introduction: Controlling the Controllers: Police Discretion and Accountability. *Policing. Volume II*. R Reiner. Andershot, Dartmouth.

Reiner R (2000). *The Politics of the Police*. Oxford, Oxford University Press.

Rodwin M A (1993). *Medicine, Money, and Morals*. New York, Oxford University Press.

Royal Canadian Mounted Police External Review Committee (1991). Conflict of Interest. Ottawa, RCMP External Review Committee.

Royal Commission into Commercial Activities of the Government and Other Matters (1992). Report. Perth, Western Australian Government Printer.

Ryle G (1997). "Scams linked to one in 10 police." *The Age*, May 14: A4.

Ryle G, L Martin, and D Adams (1996). "Police plan went wrong, says Comrie." *The Age*, June 22: 1.

Seal W and P Vincent-Jones (1997). "Accounting and trust in the enabling of long-term relations." *Accounting, Auditing and Accountability Journal* 10(3): 406–431.

Settle R (1995). *Police Informers: Negotiation and power*. Sydney, Federation Press.

Shearing C D and R V Ericson (1991). "Culture as figurative action." *British Journal of Sociology* 42(4): 481–506.

Shearing C D and P C Stenning (1987). *Private Policing*. Newbury, California, Sage.

Sherman L W (1985). Becoming bent: Moral careers of corrupt policemen. *Moral Issues in Police Work*. F A Elliston and M Feldberg. Totowa, New Jersey, Rowman & Allanheld: 253–265.

Siemensma F (2000). Conflicts of interest: The universal blindspot. General Principles. *Conflicts of Interest: The Universal Blindspot*. Melbourne, Leo Cussen Institute.

Silvester J (1995a). "Bribe scam hits police." *The Sunday Age*, November 12: 1–2.

Silvester J (1995b). "Police scandal spreads." *The Sunday Age*, November 19: 1–2.

Silvester J and R Baker (2003). "Police will face sack for improper use of files." *The Age*, October 24: 3.

Skolnick J H (1994). Police Accountability in the United States. *Keeping the Peace: Police accountability and oversight*. D Moore and R Wettenhall. Canberra, University of Canberra/Royal Institute of Public Administration Australia: 106–112.

Skolnick J H and J J Fyfe (1993). *Above the Law: Police and the Excessive Use of Force*. New York, Free Press.

Skolnick J H and J J Fyfe (1996). Rodney King and the use of excessive force: Police work and organizational culture. *Corporate and Governmental Deviance: Problems of Organizational Behaviour in Contemporary Society*. M D Ermann and R J Lundman. New York, Oxford University Press: 232–250.

Stark A (2000). *Conflict of Interest in American Public Life*. Cambridge, Massachusetts, Harvard University Press.

Stubbs J (1992). Complaints Against Police in New South Wales. Sydney, New South Wales Bureau of Crime Statistics and Research.

Sunshine J and T R Tyler (2003). "The role of procedural justice and legitimacy in shaping public support for policing." *Law and Society Review* 37(3): 513–547.

Task Force Victor (1994). Police Shootings: A question of balance. Malbourne, Australian Institute of Criminology.

The Age (1997). "Editorial: Policing the police." *The Age*, May 16: A12.

The Deputy Ombudsman (Police Complaints) (1993). Operation Iceberg: Investigation of Leaked Confidential Police Information and Related Matters. Melbourne, Office of the Ombudsman, Victoria.

The Deputy Ombudsman (Police Complaints) (1994). Investigation of police raid on the Commerce Club on Sunday 7 August 1994. Melbourne, Office of the Ombudsman, Victoria.

The Deputy Ombudsman (Police Complaints) (1995). Investigation of the police withdrawal on 2 May 1994 of charges laid against David Fox and Kenneth Richards. Melbourne, Office of the Ombudsman, Victoria.

The Ombudsman (1993). Annual Reports: Report of the Deputy Ombudsman (Police Complaints) for years ending 30 June 1992 and 30 June 1993. Melbourne, Office of the Ombudsman, Victoria.

The Ombudsman (1994). Investigation into alleged excessive force by Victoria Police against demonstrators at the Richmond Secondary College. Melbourne, Office of the Ombudsman, Victoria.

The Ombudsman (1995). Annual Report of the Ombudsman, incorporating the report of The Deputy Ombudsman (Police Complaints), 1994–95. Melbourne, Office of the Ombudsman, Victoria.

The Ombudsman (1997a). Annual Report of the Ombudsman. Melbourne, Office of the Ombudsman, Victoria.

The Ombudsman (1997b). The Maryborough Police Investigation. Melbourne, Office of the Ombudsman, Victoria.

The Ombudsman (1998a). Allegations Raised Concerning the Activities of the Operations Intelligence Unit and Other Related Issues. Melbourne, Office of the Ombudsman, Victoria.

The Ombudsman (1998b). Operation Bart: Investigation of Allegations Against Police in Relation to the Shutter Allocations System. Melbourne, Office of the Ombudsman, Victoria.

The Ombudsman (2001). 2000/2001 Annual Report: Twenty-eighth Report of The Ombudsman. Melbourne, Office of the Ombudsman, Victoria.

The Ombudsman (2003). Annual Report of The Ombudsman. Melbourne, Office of the Ombudsman, Victoria.

Thomas P G (1998). The changing nature of accountability. *Taking Stock: Assessing Public Sector Reforms*. B G Peters and D J Savoie. Montreal, Canadian Centre for Management Development and McGill-Queen's University Press: 348–393.

Topping I (1997). "Police officers and membership of organisations." *New Law Journal* 147: 63–65.

Tyler T R (1990). *Why People Obey the Law*. New Haven, Yale University Press.

Tyler T R (2004). "Enhancing police legitimacy " *Annals of the American Academy of Political and Social Sciences* 593: 84–99.

Uhr J (1993). "Redesigning accountability: From muddles to maps." *Australian Quarterly* 65(2): 1–16.

Victoria Police (1988). Annual Report 1987-88. Melbourne, Victoria Police.

Victoria Police (1989). Annual Report 1988-89. Melbourne, Victoria Police.

Victoria Police (1990). Annual Report 1989 - 90. Melbourne, Victoria Police.

Victoria Police (1991). Annual Report 1990–91. Melbourne, Victoria Police.

Victoria Police (1992). Annual Report 1991-92. Melbourne, Victoria Police.

Victoria Police (1993a). Annual Report 1992 - 93. Melbourne, Victoria Police.

Victoria Police (1993b). Discipline Procedures Manual. Melbourne, Victoria Police.

Victoria Police (1994). Annual Report 1993 - 1994. Melbourne, Victoria Police.

Victoria Police (1995). Annual Report 1994 - 1995. Melbourne, Victoria Police.

Victoria Police (1996a). Annual Report 1995 - 1996. Melbourne, Victoria Police.

Victoria Police (1996b). Project Guardian: Detection and Prevention of Corrupt or Unethical Behaviour. Options & Recommendations Paper. Melbourne, Victoria Police.

Victoria Police (1996c). Project Guardian: Ethical Standards Department. Options & Recommendations Paper. Melbourne, Victoria Police.

Victoria Police (1996d). Project Guardian: Ethical Standards Department. Final Report. Melbourne, Victoria Police.

Victoria Police (1996e). Project Guardian: Options & Recommendations Paper. Review of the Discipline System. Melbourne, Victoria Police.

Victoria Police (1997). 1996 – 1997 Annual Report. Melbourne, Victoria Police.

Victoria Police (1998a). 1997 – 1998 Annual Report. Melbourne, Victoria Police.

Victoria Police (1998b). *Code of Conduct*. Melbourne, Victoria Police.

Victoria Police (2003). "Greater accountability of members accessing the Victoria Police LEAP data system." *Media release*, October 10.

Victoria Police (2006). Conflict of Interest. *Best Practice DVD and Training Kit* Melbourne, Ethical Standards Department, Victoria Police.

Victoria Police (undated). *Ethics and Professional Standards*. Melbourne, Victoria Police.

Walker S (1993). *Taming the System: The Control of Discretion in Criminal Justice 1950–1990*. New York, Oxford University Press.

Werhane P and J Doering (1992). "Conflicts of interest and conflicts of commitment." *Professional Ethics* 4(3&4): 47–81.

Wood J (1996). Royal Commission into the New South Wales Police Service: Interim Report. Sydney, Royal Commission into the New South Wales Police Service.

Wood J (1997a). Royal Commission into the New South Wales Police Service: Final Report. Volume I: Corruption. Sydney, Royal Commission into the New South Wales Police Service.

Wood J (1997b). Royal Commission into the New South Wales Police Service: Final Report. Volume II: Reform. Sydney, Royal Commission into the New South Wales Police Service.

Wood J (1997c). Royal Commission into the New South Wales Police Service: Final Report. Volume III: Appendices. Sydney, Royal Commission into the New South Wales Police Service.

Wueste D E, Ed. (1994). *Professional Ethics and Social Responsibility*. Lanham, Maryland, Rowman and Littlefield.

Young M (1998). Conflict of Interest: Selected Issues. Ottawa, Parliamentary Research Branch, Library of Parliament.

Young M (2002). Conflict-of-Interest Rules for Federal Legislators. Ottawa, Parliamentary Research Branch, Library of Parliament.

Index

abuse of office, 46, 51

alcohol and gaming, 9, 44, 58, 119, 130, 138, 141, 158, 187, 188, 194, 236, 241, 258

bribery, 47

brothels. *See prostitution*

Canada, 117

Committee on Standards in Public Life, 19

complaints against police, 12–16, 64, 67, 265

    vexatious or unfounded, 122, 127, 149, 160, 161–62, 179, 195, 196, 240, *See also public perceptions, misperceptions*

confidential information

    release of, 5, 38, 43, 44, 48, 64, 111, 126, 139, 143, 183, 214, 215, 217, 223–34, 244–45

    inadvertent, 233–34

    information about criminal histories or investigations, 228–32, 232, 245

    security and management, 216–18, 224, 227, 244

    use of, 48, 123–24, 125, 135–36, 214, 216, 218–23

conflict of interest

    actual, 249

    and breach of duty, 5, 7, 29, 38, 39, 40, 53, 63, 104–5, 111–12, 112, 122, 139, 152, 210, 212, 217, 221, 222, 226–27, 244, 246, 249–50, 251–52, 257

        action against opposing party, 167–79

        delaying police processes, 162–63, 164–67

        failure to act, 157–64

    and corruption, 4–7

    apparent, 29, 33–37, 38, 39, 249, 252

    context of complaints, 56, 243–44

    definition, 17–18, 18, 29–40, 249–50

    latent, 32–33, 122, 249

    potential, 29–32, 37

    regulation and enforcement, 23–24, 35, 36, 58, 118, 132, 144, 146–50, 169, 181, 214, 225, 226, 246, 251, 253–59, 257–58, 259, 263, 265, 266–67

    types, 40–48

        in policing, 48–53